Navigating the Aspirational City

Spotlight on China

Series Editors

Shibao Guo (*University of Calgary, Canada*)
Yan Guo (*University of Calgary, Canada*)

International Advisory Board

Yanjie Bian (*University of Minnesota, USA*)
Qing Gu (*University of Nottingham, UK*)
Ruth Hayhoe (*OISE/University of Toronto, Canada*)
Khun Eng Kuah-Pearce (*Monash University Malaysia, Malaysia*)
Baocun Liu (*Beijing Normal University, China*)
Allan Luke (*Queensland University of Technology, Australia*)
Gerard A. Postiglione (*University of Hong Kong, Hong Kong*)
Barbara Schulte (*Lund University, Sweden*)
Rui Yang (*University of Hong Kong, Hong Kong*)
Qiang Zha (*York University, Canada*)
Jijiao Zhang (*Chinese Academy of Social Sciences, China*)
Li Zong (*University of Saskatchewan, Canada*)

VOLUME 6

The titles published in this series are listed at *brill.com/spot*

Navigating the Aspirational City

Urban Educational Culture and the Revolutionary Path to Socialism with Chinese Characteristics

By

Lorin G. Yochim

BRILL
SENSE

LEIDEN | BOSTON

Funding for this book was provided in part by the 2017 Comprehensive Discipline Construction Fund of the Faculty of Education, Beijing Normal University (No. 00300-312231103) and the Social Sciences and Humanities Research Council of Canada.

Cover illustration: Photograph by Lorin G. Yochim

All chapters in this book have undergone peer review.

The Library of Congress Cataloging-in-Publication Data is available online at http://catalog.loc.gov
LC record available at http://lccn.loc.gov/2018033029

ISSN 2542-9655
ISBN 978-90-04-38124-7 (paperback)
ISBN 978-90-04-38125-4 (hardback)
ISBN 978-90-04-38126-1 (e-book)

Copyright 2019 by Koninklijke Brill NV, Leiden, The Netherlands.
Koninklijke Brill NV incorporates the imprints Brill, Brill Hes & De Graaf, Brill Nijhoff, Brill Rodopi, Brill Sense, Hotei Publishing, mentis Verlag, Verlag Ferdinand Schöningh and Wilhelm Fink Verlag.
All rights reserved. No part of this publication may be reproduced, translated, stored in a retrieval system, or transmitted in any form or by any means, electronic, mechanical, photocopying, recording or otherwise, without prior written permission from the publisher.
Authorization to photocopy items for internal or personal use is granted by Koninklijke Brill NV provided that the appropriate fees are paid directly to The Copyright Clearance Center, 222 Rosewood Drive, Suite 910, Danvers, MA 01923, USA. Fees are subject to change.

Brill has made all reasonable efforts to trace all rights holders to any copyrighted material used in this work. In cases where these efforts have not been successful the publisher welcomes communications from copyright holders, so that the appropriate acknowledgements can be made in future editions, and to settle other permission matters.

This book is printed on acid-free paper and produced in a sustainable manner.

CONTENTS

Preface	vii
List of Figures and Tables	ix
Chapter 1: Scoping Chinese Educational Culture	1
Research Problem & Questions	2
Third-Tier City, First-World Problems	6
An Urban Educational Culture of Familial Aspiration	6
Education, Family, City, Culture	7
Conceptualizing Educational Culture	20
Organization of the Book	21
Chapter 2: The Heavy Burden of Revolution	25
Jianfu: Lightening the Heavy Burden	26
Jianfu in the Early Revolutionary Period	27
Jianfu in the Great Proletarian Cultural Revolution	33
Chapter 3: The "Reform" Era & the Emergence of the Aspirational Cité	43
The Emergence of the Aspirational Cité	44
Jianfu: A Flexible Policy	52
Chapter 4: Building an Aspirational City	57
The Utopian Scheme of San Nian Da Bianyang	59
Tangible Effects of Renovation	64
Educational Institutions for the Aspirational City	77
Chapter 5: Educating Children in the Aspirational City	83
The Parents	84
Beliefs and Activities of Middle-Class Urban Parents	92
Chapter 6: Making One's Way through the Field of Urban Educational Culture	103
Negotiating & Navigating: The Logic of China's Urban Educational Culture	103
Jianfu Reconsidered	112
Negotiating & Navigating Educational Culture	116
The Aspirational Family?	120

CONTENTS

Chapter 7: Urban Educational Culture Revisited	123
Renovation and Desire in 2017	127
Appendix A: Methodological Preliminaries and Specifications	133
Metatheoretical Preliminaries	134
Methodological Specifications	135
Scoping Orders of Worth	144
Scoping the City	148
Scoping Parents' Beliefs and Practices	150
Appendix B: Documents Used in Corpus Analysis	153
References	161

PREFACE

"New" Chinese cities reconstructed since the early 2000s house a middle-class disposed to collect and activate stocks of economic, social, and cultural capital. They do so in a geography that acts as a complex of spaces within which citizens are subject to myriad forms of pedagogic action. This project has shifted the subjectivity of middle class pledges, embedded within the resurgent institution of the family, toward conspicuous consumption, social differentiation, family-level "individualization," and "projects of the self." Yet it has also sowed the seeds of its own potential destruction. Rather than contributing newly accumulated cultural capital to the building of a new socialist China, these "new Chinese" focus their energies on personal gain, with many choosing to abandon the nation in whole or in part.

This book forwards a descriptive and explanatory account of contemporary educational culture in urban China. It culminates in a description of the beliefs and practices of urban Chinese parents about how and why children should be "educated" in particular ways. These beliefs and practices are situated in relation to a historical chain of ideas about how to best educate children, and within the rapidly changing urban context within which they are produced and reproduced, renovated and transformed. Beginning with a history of Revolutionary "orders of worth" culminating in the "aspirational cité," the book details the shifting evaluative standards that define the "human capital" conditions of possibility of a developed modern economy. It goes on to describe a set of policies and practices known as *san nian da bianyang* by which the whole of one particular city has been demolished, re-built, and re-ordered. Parents' beliefs and practices, it is contended, articulate with this ideational and material context to produce what appears, at times, to be radical transformation and, at others, remarkable stability.

FIGURES AND TABLES

FIGURES

2.1.	Freedom of marriage, happiness and good luck	29
2.2.	Daddy, this is how you write this character	30
2.3.	Helping mama study culture	31
2.4.	Criticize the old world and build a new world with Mao Zedong thought as a weapon	36
2.5.	New socialist things are good	37
2.6.	Educated youth must go to the countryside to receive re-education from the poor and lower-middle peasants!	38
2.7.	Hold high the great red banner of Mao Zedong	39
3.1.	Respect yourself, love yourself, conduct yourself with dignity, improve yourself	48
3.2.	I want to be an amazing Chinese	49
3.3.	Show concern for others	50
4.1.	Shijiazhuang's new railway station	58
4.2.	Shijiazhuang city residential land use renewal map 2008–2010 (shijiazhuang shi zhufang jianshe yu baozhang guihua; shiqu juzhu yongdi gaizao fen qu tu)	59
4.3.	The process of Shijiazhuang's urban redevelopment	61
4.4.	High rise apartments rise from the rubble of dozens of urban villages demolished under san nian da bianyang	63
4.5.	Shijiazhuang's huancheng shuixi (环城水系)	64
4.6.	Another demolished village makes way for high density apartment buildings	65
4.7.	Traditional markets on the way out under san nan da bianyang	66
4.8.	High cultural facilities and high rise buildings embody the spirit of san nian da bianyang	67
4.9.	Office/hotel towers over the Hebei provincial museum and its renovated north plaza	68
4.10.	Shijiazhuang's scenic shui shang gong yuan (水上公园)	70
4.11.	Shijiazhuang's new metro system	72
4.12.	Beijiao Cun (centre) in 2010 prior to demolition	73
4.13.	Fields of flowers	75
4.14.	Shaded Forest Kingdom	76
4.15.	Spring returns	76
4.16	Front gate of SFLS	77
4.17.	SFLS fosters an international perspective in its students	78
4.18.	Central dome of Xiantianxia	81

FIGURES AND TABLES

6.1.	Parents and their children pose for photos at the gates of Tsinghua University	104
7.1.	The redevelopment of Dong San Zhuang	124
7.2.	Time goes on in Shijiazhuang	125
7.3.	"I'm elite!"	127
7.4.	Tackle difficulties; pursue excellence (gongjian kenan, zhuiqiu zhuoyue)	130

TABLES

1.1.	Bourdieu & Passeron's typology of pedagogic action	9
2.1.	Early-revolutionary era order of worth	28
2.2.	Order of worth of the cultural revolution	35
3.1.	Order of worth of the present, the aspiration cité	46
A.1.	Class-occupational structure of contemporary China	141
A.2.	Objects, data sources, and modes of analysis	143
A.3.	Comparison of codes in different modes of analysis	143
A.4.	Coding used in "scoping orders of worth"	146
A.5.	Coding used in "scoping the city"	149
A.6.	Coding used in "scoping parents' beliefs and practices"	151

CHAPTER 1

SCOPING CHINESE EDUCATIONAL CULTURE

> Research questions do not come from nowhere. In many cases, their origin lies in the researchers' personal biographies and their social contexts.
>
> (Flick, 2009, p. 98)

At the close of a sweltering summer day, friends and I have gathered for dinner. The outlay of food and alcohol is, in proper Chinese fashion, varied and generous, and matched by the capacity of the attendees to comment upon and consume them. The home in which we gather is a young one is two senses. First, neither member of the host couple that live in it is much more than 25 years old. Second, they have occupied it together for only a short time, a fact revealed by the paucity and makeshift quality of its furnishings. Each of the attendees, myself excepted, arrives not only as him or herself, but as a member of a pair. As such – as young, married Chinese men and women – what unites them in conversation as the evening progresses are the concerns and questions of parenthood, the collective anticipation of an impending if not inevitable future from which springs a lively and, from my perspective, entirely unlikely hours-long discussion of the challenges of building a family (成家 – *cheng jia*), of, more specifically, what they refer to as "family education" (家庭教育 – *jiating jiaoyu*) in contemporary China.[1]

Beyond friendship, beyond a love of food and conversation, beyond imminent parenthood, each of these couples shares the experience of living in the rapidly changing cityscape of Shijiazhuang. Like most other cities in contemporary China, this one is undergoing not only rapid growth but also what might more properly be called *radical renovation* as part of a process that L. Zhang (2010) calls a "new revolution" (p. 1).

In recent years, a rapid and massive process – at once both purposeful and chaotic – of demolition and reconstruction has lent Shijiazhuang a modified if not entirely new character. Governed ideologically and practically by a program coined *san nian da bianyang* (三年大变样 – three years complete change), the effects of renovation have been remarkable. The city is growing outward at an impressive if not alarming rate, chewing up surrounding farmland and villages as it expands. At the same time, scores of neighbourhoods, markets, and street-side commercial strips have been razed and replaced by high rise apartment buildings, giant shopping mall-style department stores, and the roadways that accommodate an explosion in private car ownership.

CHAPTER 1

Constant change has tangible impacts on my own life in the city. An absence of only six or eight months necessitates substantial revision of my mind map of the city. I need to figure out what "old" and new places should be erased or added, not to mention what revamped or newly built roads and routes will get me to my destination. For longtime residents of the city, my annual struggles must seem trivial, for it is certain that the shifting landscape of Shijiazhuang has more significant consequences for people bound to the city more tightly than me. For example, in the case of the parent-informants you will read about in this book, the manner in which they have remodelled their family circumstances has mirrored urban renovation; each has moved house, changed jobs, and/or moved a child from one school to another at least once since the study commenced. Some have done so repeatedly.

Beyond facing common material conditions as co-residents of Shijiazhuang, these are people bound together as members of a generation raised in a China far different from that which was once firmly committed to socialist means and ends. They have grown up in an era characterized by the contraction and near demise of state-guaranteed employment and welfare provision. At the same time, they have experienced the expansion of market-based opportunities and challenges, whether these be access to goods made available through the opening of global markets, the lure of emigration, or the more precarious everyday life that reform and opening up has engendered. If their parents were the children of Mao, then surely they and those aspects of their individual and collective selves – their tastes, their aspirations; their desires, their fates – are inextricably bound up with the vicissitudes of the China chiseled from the foundational stones – some would say the rubble – of Mao's New China. Children of a new of "market socialism," they are without doubt the progeny of Deng Xiaoping's China.

In this book, I describe the beliefs and practices of urban Chinese parents about how and why children should be "educated" in particular ways. I seek to better understand the shape, character, and significance of these beliefs and practices by situating them in relation to a historical chain of ideas about how to best educate children, and within the rapidly changing urban context in which they are produced and reproduced, renovated and transformed. I consider how parents' beliefs and practices articulate with this context to produce what appears, at times, to be radical transformation and, at others, remarkable stability. Throughout the book, I use the term "educational culture" to refer to what I take to be a dynamic space within which personal, social, historical, and built environment come together.

RESEARCH PROBLEM & QUESTIONS

For those convinced that the "end of history" has been upon us for the past three decades, China's rise indicates nothing less than the triumph of market capitalism. Others, unimpressed with this new "asiatic" mode of governance, hold that the emergence of an authoritarian alternative to U.S.-led capitalism provides still more evidence of the dangers of unbridled statism, the folly of cadre-led socialism, and even the surest, best proof that late capitalism is upon us. Whatever the strengths and weaknesses of these perspectives, it would be hard to argue that their concern with China is unwarranted. By virtue of its world-historical stature, its spectacular and ongoing ascent as an economic power, its role as home to nearly one-fifth of the world's population, and, last but not least, its position as birthplace of one of the world's oldest and most respected educational traditions, accurate representations of the present state of China and its peoples ought to be of profound interest to those concerned with the economic, cultural, and political future of the world.

The call to think about China and re-imagine its place in the world is being taken up with increasing vigour. China, threat to regional stability; China, saviour of the world economy; China, human rights violator; China, source of spectacular films and tattoo parlour motifs – ubiquitous, competing tropes not only underscore the centrality of the middle kingdom in policy debates, but also its growing profile as a global cultural force. Unfortunately, many of the products of this new sinology rely on analytical frameworks that derogate the complexity and dynamism of the socio-cultural landscape of contemporary China. Alternatively, they pay little attention to the broader forces that constrain and enable possibilities in circumscribed social contexts. On the one hand, we learn of one or another anthropomorphized cultural, political, and/or economic system and its prospects for bringing about a better China. On the other, we are left with an abundance of depictions of heroic individuals or collectivities struggling against this or that economic and/or cultural constraint in order to realize one or another vision for the future.

Of course not all studies of contemporary Chinese society are so crude. For example, in their studies of urban educational culture, Teresa Kuan and Andrew Kipnis demonstrate the value of non-reductive analysis. Kuan (2008, 2011) gives insight into the overbearing nurturing of mothers by first describing the lengths they go to to ensure their child's "success," and then bringing their lived experiences into relation with the commodification of culture in post-Mao market society. Apparent intensification of affective relations between mothers and children is linked to the rise of the governing discourse of *suzhi jiaoyu* (素质教育 – education for "quality") and the unintended consequences of the "one-child policy." This same strategy of in-depth description of a single setting helps Kipnis (2011) to explain the phenomenon of high "educational desire" in Chinese culture. Through a multi-faceted ethnography of the city of Zouping (Shandong Province), he determines that desire for educational attainment cuts across class and socioeconomic divides. Going a step further than Kuan, Kipnis "emplaces" the educational culture of Zouping within national and regional contexts, exploring how glorification of scholastic achievement characterizes the educational cultures of China and East Asia as a whole. Both Kuan and Kipnis answer questions about socio-cultural phenomena not only through careful exploration of a particular contemporary locale, but also by locating what is a decidedly personal, present, and local context within a wider cultural, historical, politico-economic terrain.

CHAPTER 1

As the anecdote that began this chapter implies, this research project was motivated by a pair of observations. The first of these took note of a feature of life in China that strikes native Chinese as entirely mundane. Put simply, Chinese parents spend an enormous amount of time and effort agonizing over the general course and minute details of their children's education. This is true whether we think of "education" as a more general process within which a child is "nurtured," "raised," or "socialized," or as a more specific process of "pedagogic action" by which children are systematically "schooled" in a variety of institutionalized settings (Bourdieu & Passeron, 1990). Parents seem to hover over their infants and toddlers constantly – caring, cajoling, and guiding them in a manner that some amongst them consider to be excessive, but that is more generally taken as proper education in the home. They also participate in an extraordinary range of activities in order to ensure high educational achievement and attainment. Many compare their children and have a keen sense of social competition, so they constantly seek new ways to distinguish their children from others. They appear to see such rumination and constant care as crucial, indeed, mandatory to the task of ensuring the long-term success of their children. The dim view of such behaviour is that it results from the tendency of parents to "follow trends blindly and to believe most of what they hear" (Chang, 2008, p. 82). On this view, all of this fretting and running about takes place in a society that values collectivity, tradition, and conformity above all else. But it is hard to reconcile the spectacle of acquisitiveness with a theory of cultural conformity or passivity, especially when the official position on school choice, for example, has tended to be that it transgresses official policy (Qin, 2008, p. 332). While Kipnis (2011) sees this phenomenon as the latest manifestation of the age-old cultural tendency toward high "educational desire," Kuan (2008, 2011) shows how desire and anxiety have intensified as market relations have come to dominate mainland society.

The second observation sprung from my experience of an aspect of life in China that has, like educational desire, become a tedious if unavoidable feature of urban life – constant demolition, re-development, and growth. In this respect, Shijiazhuang is far from unique, as detailed by Xuefei Ren (2013) in a broad-ranging book that discusses the advent of massive debt financing used to fund municipal improvement projects like *san nian da bianyang*. Anthropologist Li Zhang (2010) rightly calls this process a "revolution" and focuses on the substantial spatial, cultural, and political effects of the rise of private home ownership in the southern city of Kunming. Zhang links this shift away from the formerly dominant *danwei* (单位 – work unit) system of social provision to new forms of urban organization and the "lifestyle practices" that characterize an emerging middle-class subjectivity (p. 3). One of the strengths of Zhang's account of urban class formation is its focus on the fraught nature of her informants' experiences of this transition. The emerging middle-class is highly desirous of the trappings of a consumerist lifestyle and of privacy and comfort, not to mention distinction from the lives and lifestyles they seek to leave behind (see also Hanser, 2005, 2007). Where aspiring to seclusion and difference are the lodestones of the new middle-class, protection of the achievements toward these ends means that they are also forced outward into public spaces. Notable for my purposes, Zhang's study is sensitive to the reconfigured moral order of this new urbanity, especially the ways in which people and places are evaluated and justified.

Inspired by the work of Kuan, Kipnis, Zhang, and Ren, in this book I aim for a detailed, layered account of urban China's educational culture. In the chapters that follow, I describe and explain this culture with reference to the twin spectacles of educational desire and urban renovation. Taking studies like theirs as models, I use the perspectives and tools of ethnography to study a single city in north-central China – Shijiazhuang. While my empirical focus is only one city and my aim to respect the specificity and complexity of the lives and experiences of the parents of this city, I also frame the study as *critical* ethnography. Here I understand critical as a rejoinder to remain cognizant of the relations that bind personal to cultural, present to past, and local to national and global. Therefore, I examine the educational culture of this city by considering three questions corresponding to three analytically distinct but inextricably linked levels.

First I ask, how do Shijiazhuang's middle-class parents conceive of "education" and go about getting such an education for their children? What aims and purposes do they hold to be key to an appropriate education for their child? At this level, I pay close attention to the perspectives of parents and, in particular, to the ways in which they conceive of "education," as well as the activities they engage in to pursue an education thus conceived.

Second, I pay careful attention to the following question: how do parents' conceptions, aims, and purposes articulate with precepts, prescriptions, and propositions that circulate more broadly in Chinese culture? I explore the specific content of national educational culture by compiling a history of "orders of worth" (Boltanski & Thévenot, 2006). I begin this history somewhat arbitrarily in and around the year 1950, and show how each of these orders provided direction to the people of the day. Each provided guidance in terms of what kinds of things, what sorts of people, and what ways of living and learning were more or less good and/ or desirable (Boltanski & Chiapello, 2007). I suggest that this history culminates in the emergence of the aspirational *cité*, an order of worth shot through with evaluative standards that define the "human capital" conditions of possibility of a fully developed modern economy.

Third, I turn my eye on the material environment of the city and ask, how are parents' ways of thinking and acting enabled and constrained within the new material and spatial orders emerging out of the renovation and growth of Shijiazhuang City? I probe the policies and practices of Shijiazhuang's urban renovation by describing a set of tangible effects of particular relevance to extant education culture. My overall aim in doing so is to reconstruct how the aspirational *cité* and the built environment of Shijiazhuang have come together at a particular moment in time and the ways in which this ideational-material configuration articulates with the educational ideas and practices of Shijiazhuang's emerging middle-class.[2]

CHAPTER 1

THIRD-TIER CITY, FIRST-WORLD PROBLEMS

The Shijiazhuang I encounter in 2017 is a far cry from the somewhat backward, dingy city I moved to in 2002. It was then and remains a third-tier city, one that, while much modernized, remains a relative backwater compared to its larger counterparts like Beijing and Shanghai or even regional comparators like Qingdao. I am here this time on a more modest mission than that which drew me to Hebei province fifteen years ago. This time around I am meeting old friends and research informants, having a look at the city's still under construction but partly operational metro system, and taking new photos for the imminent publication of the book you are reading.

Meeting with these folks in this city makes me realize how time and *a time* has passed. I've known them and the city for about fifteen years now and seen both change immensely. For these parents, the joy of a newborn's arrival has given way to the anxiety of school choice, the pressure of weekend training classes, and the trials of graduation examinations. For some the process has been one of expectations met or exceeded; for others, disappointment has accompanied the realization that the reality of their only child's passage through a highly competitive education system will be less successful than they once hoped and dreamed.

These triumphs and failures, it should be noted, are closely connected to the city itself. Shijiazhuang is a third-tier city in one of China's most populous provinces, meaning that students who graduate from its schools face tougher entrance requirements to the nation's top universities, themselves a virtual guaranteed path to upward mobility. Put simply, not every child will make it to that level.

What I learn on this trip, however, is that this is no longer the end of the line for them or their parents. Indeed, fifteen years of development in China are mirrored in Shijiazhuang. The prospects for its residents – economically, educationally – are far more diverse and promising in 2017 than 2002. For Lao Dong, who I meet for coffee at a Starbucks location in Shijiazhuang's hippest new mall, changes in economic structure and educational culture mean that stress over his daughter facing the *gaokao* (高考 – university entrance exam) has been alleviated by the possibility of overseas study. When we last talked, his daughter was entering high school and hoping to test highly enough to attend a desired local option rather than moving to nearby Tianjin. Now, rather than him seeking my help as an English tutor for his daughter, it is his daughter who directly engages me as a source of advice on how to complete her application to study in English in a Japanese university. In the new Shijiazhuang and within this one family of means, aspiring to study abroad has taken the place of Tsinghua dreams.

AN URBAN EDUCATIONAL CULTURE OF FAMILIAL ASPIRATION

It was my sense of this shift that led me the research questions above, and to the analysis that forms the core of this book. In the chapters that follow, I examine how Chinese cities re-constructed since the early 2000s house a nascent middle-class disposed to collect and activate stocks of economic, social, and cultural capital. They are aggressive in their attempts to "better" both themselves and their children, with the aim of improving the material security of the family as a whole.

The multilayered project of creating these new middle-class, consuming subjects began with the gradual construction and dissemination of a moral order comprising a set of precepts, prescriptions, and propositions that were subsequently translated into new, post-socialist urban spatial forms. This new urban geography now acts as a collection of pedagogical spaces, a classroom writ large within which the kinds of subjects imagined in the new moral order are subject to myriad forms of pedagogic action.

This project, successful as it has been at shifting the subjectivity of middle class pledges toward conspicuous consumption, social differentiation, family level "individualization," and "projects of the self," also sows the seeds of its own destruction. New middle class subjects, embedded within the resurgent institution of the family, absorb and attempt to live out the precepts, prescriptions, and propositions of an aspirational *cite*,[3] and, further along, deploy them to evaluate the newly built aspirational city.[4] As they do so, they find this new order lacking. While these new subjects are imagined to be the foundation of a new China, they give every indication of a trajectory of radical liberation – both emotionally and often physically – from the nation building necessities of the past. Rather than contributing their newly accumulated cultural capital to the building of a new socialist China, they focus their energies on personal gain, with many choosing to abandon the "new" China in whole or in part.

EDUCATION, FAMILY, CITY, CULTURE

The theoretical terrain staked out by these claims is expansive. It encompasses a specific set of claims about education, families, cities, culture, and the relations that bind them that challenges commonly posited understandings of social order in contemporary China. In the following four subsections, I briefly outline the theoretical and empirical inheritance that informs this analysis and the approach I took to the research, beginning with a discussion of "education" and its conceptualization in contemporary China.

Education

It would be difficult to discuss the beliefs and activities of families in any modern society without addressing the topic of education. This is perhaps no more true than in China, a country in which child-rearing, public education, and schooling practices are of overriding concern to political leadership and everyday folk alike. The pervasiveness of this concern for all things education, what I have already

CHAPTER 1

described (pace Kipnis, 2011) as "educational desire," led me to rely on Bourdieu and Passeron's (1990; see Table 1.1) typology of "pedagogic action."

I find this typology valuable for three reasons. The first is that it includes "family education" as a discrete domain of educational practice that occurs in and through the family. The institution of the family is seen to be one in which a distinctive form of pedagogic action takes place, an inclusion of direct utility given my focus on the beliefs and practices of parents. The second reason is that these spatially defined domains set Bourdieu & Passeron's typology apart from more common discourses on education that favour terms such as "formal," "informal," and "non-formal" education/learning, a practice that privileges mode of education/learning (Burns, 2001; Malcolm, Hodkinson, & Colley, 2003; OECD, 2013; Schugurensky, 2000; Werquin, 2007). By contrast, Bourdieu & Passeron's distinctions privilege *place* over *mode*. The third reason for using this typology is that it distinguishes a private domain of education (the family) from public (diffuse, institutionalized) domains, while preserving the formal/informal (institutionalized/diffuse) distinction.

Each of these pedagogic domains come into play when one considers the present shape of education in China, which owes much to the broader trends that have shaped the country since the death of Mao Zedong and the subsequent reorientation of state policy under Deng Xiaoping and successors Jiang Zemin, Hu Jintao, and Xi Jinping. The scope of this reorientation has been as inclusive in terms of its effects on the lives of all Chinese citizens – whether urban or rural, professional, or peasant/farmer – as it has been aggressive in its pursuit of the complete 'renovation' of the nation and its people (Anagnost, 1997). The ostensible starting point of reform was the rise to power of Deng Xiaoping, who raised to the pinnacle of the political agenda what both Mao Zedong (in 1965) and Zhou Enlai (in 1975) had identified as the crucial goals of socialist development (Shen, 1994, p. 61), that is, the "Four Modernizations" in "agriculture, industry, science and technology, and national defense" (Henze, 1987, p. 252). These general goals were spelled out as a set of aims designed to improve an all-encompassing yet ill-defined "quality" (Henze, 1987, p. 253).

It might seem obvious that the success of such a totalizing program of modernization would be linked institutionalized forms of education, but it was not until 1974–1975 that this tie was made explicit (Henze, 1987, p. 253). It was Deng Xiaoping who agitated for an "interpretation of education as a productive force" (p. 253) and as having a central role in preparing the country for its transformation (Paine, 1992; Shen, 1994). Deng has taken his place as the great leader of China's resurgence in the late 20th century, but his positioning of education at the centre of this program is hardly *sui generis*. Indeed, the voices of 19th century reformers echo loudly in his words. That earlier generation was also concerned that a protracted era of subordination to Western powers was the result of a lack of "advanced talented people…versed in the knowledge of Western science and technology" (Zheng in Shen, 1994, p. 58). Schools, they

8

Table 1.1. Bourdieu & Passeron's typology of pedagogic action

Type of pedagogic action	Pedagogic action is exerted by
Diffuse education	"all the educated members of a social formation or group" (Bourdieu & Passeron, p. 5)
Family education	"the family-group members to whom the culture of a group or class allots this task" (p. 5)
Institutionalized education	"the system of agents explicitly mandated for this purpose by an institution directly or indirectly, exclusively or partially educative in function" (p. 5)

argued, ought to be the source of the nation's strength, as they were in Western countries (Shen, 1994). The connection between the West, modernity, and science and technology is present one hundred years before the opening-up, as is the invocation of quality – in the descriptors *ren cai* (人才) and "talent" – as critical to raising of the nation to the level of the other.

In order to better understand the specific actions that the general goals of post-Mao reform set in motion, one must recognize that China was emerging from a "disastrous period of ideological fanaticism, economic depression, and national isolation known as the [Great Proletarian] Cultural Revolution" (GPCR) (Shen, 1994, p. 57). It would be difficult to overstate the effects of that period of time on both individual citizens and the national psyche. The GPCR by design attempted to dismantle the foundations of Chinese society, including the family, educational institutions and, indeed, culture itself (Barendsen, 1975, p. 6; Fan, 1990). Knowledge of the sweeping effects of the GPCR also helps one better understand the comparative and self-critical nature of reform following the repudiation of the Gang of Four. Where past revolutionary struggles were justified by reference to a superior other or the ghost of an inferior Chinese self – as in the Great Leap Forward's battle to rectify China's lack of industrial capacity relative to the USSR or Western nations; or the GPCR's determination to root out, amongst other evils, remnants of the feudal self – so, too, has the course of 'opening-up' been initiated and propagated as a battle against those things that made China 'underdeveloped' and, by definition, less 'modern' than 'developed' nations (Henze, 1987, 1992). One might argue that this sense of inferiority has been consciously nurtured as a locus of common struggle. Regardless of its origin and role, the invocation of Chinese inferiority inextricably ties the notions of modernization, development, and quality together. According to Henze (1992), the equation of the first two concepts was central to Deng's vision (p. 104). But in order to understand the thrust of policy in the reform era, one must realize that development *qua* modernization was to be achieved through the 'renovation' of the population itself; poor quality of peasants, teachers, or any other identifiable group appropriate to the sector under discussion, was deemed responsible for the failure to 'progress,' as opposed

CHAPTER 1

to an unfortunate result of underdevelopment (Anagnost, 1997, 2004; Fan, 1990; Henze, 1992; Xinhua, 1987). Anagnost (1997) argues that policy implementation in the reform era may be analyzed as a set of practices by which the government has subjected the population itself and, by extension, the individual bodies it comprises, to processes designed to elevate quality. Positioned thus, education becomes a technology for overhaul of the social body and removal of barriers to modernization.

Perhaps the most telling feature of educational reform following the GPCR is the disappearance of the "zero-sum," "moderate" versus "radical" politics that characterized public discourse during the revolutionary period, most strikingly so in the Cultural Revolution (Rosen, 1984, p. 65). In line with the goal of refocusing the nation's economy on science and technology, reform era policy took on a strikingly pragmatic tenor. 'Quality' loomed large in this vision, and a number of concrete measures signaled that much of the road ahead would be paved with well-worn stones of the past, as indicated by the re-introduction of examinations, diversity in types of schools, and key-point schools (Fan, 1990; Hu & Seifman, 1987; Rosen, 1984, pp. 66–67). Further developments have involved new curricula and reorganization of primary, secondary, and higher education (Rosen, 1984, pp. 66–67). And while reform to primary and higher education systems have been relatively uncontroversial, the same cannot be said for secondary schools. If the popularization of primary education has been widely accepted, and the restoration of higher education a necessary but not sufficient condition of success of the Four Modernizations, then changes to secondary schools have been most problematic, especially considering the ways in which they were to be returned to their role as a proving grounds for those striving to be admitted to universities (p. 65). But despite the fact that this system was compromised by unfair promotion, that which emerged following the closure of schools at the outset of the GPCR was plagued by a new type of preferential treatment – this time in favour of a new elite, the children of cadres (p. 70). Pre-GPCR tensions, never fully resolved, were thus re-instated and intensified (p. 71) in Deng era reforms. In the absence of critical analyses separate from the viewpoints of GPCR radicals or an appreciation of the role of social and cultural capital in educational attainment, and especially given the disaster that the GPCR represented, little could be said to counter the resurrection of the elitist features of the old system.

Given the goals laid out by Deng and his successors, it is not surprising that discussions of China's educational reform have tended to comprise evaluations of its effectiveness vis-à-vis economic modernization (Adamson, 1995; Bray & Borevskaya, 2001; Chan & Mok, 2001; Fan, 2006). Also important is the question of schools' success in instilling the values deemed necessary to replace the normative orders of Mao's time, the development of "civilized citizens" in accord with the "innumerable…[and] diverse…ways of acting, doing and being – from bodily functions to governing the people" prescribed and described in post-Mao "civilization theory" (Dynon, 2008, p. 109). Critical scholars of education tend to link modernization and educational reforms with social stratification, concerning themselves with how commodification and the now-dominant discourses of "civilization" and *suzhi jiaoyu* (素质教育 – education for quality) (Anagnost, 2004; Kipnis, 2006; Kuan, 2008, 2011; Woronov, 2008) have shifted policy away from universal access and toward differential provision.

This account of the course of educational reform since the inauguration of reform and opening up is obviously partial. Much more could be said about matters of curriculum reform (L. Guo, 2012; Guo, Guo, Beckett, Li, & Guo, 2013; Huang, 2004; Jones, 2002; Yochim, 2012), teacher development (Guo, 2005; Paine, 1990; Wang & Paine, 2003), popularization (Rosen, 1984), rural education (Yang, 2002), globalization (S. Guo, 2012; Y. Guo, 2012), and, in particular, the various forms of inequality that have sprung up under the quasi-market educational system of socialism with Chinese characteristics (S. Guo, 2012; Li, 2012; Yang, 2006; Zeng, Deng, Yang, Zuo, Chu, & Li, 2007). Such matters will inform the analysis undertaken in Chapters 2 and 3, but for now my aim has been to sketch an outline of the educational matters of most concern in this research, that is, the shifting moral and cultural foundations that undergird the forms of family, diffuse, and institutionalized education that have emerged in the past three decades. Each of the final group of critical scholars listed in the previous paragraph also places such concerns at the centre of his/her research. From a methodological perspective, they give pride of place to the perspectives of parents. In terms of theory, this has resulted in the positioning of parents and, more specifically, the institution of the family at the nexus of state-sanctioned culture and diffuse/institutionalized forms of pedagogic action. In the next section, I outline the significance of this move and indicate how and why in this research I attempt to emulate it.

The Family

My focus in this book is on conceptions of education and educational practices. With respect to the latter, my focus may run counter to the reader's expectations. I am less concerned with what goes on in China's schools, and more with the role of the family in the overall educative process. I am particularly concerned to show how the resurgent institution of the family mediates the educational dynamics of contemporary China. The evidence for and significance of this resurgence will become clear as the book progresses. For now, though, it will suffice to say that I take the family to be the central institution of Chinese society both historically and, despite a series of challenges to its authority, presently. The centrality of the family was on Lin's (2000 [1936]) mind when he considered social order in Chinese society more than eighty years ago. He held that the simple truth of the "Chinese nation" is that it comprises a fundamentally "selfish" citizenry, an individualistic people lacking a sense of "social-minded[ness]" (p. 169). The full significance of this curious diagnosis becomes clearer when one realizes that he does not propose a society founded upon the autonomous individual. Rather, the "individual" in Lin's

CHAPTER 1

sociology is subsumed under a notion of "family," and "family-minded[ness]" is the fundamental quality of "the Chinese" (p. 169). Whether or not the conflation of individual and family is sustainable either ontologically or empirically is uncertain, but it provides a compelling explanation for the apparent collectivity one witnesses in Chinese society, particularly in the educative projects of families.

The family as both a bridge to institutional education and as an educative institution in its own right have long been recognized in sociologies of "Western" education and the family. Skepticism about the positive role of the family in relation to schooling stands alongside recognition of its powerful influence as an agent of family education. As Musgrove (1966) noted at the height of historical conservative panic over the family's decline (Cohen, 1972), "the family still exerts a powerful influence on the prospects, capacity for development, and life-chances of the young" (Musgrove, 1966, p. 1). Recognition of the persistence of the family as a socializing agent was, for Musgrove, a necessary step if the problem of schools' failure to moderate "the influence of family background…when necessary" (p. 1) was to be somehow fixed. Musgrove's faith in the state to set up institutions capable of "[enabling] the individual to achieve the fullest development of which he is capable; to further the cause of social justice by eliminating the influence of 'birth'; and to promote a more unified and cohesive society" (p. 1) was not shared by the generation of critical scholars who would rise to prominence in the decades following this declaration, but his diagnosis of the continued salience of the family certainly was. For a generation of theorists of social reproduction skeptical of the liberal school as social equalizer (Giroux, 1983), the family played a vital role in the positioning of its wards in the social structure of the society of which it was a part. The most compelling of such theorists posit the influence of family cultures, themselves grounded in class positions, as the missing link that explains the relative success of students (see, for example, Willis, 1977; Bowles & Gintes, 1976; Bourdieu, 1990). Recognition of the special role of the family is not, of course, the exclusive domain of critical scholars. Coleman and Hoffer (2010), for example, would mine the stores of social capital held in the family and convert them to human capital via the agency of institutionalized education.

Critical or not, that the family as an institution should have such power resonates with Durkheim's historical view of the family as essentially functional, if not with his ultimate pessimism about the capacity of the modern family to fulfill its modern role (Lammana, 2002). For Durkheim, each version of the family had its own expression of solidarity culminating in the "affectional ties of the modern family" (Lammana, 2002, p. 47). The "modern" family is primarily held together by affective bonds and oriented toward individual freedom, despite the fact that some remainder of earlier forms is retained in the authority wielded by the father over his immature children, though this authority primarily functions to allow for the nurturing of the minor child (p. 52). Precisely because of its grounding in affective relations and its susceptibility to particularistic norms, Durkheim was skeptical of the family as an institution of moral education (pp. 124–125), a view that stands him in sharp contrast to other

"French" views. For Althusser (1970), the role of the family as educative institution is complementary to the aims of the capitalist state, and crucial to his theorization of "ideological state apparatuses," (ISAs) a collection of institutions of the state that function primarily through the transmission of ideology rather than repression and, thus, serving to reproduce the relations of production. For Bourdieu (1986) the class reproductive role of the family is accomplished mainly through the transmission of various forms of capital, economic inheritance being only one of a list that includes social and cultural capital, the latter crucially facilitated by another ISA, "the educational ISA (the system of different public and private 'schools')" (Althusser, 1970, "The State Ideological Apparatuses"). Both Althusser and Bourdieu betray the influence of the classical tradition beginning with Engels (1884), in which the monogamous family was a crucial element of capitalist order, one that ensured the secure ownership and transmission of private property by inheritance. The classical tradition was not, of course, silent on the question of the Chinese family. Weber, in keeping with his Protestant ethic thesis, found the Chinese form of kinship to be one of many institutional barriers to the development of capitalism. This was especially apparent in the way that families, contrary to principles of rational management of interests, invested in education as a means to install family members in higher office to ensure favourable treatment (Yang in Weber, 1951, p. xxvi).

Due to the rapid rise of China as an economic power, not to mention the theoretical inheritance just mentioned, it is not surprising that much research focusses on cultural and institutional factors that might explain the country's recent success. This question certainly lay behind early classical work that sought answers for the rise of capitalism in Europe over other potential sites. Marx (1973 [1857]) believed that an "asiatic mode of production" stood as a waypoint on the road to capitalism and, perhaps most famously, Weber (1951) found, among other factors, Chinese religious orientations to be at fault. In more recent work, China's seat at the pinnacle of economic development in the 19th century is seen to result from institutional stability, bureaucratic efficiency, and an earlier "industrious revolution" that later stood as a barrier that delayed a subsequent industrial revolution (Sugihara in Arrighi, 2007). Indeed, responding to a long period of economic stagnation, the collectivizing Chinese family was seen as inimical to economic development, with its care for all and supposed lack of incentives (Clark Kerr in Whyte, 1996). Filial piety and deference to tradition also seem to work against the potential for creativity and entrepreneurship. The family enterprise in particular was viewed as inefficient and insular and, thus, fundamentally opposed to the kinds of association necessary to the development of a virtuous economic cycle. To simplify, to borrow Whyte's (1996) terms if not his conclusions, the Chinese family worked to stifle innovation, and Chinese firms failed to incentivize entrepreneurship and industriousness.

In more recent years, the question of the role of the institution of the family in China's stasis and/or change has taken centre stage. A massive literature has developed around questions of the role of the "Chinese family firm," particularly the suitability of this institution to capitalist development (Wong, 1985). As

CHAPTER 1

Whyte (1996) details, theorists of Chinese society once saw the Chinese family as an obstacle to development, as did, to some extent, Mao Zedong, whose criticisms of traditional order and legal reforms did much to drag Chinese family relations into the modern era. Often seen as a conservative institution resistant to change, particularly economic change, theorists of this era have begun to focus instead on the role of families in facilitating development (Whyte, 1996). The "educational desire" (Kipnis, 2011), for example, that is a powerful feature of Chinese society is directly attributable to the values and norms of the Chinese family. Loyalty and piety, put simply, are "a very strong source of motivation and performance" (Whyte, 1996, p. 9).

Such arguments mirror earlier ones over the role of the Chinese family – indeed, it's very survival – in the Communist Revolution. It is clear that certain features of the traditional family did come under severe criticism at different points before and during the Revolution (Whyte, 1973). Women's subordination was an early target of reform, and the authority of parents was severely challenged in the Cultural Revolution. On the other hand, it seems equally clear that the family has been seen, by necessity, as an ally of Revolution as much as foe, something that the Party would seek to "sustain and nourish" (Whyte, 1973, p. 1). The early years of reform and opening up provide perhaps the most obvious of institutional reforms that relied on the strength of the traditional rural family. The household responsibility system has been largely credited with restoring the entrepreneurial vigour of the rural family in the 1980s (Whyte, 1992), and much was made of the stability provided by the family when mass layoffs hit the manufacturing sector in the crisis of 2008 (Whitehouse, 2009). Today, as then, the Chinese family remains a crucial site for the fostering of the kinds of citizens vital to the success of the nation. Indeed, through incitements detailed in Chapter 5 under the guise of "family education," it is clear that the family is seen as a partner in the development of the "human capital" that is the primary goal of the new *National Plan for Medium and Long Term Educational Development, 2010–2020* (china.org.cn, 2004; Ministry of Education, 2010; People's Daily, 2000; Wu, Zhu, Chen, & Liu, n.d.). Far from being a barrier, the family is an incubator for the capacities and dispositions that define a reconfigured human capital under socialism with Chinese characteristics.

At the same time, these moves within China must be considered in the context of globalization. As time-space compression (Harvey, 1989) brings about a world more tightly connected through information technologies, high-speed travel, and globalized trade activity, the role of the family as "mediator between private and public" (Berger & Berger in Edgar, 2003, "New forms of state and family agency") would appear to be in question. A world constructed by growing ranks of free, "reflexive moderns" (cf. Beck, Giddens, & Lash, 1994) is supposedly less constrained by both state and family. There is a certain emotional (would that we were all freed from constraint!) and explanatory appeal to this vision of today's world. After all, it is certainly the case that a large number of people are globally mobile and detached from the geographical and political constraints that once held them in place. At the same time, the notion that "collective and group-specific sources of meaning...in industrial society and culture are suffering from exhaustion, break-up, and disenchantment" (p. 7) seems something of an overstatement given other aspects of the empirical present, not to mention an iteration – with a positive normative spin – of an observation Durkheim (1893) made more than a century ago. Withdrawal of the state from social provision under neoliberal logic and the unequal distribution of the capacities required to prosper in such a world means that new forms of solidarity must and do take shape, and they are "multiple, highly diversified, following the contours of each culture, and of historical sources of formation of each identity" (Castells, 1997, "Our World, Our Lives"). Whether the inadequately reflexive take shelter in religious fundamentalism or "freemen" movements (http://freemanontheland.com), reflexive modernization, to the extent that it has so far brought any of its positive promises for liberation to some, has also fostered protective spheres both local and extra-local. Though it has not been fashionable to say so, it seems clear the family is one of these local spheres, one that continues to be worthy of attention for a number of reasons, not least of which is the rising prominence of resurgent East Asian powers like China. To say so is to recognize the inherent Western bias in much of the sociology of the family (Edgar, 2003), if not to indict the notion of individualization and reflexive modernity as false altogether.

But despite Lin's counterintuitive notion of the family as individual, it would be wrong to conclude that individualization is not an aspect of the historical trajectory of the Chinese family. As already mentioned, beginning in 1949, socialist modernization had already made a radical attempt to disembed the family from its seat in "communal and/or lineage structure[s]" (Yan, 2011, p. 209). It is also the case that privatization *qua* individualization was accelerated with the shift to market-oriented reform (p. 210; see also Kleinman et al., 2011; Yan, 2010). Indeed, a raft of policy changes in both rural and urban settings have the effect of "freeing" matters of everyday life from state control (Ong & Zhang, 2008; Whyte, 1992, 2008; Yan, 2010, 2011). This certainly seems to be the case with respect to choice of location of family home and school, not to mention, to the extent that positioning in the labour market allows it, place of work. The return of such decisions, once largely under the control of work units and other government authorities, to the home places the Chinese family in the role of what Boulding (1983) has called "familia faber," a theoretical move that makes it possible to see the family as a constructor of social reality. More than mere pawn of globalization or institutional dope to be manipulated at will by the overwhelmingly modern state, *familia faber* is one capable of collective action, of reading and adapting to extant conditions and, indeed, of manipulating and transforming social reality (Boulding, 1983).

Foregrounding the family as "maker of the future" demands attention to "intrahousehold interaction with interhousehold interaction in community settings" (p. 258). My concerns in this book are narrower than this, that is, the interaction of families with broadly circulating ideas, many of which take material and spatial form in the built urban environments in which they live. I also want to shift slightly Boulding's concept. Rather than taking the family as an agent capable of action in and for itself, I propose to see it as a crucial domain within which the experiences and actions of individuals take place. In this conceptualization, *familia faber* retains its value as a space of "family agency," one that facilitates some strategies that are "progressive" and others that are essentially protective and conservative. But it also allows me to pay heed to "the family as a process of individual experiences, that is, the lived experience of family life" (Yan, 2011, p. 208). After all, it is individuals who, empirically, accomplish the deeds and duties of everyday life, even if they do so, paraphrasing Ong and Zhang (2008), "regulated and framed within" the relatively protected space of the state and the family institution (p. 1). As Boulding points out with respect to newcomers to boomtowns in the US, the reconstruction of the individual and collective social lives of family members is an active process. Still, I would rather say, channeling Marx, that this new social reality is forged from materials given rather than chosen. In my work, Boulding's notion of the *familia faber* creating social reality in the boomtown has been particularly illuminating. In many ways, the radical reconstruction of Chinese cities in the context of the country's explosive economic growth has made all urbanites newcomers re-constructing the social realm by necessity from whatever material and cultural resources are at hand. Urban folk did not ask to be newcomers, but many appear to have taken up the task of reconstruction with vigour.

The City

Where the "boom" in "boomtown" might suffice to evoke the explosive growth seen in today's urban China, the compound's unfortunate other half – "town" – seems laughably inappropriate to a description of Chinese cities. Already massive and crowded by the standards of most other countries, urbanization, growth, sprawl, and redevelopment are turning them into the polar opposite of the entities to which even the most generous understandings of the word town refer. In many ways, it is this removal from common experience and, by extension, from common application of terms that made this research difficult for me. Doing the work of social science is commonly understood to mirror de Certeau's (1984) description of the totalizing gaze of the elevated observer, where "seeing Manhattan from the 110th floor of the World Trade Center" makes an "urban island" of the rich life of the city, "a sea in the middle of the sea" (p. 91). But Shijiazhuang offered no World Trade Centre to "lift me from its grasp" (p. 92). Had it done so, any potential "erotics of knowledge" derived from "seeing the whole" would likely have been interrupted by the ever-present shroud of smog that obscures the city (p. 92). Forced to experience this city from "below the thresholds at which visibility begins" (p. 93), I was nevertheless removed from many of the necessities of life faced by the "real" residents of Shijiazhuang, a fact that accounts for my initial apprehension of the city as spectacle (cf. Bourdieu, 1977; Debord, 1994 [1967]).

Still, the outsider's standpoint, which introduces a distance from necessity (Bourdieu, 1977) that, while a barrier to direct access to the insider's intimate knowledge of social reality, is also a condition of possibility of social scientific knowledge. The shock of my experience of the city as spectacle forced me to see things as an insider might not, convincing me that the transformation of the city must be somehow related to changes in the ways in which people work, live, and relate. As Harvey (1988) puts it, "any general theory of the city must somehow relate the social processes in the city with the spatial forms the city assumes" (p. 23). Relating the two in this way involves taking Mills' (1959) exhortation to develop the capacity to "understand the larger historical scene in terms of its meaning for the inner life and the external career of a variety of individuals" (p. 5) to its logical conclusion, that is, to develop a complementary capacity that Harvey (1988) calls the "geographical imagination." Ideally, such a capacity "enables the individual to recognize the role of space and place in his own biography" and, of particular relevance to my research project, "to recognize how transactions between individuals and between organizations are affected by the spaces that separate them" (p. 24).

Unsurprisingly, Harvey's (1988, 1989, 2000, 2001, 2003, 2005) body of work proved a rich repository of concepts for my own project of geographical imagination, among them "spatio-temporal fixes" (2005) and "accumulation by dispossession" (2001, 2005). Equally importantly, each of these concepts also attaches to a more general notion that urban renovation and cultural change are necessarily linked (1988, 2003). Two of Harvey's works are particularly enlightening with respect to the latter relation. In *Paris, Capital of Modernity* (2003), he writes in detail of Hausmann's transformation of that city, and on its effects on the artistic output of authors from Balzac to Flaubert to Baudelaire, drawing especially on the struggles of such authors to capture the essence of life in the putative "creative destruction" (p. 1; cf. Marx & Engels, 1848; Schumpeter, 2003 [1943]) of mid-19th century Paris. *Spaces of Hope* (2000) brings a similar analysis to the new world and into the present. The redevelopment of decaying industrial Baltimore highlights these processes at work as capital investments both public and private prepare the ground for future capital accumulation (spatio-temporal fixes), bowl over entire well-established if ailing communities (accumulation by dispossession), and construct city spaces representative of a reconfigured, re-classed cultural milieu (cultural change). For those familiar with the transformation of Beijing into an Olympic city or with the general situation in the urban China of today, the notion that processes of creative destruction are underway as various levels of government team up with local capitalists to "bludgeon...[the country] into modernity" (Harvey, 2003, p. 2) will not be hard to accept. Certainly "the annihilation of space" (p. 47) described in this research fits, and I strive to demonstrate the importance of the accompanying obliteration of time in the lives of those residents of Shijiazhuang City whose prospects seem brightest.

In recent years, the transformation of China into an urban society and the conversion of the urban spaces that now house the majority of Chinese citizens have

CHAPTER 1

been an object of interest to increasing numbers of social scientists. Urban poverty is one unfortunate consequence of urbanization and redevelopment, but it has received relatively little attention, not surprising given that the negative consequences of urban-rural migration, layoffs from the SOE sector, and the marketization of real estate generally are relatively recent (Appleton & Song, 2008). Absolute poverty aside, "class-income inequality" has emerged in China's newly marketized cities, in part due to the expiry of a social system that distinguished cadres from workers through differential access to privileges rather than income (Bian & Gerber, 2008; Davis, 2003; Wang, 2003). The extent to which the rise of inequality has been inevitable is a matter of some debate, but it is clear that the shift to a marketized, consumption-based economy has made economic capital the prime driver of social differentiation, meaning that the urban class structure has become increasingly differentiated (White, Wu, & Chen, 2008; Bian & Gerber, 2008).

Combined with Harvey's insights, such examinations have helped me bring order to the spectacle of urban renovation that I initially experienced only as chaos. In particular, they have helped me to understand how economic reform is linked to the rise of any number of urban phenomena, including the difficulties faced by rural-urban migrants and forms of social differentiation such as community "gating" (Liang, Luong, & Chen, 2008; Huang & Low, 2008; Ren, 2013; Wu & Rosenbaum, 2008; Zhou & Cai, 2008). Many of these elements of the urban scene point in the direction of culture, the conceptualization of which I turn to now.

Culture

Culture is one of the two or three most complicated words in the English language. (Williams, 1983, p. 87)

Cultural theorist Raymond Williams (1983) famously proposed an "ordinary" conception of culture – of culture as surrounding us in our everyday lives; of culture as consisting in everything a given group of people do, feel, and see. The value of this conception of culture is that it disputes a definition this restricts its meaning to the realm of art and formalized learning, especially of the "high" variety (p. 93). The latter had its origin in animal husbandry and agriculture, practices within which one "cultured" or "cultivated" something, whether animal or plant (p. 87). Williams did not deny that culture includes the sense of culturing or cultivation the finest of things, but he also recognized a more generalized notion of culture as "a whole way of life," as a collection of "common meanings" that bind us each to the other (p. 93). Both high and common culture comprise two aspects, the first having to do with what is known and passed on from one to another, from one generation to the next, that is, that which inhabitants of a culture receive through socialization, indoctrination, or other means. The second aspect relates to the sense in which a culture is always also coming into being, an entity within which new "observations, comparisons, and meanings" are being made and remade (p. 93). A society is made by its members, its shifting terrain the outcome of "an active debate and amendment under the pressures of experience, contact, and discovery" (Williams, 2002 [1958], p. 98). Culture, then, concerns both observable "things" and processes simultaneously oriented to the past and the future, and its analysis is necessarily a matter of clarification of "the meanings and values implicit and explicit in a particular way of life" (p. 48).

A second theorist, Margaret Archer (1985, 1996) also informs my understanding of "culture" by alerting me to a common feature of its use, specifically the notion that culture consists in "strong and coherent patterning" (1985, p. 335). To be sure, culture presents itself to observers and insiders alike as a more or less consistent set of interrelated beliefs and practices, despite that it is equally easy, upon reflection, to perceive inconsistency, disagreement, and conflict between any given supposedly powerful and coherent element. In Archer's terms, this conception of culture posits a system with a "uniform ethos, a "symbolically consistent universe" (1996, p. xvii) that is binding upon members of a culture (1985, p. 343). It can be safely assumed, that is, that culture organizes people and things together under a common, unitary system. The problem with this assumption is that it leads to analyses that, in searching for coherent "wholes," tend to ignore not only incoherent fragments (p. 335), but also the role of the actual practices of discrete individuals – not to mention the collective activities of identifiable groups of people – in reproducing or transforming culture. Rather than examining culture as a coherent whole, Archer urges us to consider it through "analytical dualism," by which she means that we ought to consider its systemic content separately from its causal relationships (1996, p. xvii). This involves, first, thinking of culture as a "world of ideas" (p. xvii) comprising "intelligibilia…[with] the dispositional capacity of being understood by someone" (p. xviii). Culture in this sense is a system of logically related propositions, the analysis of which involves the search for and description of those relations that may be consistent or contradictory. Second, it involves considering separately the contingencies of the realm of "socio-cultural interaction" (p. xxiv) in which everyday folk show themselves "willing or able to grasp, know or understand" the propositions given them by the cultural system (p. 104). This aspect of culture might be described as the realm of 'real life culture,' spaces of socio-cultural interaction in which the propositions of the cultural system hold more or less force, and the field upon which potential cultural change is foregone or realized.

Archer (1985) demonstrates how making a distinction between "cultural system integration" and "socio-cultural integration" (p. 338) produces analytical possibilities often missed. With respect to the former, the analyst pays attention to "the degree of internal compatibility between the components of culture" (p. 336). With respect to the latter, what is important is "the degree of social uniformity produced by the imposition of culture…by one set of people on another" (p. 336). In this book, for example, one might find a high degree of coherence in what I identify in Chapter 3 as the "order of worth" that orients policy at the level of the Party bureaucracy in contemporary Chinese society, but a low degree of consensus in terms of the way

CHAPTER 1

that contemporary Chinese actually govern themselves in the built environments of China's cities. Certainly this would help to explain the significant gap between government policies designed to provide educational opportunity on a more or less equal basis, and the rather obvious ways in which Chinese parents pursue opportunity and distinction. Policies that promote universal high quality education, that is, have little force where parents are willing and able to pursue means that produce fragmented, unequal outcomes.

CONCEPTUALIZING EDUCATIONAL CULTURE

These conceptions of education, families, cities, and culture, along with cultural analysis based on analytical dualism allow me to reconsider the anecdote that opens this chapter. It would be tempting – and has proven so for too many popular and academic observers of China – to gasp in horror at the apparently out of control educational desire of Chinese parents and the disintegration of egalitarianism that it appears to indicate. While I share this instinctive revulsion, the purpose of this work is to see things differently, beginning with the research questions stated above.

As those questions suggest, it is possible to gain a clearer sense of the shape, scope, and trajectory of urban China's educational culture by asking people what they know and believe, but also by attending to the activities they engage their children in and the kinds of choices they make in terms of where such activities are pursued. Here the perceptions and experiences of parents are crucial to this study, as are the ways in which they 'live' these understandings, those aspects of their lives accessible to an outside observer that are not easily penetrated by those immersed in the hustle and bustle of everyday life.

But even the notion that particular beliefs lie beneath everyday action suggests that more can be discerned of educational culture than that which can be verbalized or observed in the activities of people. At another level of abstraction, elements of Chinese educational culture can be discerned by searching in the broader culture for propositions and precepts that can be examined in terms of logical relations (cf. Archer, 1996).

In order to get a sense of the cultural system that such propositions and precepts comprise, it is helpful to establish the history of contemporary culture, that is, to examine that from which the culture of the present emerged. To propose doing so in the case of China is to set out a potentially long period of time and possible objects of study that is perhaps unachievable in a relatively short document. Therefore, my survey of historical origins has been limited in scope, but has proved productive *vis-a-vis* answering the core questions in the study and, I hope, will counter a trend in the study of Chinese culture.

With respect to educational culture, it is my general feeling that observers of Chinese education have offered much in the way of descriptions of the spectacle of that cultural sub-field. But they have also been excessively concerned to locate the genesis of contemporary education culture – and, *inter alia*, political culture and interpersonal relations – in Confucian and/or other "ancient" religio-philosophical systems. As valuable as such insights are, this focus on ancient roots has the effect of derogating the role of other systems of thought, especially those – both past and present – that amount to direct attacks on ancient tradition.[5] It goes without saying that some of these are part of a political project to delegitimize Maoism and, by doing so, the Chinese Communist Party itself. More importantly, however, efforts to incorporate Maoism or contemporary Chinese capitalism into the ancient tradition are particularly acute instances of the desire to re-integrate disparate movements into a cultural whole (see, for example, Hofstede & Bond, 1998; Peng, 1997), as are contemporary elisions of the socio-politics of Maoism and the present political formation as essentially one of a kind, "totalitarian" governance. Having said this, it is not my goal to propose a *sui generis* revolutionary educational history and culture utterly disconnected from ancient tradition. But my unease with projects of political de-legitimation and cultural reunification lies behind the research questions that structure this study. In the chapters that follow, I am most concerned with exploring the revolutionary roots of contemporary urban educational culture.

Approaching this topic from the two perspectives I have just described – the first corresponding to Archer's realm of *socio-cultural interaction,* the second to her conception of *cultural system* – leaves out what I suggest is a crucial component of the educational culture of contemporary urban China. Standing between everyday actors and high-level propositions and precepts lies an environment that straddles the material and the ideational – the city itself, the collection of places, relations, and institutions within which urban residents live their lives. My claim here is that an urban space structures or conditions the lives of its residents in at least two ways. First, the physical city – its streets, sidewalks, alleyways, neighbourhoods, buildings, and squares – presents to residents a particular set of opportunities and constraints, an assemblage that conditions in a non-determinative way the course of daily life. Second, the city is a pedagogical space. Neither institutionalized nor diffuse in Bourdieu and Passeron's sense (see Table 1.1), it is, rather, a classroom writ large within which a pedagogy of everyday life takes place.[6] Each of these dovetails with deCerteau's (1984) descriptions of the manner in which the urban resident "walks in the city," both guided by the "strategies" of the urban planner and resisting, through "tactics" efforts to plan and design the course of everyday life. In Archer's terms, the city is intelligible – either actively or passively "read" and more or less perfectly understood or accepted – to its occupants, and, thus, can be understood as both part of the cultural system and a space of socio-cultural interaction.

ORGANIZATION OF THE BOOK

My analysis of the educational culture of Shijiazhuang begins in Chapter 2 and continues into Chapter 3 with an overview of changes in the educational cultural system of China as a whole. Taking as an object of analysis a series of calls to *jianfu* (减负 – lighten students' heavy burden), I show that, despite rhetoric that

CHAPTER 1

sometimes suggests the opposite, the Party/government since 1950 has unwaveringly pursued the aim of modernization/development. This is not to suggest that it has always done so in precisely the same way. Indeed, it has changed vehicles if not course in response to political ruptures and as structural and cultural conditions have changed. Educational policy has tended to be seen to mirror more or less precisely this history of rupture, most convincingly in the frameworks of Sautman (1991) (politicization, hyperpoliticization, depoliticization) and Pepper (1996) (regularization/deregularization). Where such authors highlight discontinuity, I seek theoretical purchase in those aspects of society and culture that have proved durable. The surprisingly resilient policy of *jianfu* is a case in point and provides insight into the prevailing educational culture of each period within which it was pronounced. Drawing on Boltanski and Thévenot's (2006) notion of "orders of worth," I demonstrate how at the core of each iteration of *jianfu* lies a renovated vision of the ideal student/citizen. This series of visions, I suggest, culminates – if temporarily – in the "aspirational cité," an order of worth that orients the efforts of today's parents.

Whereas in Chapters 2 and 3 I establish the order of worth that orients the nurturing of the contemporary Chinese student-citizen, in Chapter 4 I look at how the leadership of Shijiazhuang City and Hebei Province is pursuing a strategy that aims to create the material conditions of possibility of the society envisioned in the aspirational cité. To bring theoretical focus to what is largely a descriptive account of Shijiazhuang, I consider the overarching policy framework, *san nian da bianyang* (三年大变样 – three years complete change), that orients the city's efforts to promote and accelerate urbanization and to bring into being a city with a completely new image. I highlight a set of five effects of *san nian da bianyang* of particular relevance to the ways in which parents conceive of and pursue their educational projects. I theorize that, to the extent that the reconstruction of Shijiazhuang has been total, urban renovation is constructing an "aspirational city" that favours those parents best positioned to rear children to become the kinds of good persons conceived of in the aspirational cité.

Chapter 5, *Life in the Aspirational City*, shifts the focus of the study from the cultural system to the domain of socio-cultural interaction. In this chapter, I dwell on the beliefs and activities of contemporary parents by relating the perspectives and experiences of a number of families. I pay attention to how these parents conceive of "education" and the things they do to nurture, cajole, school, and otherwise create an environment conducive to rearing a child that embodies these understandings. I position these stories in relation to the emergence of the aspirational cité as described above and consider the extent to which the beliefs and activities of middle-class parents are informed by the precepts, prescriptions, and propositions of the aspirational cité. I theorize that those best positioned to "succeed" are those best able or most disposed to align themselves with the kinds of preferred persons, knowledges, and learning styles promoted in the *aspirational cité*. These people overwhelmingly – if not completely – experience the new, aspirational city of Shijiazhuang as legible, empowering, and satisfying. Others find themselves less impressed with or invested in this new environment, finding the aspirational city to be frustrating, to be lacking in important ways, or to be simply distasteful.

In Chapter 6 I bring together the observations of the previous three chapters through what I hope are acts of creative and comprehensive theory building. Chapters 2 through 4 deal separately and systematically with three different aspects of Chinese educational culture, the first two with elements associated with Archer's (1986, 1996) "cultural system," the third with a realm of "sociocultural interaction." In brief, these chapters dwell on, respectively, ideas about education and society (Chapters 2 and 3), material manifestations and effects of those ideas in the urban setting (Chapter 4), and the ways in which parents think about and act to "educate" their children (Chapter 5). Chapter 6 is dedicated to proposing a more general theory of how ideational (i.e., the aspirational cité) and material-ideational (i.e., the aspirational city) edifices articulate with the beliefs and activities urban middle-class parents

NOTES

[1] For the sake of simplicity, I use "China" to refer to the Mainland of the People's Republic of China throughout. "Chinese" is a regrettable shorthand, but one that is useful as a way to refer to the culture of the dominant ethno-racial group ("Han") of the PRC. My use of these terms is not meant to endorse or diminish the political claims of Tibetans, Uyghurs and other minority populations residing within or outside of the contiguous territory of the PRC.

[2] This sentence is a paraphrase of Harvey (2003): "My aim…is to reconstruct…how capital and modernity came together in a particular place and time, and how social relations and political imaginations were animated by this encounter" (p. 18).

[3] Chapters 2 and 3 are dedicated to developing this concept. For the time being, the reader's patience is appreciated.

[4] The concept of "aspirational city" is developed in Chapter 5.

[5] This critical tradition is obviously long, but I have in mind critiques such as the liberal-democratic New Culture Movement of the early-20th century and the radical *pi lin pi kong* (批林批孔 – Criticize Lin, Criticize Confucius) campaign of the Cultural Revolution.

[6] I have applied the idea of "pedagogy of everyday life" in a series of photo essays that can be viewed at http://vocationoftheheart.wordpress.com/tag/pedagogy-of-everyday-life-2/

CHAPTER 2

THE HEAVY BURDEN OF REVOLUTION

> Postsocialist changes are not simply about the privatization of the economy or market liberalization but also about the making of new kinds of persons and class subjects.
>
> (L. Zhang, 2010, p. 13)

The evening with friends described in Chapter 1 is now years in the past. Had I known at that time that I would soon find myself in a similar position to my dinner companions – a spouse to a Beijing-born woman of this same generation; father to a first-born, only-grandson – perhaps I would have felt more invested in the topic of conversation and obliged to contribute. Perhaps there was much practical knowledge to be gained that night, familiarity with which would have left me better-equipped to inject my own thoughts into my father-in-law's not infrequent lectures on fatherly duty, or to defend myself against matter-of-fact accusation of "poor parenting" occasionally leveled by my parents-in-law.

But at this point I should clarify the links between this research and personal biography. The field research upon which this book is based coincided with my immersion in and assimilation into the lifeworld of a Chinese parent. Where immersion speaks to the more commonplace demands of ethnographic research, assimilation invokes the practical and affective demands of life in an extended Chinese family. The contingencies of personal life have meant that, in many ways, this research unfolded not only as a sating of my curiosity about a cultural other, but also as a process of defamiliarization of personal and cultural origins. Whatever my contribution – or lack thereof – to the conversation on that night in Shijiazhuang, during the fieldwork phase of this project, matters of family and child-rearing were very much on my mind.

The analysis presented in this chapter is an effort to familiarize the reader with the educational culture of China and how it emerged in its present form. I use official declarations of a policy known as *jianfu* as a springboard to an examination of changes in China's educational cultural system (Archer, 1986) since 1950. Doing so requires that I paint a clearer portrait of the contexts surrounding each declaration of *jianfu*. Obviously there are a number of helpful sketches already available, the most convincing and comprehensive of which is Pepper's (1996) history of 20th century Chinese education. The empirical scope of this chapter is much narrower than Pepper's, and I aim to further tighten the analysis by bringing into play Boltanski and Thévenot's (2006) notion of "orders of worth."

CHAPTER 2

JIANFU: LIGHTENING THE HEAVY BURDEN

From my earliest days in China, I found confusing and distasteful the kind of pressure-parenting exhibited by many Chinese parents in the form of willing their children to *chengji hao* (成绩好 – be a high achiever in school) and *kao gao fen* (考高分 – score high marks). My confusion flowed from my understanding that China is a socialist country, one committed to communal, egalitarian approaches to development. But the spectacle of contemporary Chinese society and especially the activities of parents defied my expectations. Feelings of distaste flowed not only from my upbringing in a relatively laissez-faire, rural working-class home environment, but also from a professional *habitus* – fostered through several years of training and practice – that positively disposed me toward liberal/progressive forms of education and schooling. My take was affirmed by a policy that aimed to bring educational practice in line with broadly accepted educational theory.

I wasn't aware when I first arrived, however, that China's education sector was operating and reforming under the influence of *jianqing xue sheng guo zhong fu dan* (减轻学生过重负担 – *jianfu*, for short), a general directive and a set of mandated practices that aimed to "lighten students' heavy burden." The policy was all the rage (and outrage) in the early 2000s and made for an interesting if readily dismissed topic of discussion in a focus group I assembled a few years later when I conducted research toward completion of my master's degree (Yochim, 2006). As one of the groups' participants put it, "I think *jianfu* is impossible." By then, *jianfu* had, by any objective measure, failed to reduce students' workload. The future may yet supply the fertile material and cultural soil upon which something resembling *jianfu* might take root. But for now, *jianfu* has not proven itself capable of standing up to either the objective scarcity of high quality educational opportunity or the overwhelming educational desire so central to Chinese educational culture.

The failure of *jianfu* despite its apparent virtues raises questions about the policy's meaning and significance. Why attempt a policy that appears to have had little possibility of succeeding, not to mention minimal support amongst those with the institutional power to buoy or scuttle it? On the other hand, it is not hard to find evidence that, despite the notable educational achievements of the Chinese state in the latter half of the 20th century (CERNET, 2005; Cheng, 1990; Cleverly, 1991; Fan, 1990), the prospect of substantive change in China's education system is typically met with a range of responses. With respect to efforts to reduce students' workload, the mood of Deputy Minister of Education Chen Zhili (2000) was strictly optimistic: "as the new [millennium] begins, the ministry of education convenes its first conference – today's 'lighten students' heavy burden work meeting' videoconference; this suffices to speak clearly of our determination and the importance we attach to this work." Experienced middle school teacher Wang Dian (Interview, November 12, 2005) was a *jianfu* fatalist: "the society is developing. And everybody including the old, the young, and the students must work hard. Everything is developing! So, I think *jianfu* is impossible." Most telling, perhaps, was the cynicism of a commentator on a popular education website: "Why is that when China tries to '*jianfu*,' God laughs?" (Liang, 2007). Beyond demonstrating that policy making and implementation in China is more problematic and contested than is often taken to be the case, each comment evokes the long and troubled history of the desire to reduce students' workload.

Interestingly, early on in Vice-Minister of Education Chen's speech we learn that the phenomenon of over-burdened students is an enduring one for all segments of society, raising further questions about the wisdom of the work conference she is addressing: "The heavy burden of the middle school students is a chronic problem that has long plagued China's basic education, and has always been a primary concern of all segments of society and of the people." Indeed, if Chen's determined optimism in 2000 seems misplaced given Wang's and Dian's respective evaluations of *jianfu* five and seven years later, she needn't be judged harshly, for the desire to reduce student workload had been expressed on at least two earlier occasions by none other than Mao Zedong, first in the early-1950s and once again in the mid-1960s (CERNET, 2001; Chen, 2000). It is to these earlier expressions I now turn.

JIANFU IN THE EARLY REVOLUTIONARY PERIOD

In 1955 the State Education Commission made solving the problem of students' heavy workload a priority (CERNET, 2001), an announcement best understood in the context of the prolonged commitment of Mao Zedong himself to the project. Indeed, Mao's legendary ambivalence toward ungrounded intellectual activity in general and schooling in particular was clear as early as 1942 in his talks at Yan'an on literature and art:

> I came to feel that compared with the workers and peasants the unremoulded intellectuals were not clean and that...the workers and peasants were the cleanest people and, even though their hands were soiled and their feet smeared with cow-dung, they were really cleaner than the bourgeois and petty-bourgeois intellectuals. (Mao, 1967 [1942], p. 74)

By 1953, Mao's audience and topic were different, and, from the perspective of guidance for specific policy, the message had become more positive vis-à-vis the role of schooling: "at present the classes in junior middle schools take too much of the students' time, and it would be preferable if they were cut down to suitable proportions" (Mao, 1997 [1953], p. 97). This was not the unbridled anti-intellectualism that was to mark the Great Proletarian Cultural Revolution (GPCR). Rather, Mao's concern stemmed from a need to recognize the hard work of youth in bringing about the Revolution and the resulting neglect of both traditional study (in favour of political education and prosecuting the wars of liberation) and all-around health. This would need to change if the socialist reconstruction of China was to succeed in the long-term (see also Löfstedt, 1980, p. 72). It was in this context that *jianfu* became necessary; the Revolution would fail if it didn't "[make the] new kinds of persons" (L. Zhang, 2010, p. 13) needed for the socialist reconstruction of the nation.

CHAPTER 2

Table 2.1. Early-revolutionary era order of worth

Reference to	Descriptors
Common good	• building a new socialist motherland • development and modernization of both agriculture and industry • pragmatism oriented toward balanced economic development
Persons and relations between persons	• workers = those contributing in multiple domains (e.g., factory, field, home, classroom) toward socialist reconstruction • healthy, strong, courageous, active, persevering, optimistic, caring, • valorization of peasants, workers, soldiers as seen in artistic representations of Mao's thought along with denigration of intellectuals, who are nonetheless key to modernization
Knowledge	• balance of scientific and revolutionary (political) knowledge • knowledge ought to be oriented toward practical problems in rationalistic/scientific manner • rich cultural heritage should be enjoyed by all • literacy is seen to be the most significant educational goal of the revolution at this time.
Teaching/learning styles	• good teaching is rapid, systematic, and oriented to the solution of practical problems • memorization and speed • Figures 2.2 and 2.3 illustrate a new egalitarianism: citizens of all ages and social locations can be teachers and should be accepted as such

The moulding of new kinds of people, however, did not proceed aimlessly. In the early revolutionary period, conceptions of good persons were tightly linked to notions of labour and labouring. Good people were first and foremost *workers* (in all domains) in the cause of socialist reconstruction. Surprisingly, and in contrast to later positions taken by the state, the official attitude toward "class enemies" such as intellectuals and capitalists was relatively generous. Those pushed into these categories were still seen as key to modernization and retained a degree of respectability, however tenuous and ultimately temporary (Hsu, 2008; see also Mao, 1967 [1942]). Marginalized class enemies aside, depictions of good persons at the time made clear that not just any worker would do. Moral tales of model workers abounded. In one of these, Miss Sung, a young woman of limited education, bravely faces the opposition of older women to the education of their daughters and daughters-in-law, and eventually wins these elders to the cause of eliminating illiteracy (CWI, 1952b, p. 12). Miss Sung, like other model teachers, was a dedicated investigator and solver of the practical problems that stood in the way of socialist reconstruction. These teachers were not like those of times past:

THE HEAVY BURDEN OF REVOLUTION

Gone were the authoritarian, self-centered pedagogues I remembered from my own schooldays. Gone too was the reticence of the children toward the teachers, based on fear of authority, and the individualistic spirit among the pupils themselves. In their place were warm friendliness and an atmosphere of cooperation and good teamwork. (Pan, 1955, p. 13)

The main change, however, is in the teaching – which is richer in content and more practical in spirit. (CWI, June, 1955, p. 13)

Those deserving of the label "teacher" were not always employed as such in the formal education system. Dedication to the cause of reconstruction, high productivity, selflessness, inquisitiveness, ingenuity, cooperativeness – all were attributed to those to whom the title "teacher" could be applied. New and faster methods to eliminate literacy were attributed to workers like Chi Chien-hua, "a rank-and-file cultural

Figure 2.1. Freedom of marriage, happiness and good luck (Yu, 1953). Retrieved from http://chineseposters.net/themes/marriage-law.php, IISH/Stefan R. Landsberger collections. Reprinted with permission

29

CHAPTER 2

worker of the People's Liberation Army" (CWI, 1952e, p. 42). Such workers gladly taught what they knew and their examples were followed.

Indeed, such simple acts of emulation were seen as crucial to the industrialization of the motherland, as the example of lathe operator Ma Heng-chang illustrated (CWI, 1952a, pp. 24–25). The dedication and cooperative spirit fostered under his leadership became the model for the operations of more than 6000 production teams. A manual labourer, the elderly Chu Yun-kang, was lauded for his productivity, even as his achievements were duly rewarded and his techniques taken up by others (CWI, November–December, 1952f, p. 16). A "teacher," put simply, was the kind of good person that *ought to be learned from*.

The daily tasks associated with socialist reconstruction were physically and mentally demanding. Thus, the project would be unachievable in the absence of

Figure 2.2. Daddy, this is how you write this character
(Zhu, 1954). Retrieved from http://chineseposters.net/posters/e13-710.php,
IISH/Stefan R. Landsberger collections. Reprinted with permission

THE HEAVY BURDEN OF REVOLUTION

workers in good physical and psychological health. A population of such workers was to be fostered in part through a new "physical culture" that would be created by training "men and women who are healthy, strong, courageous, active, persevering and optimistic in spirit" (CWI, 1952d, p. 40). As in other domains, this new purpose for "national physical culture" was contrasted with that which it would replace – the physical culture encouraged under the fascism of the Guomindang,[1] a form of "sports degraded by commercialization," used to "train fascist bullies," and characterized by the brutalization and injury of opponents (p. 40). The new physical culture was meant to be, as one might expect, "truly of, for, and by the people" (p. 40).

As these tales of productive model teachers and workers implied, good persons ought to relate to one another in particular ways, as they did, apparently, in the "new" city of Chongqing,[2] where everything was said to have changed after 1950

Figure 2.3. Helping mama study culture
(Yu, 1956). Retrieved from http://chineseposters.net/posters/e15-382.php,
IISH/Stefan R. Landsberger collections. Reprinted with permission

31

CHAPTER 2

(Cheng, 1952). No longer ill-natured and quarrelsome, their bonds cast off, people were "most polite and helpful to one another" (p. 49). As in the stories above promoting the links between collective labour, innovation, and productivity in factories, a collective spirit was the order of the day in bringing about new socialist cities. Indeed, the new people of New Chongqing were not merely friendly; they held "violence and vituperation" in contempt (p. 49). Such relations were to be generalized in New China, as each of Figures 2.1 to 2.3 seek to portray. These new relations between persons ran contrary to traditional norms: Figure 2.1 depicts a man and woman as equals in marriage; Figure 2.2 glorifies a father happy to be corrected by his eager son; in Figure 2.3 the sight of a mother accepting the tutelage of her daughter appears both desirable and natural.

These images typify the broad movement to cast off traditional roles and divisions in all fields. Manual labourers were no longer to be held to a restricted notion of production. Despite the veneration of practical knowledge (i.e., knowledge oriented toward solutions to quotidian problems of industrial or agricultural production), other forms of knowledge, especially that expressed in the rich cultural heritage of the motherland, were to be made available for the enjoyment of all. Indeed, workers normally engaged in practical production were shown to have much to offer as cultural producers, as did the humble Kao Yu-Pao, "soldier-writer of new China" (CWI, 1952c, pp. 40–41; see also Shen, 1952). Cultural production, despite the veneration of such figures and formal declaration of the need for "raising of the cultural level of the People" (CCP, 1949, Article 41), remained fundamentally instrumental. Artistic expression was not valued for its aesthetic qualities or other altruistic ends, such as the happiness of workers. Rather, cultural activities and products were tightly connected to "the training of personnel for national construction" (Article 41). Widespread production and consumption of culture was meant "to awaken their political consciousness, and to enhance their enthusiasm for labour" (Article 45).

> The basic principle for the economic construction of the People's Republic of China is to develop production and bring about a prosperous economy through the policies of taking into account both public and private interests, of benefiting both labour and capital, of mutual aid between the city and countryside, and circulation of goods between China and abroad. (CCP, 1949, Article 26)

In retrospect, an overarching concern with balanced or all-around development of citizens was as central to the new regime as it is to today's leaders, though the qualities seen to constitute a developmentally balanced individual have certainly changed. In the early revolutionary period, each individual was inextricably bound to the broader project of creating a "quality" population both "red and expert" (Mao, 1977 [1957], p. 490). But it was a relatively broad notion of what the balanced person ought to be and do, and embraced what appear to be a number of highly progressive principles. Balance was inherent in the principles put forward in codes of conduct such as the "Rules of Conduct for Primary School Students" (Ministry of Education, 1980 [1955]):

Endeavour to be a good student; good in health, good in study and good in conduct. Prepare to serve the Motherland and the people...

Respect the principal and the teachers...

Respect and love your parents. Love and protect your brothers and sisters. Do what you can to help your parents...

Eat, rest and sleep at regular hours. Play and take exercise frequently to make your body strong. (p. 84; also in Spring, 2006, p. 92)

While the code did address the pressing tasks of the revolutionary present, traditional values were not seen to be incompatible. Exhortations to respect teachers and parents, for example, expressed the importance of balance and figured prominently in propaganda campaigns. Figures 2.2 and 2.3 demonstrate a balance of revolutionary and traditional culture; children teach their elders in dramatic role reversals made natural by the respectful manner of the interaction. Indeed, both new and traditional values such as those promoted in the rules of conduct suffused the legal and propaganda materials of the day. The new marriage law of 1950 and its provisions, for example, codified not only the equality of men and women in marriage, but also the obligation of married couples to care for elders: "Parents have the duty to rear and to educate their children; the children have the duty to support and to assist their parents. Neither the parents nor the children shall mistreat or desert one another" (Marriage Law, 1975 [1950], p. 7).

As Table 2.1 shows, *jianfu* in the early revolutionary period was not a matter of reducing workload *per se,* or with students' freedom from the oppression of externally imposed tasks, although it clearly appealed to the emotions of parents who might feel guilty at driving their children to ever greater scholastic and social heights. Rather, *jianfu* was more concerned with renovating the physical and psychological makeup of the population.

The policy went hand-in-hand with a broader revolutionary program that aimed to create the institutional (i.e., family, school, workplace, etc.) conditions of possibility of a new, socialist citizenry – of children respectful of parents and elders; of parents respectful of the future potential of the nation embodied in their children; of citizens concerned with and willing to work toward the uplift of their fellows; of students of all kinds willing to work collectively to solve practical problems of production; of willing teachers dedicated to collaboration with their students – each and every one dedicated to building a meaningfully socialist motherland.

JIANFU IN THE GREAT PROLETARIAN CULTURAL REVOLUTION

The lowly are most intelligent; the elite are the most ignorant. (CWI, 1975, Cover)

In 1964, a bulletin of the Revolutionary Ministry of Education Provisional Working Group identified "three excesses" related to "the phenomenon of primary and middle

CHAPTER 2

school students' heavy burden...: too many types of courses, too many after-school assignments, too many tests and examinations" (CERNET, 2001). It also identified a cause for the phenomenon in a "unilateral mentality of pursuit of higher levels of education" (CERNET, 2001). As in the early-Revolutionary period, the call to *jianfu* was closely associated with the agitations of Mao, evidenced in a directive to Minister of Propaganda Lu Dingyi:

> The burden of students is too heavy and has a negative effect on their health. Also, much of their studies are useless. I recommend that all activities be cut by one third. Please invite representatives of the teachers and officials to discussions on how to put this recommendation into practice. (Mao, 1965 in CERNET, 2001)

Penned on the occasion of his reading of a report that sounded the alarm on increased stress and declining health amongst Beijing normal school students, this response is notable for its denigration of study, a harbinger of the most extreme anti-intellectual moments of the Cultural Revolution.[3] A second directive provides more specific evidence of Mao's intentions:

> The students are in a similar position. Their studies are their chief work; they must also learn other things. In other words, they ought to learn industrial, agricultural, and military work in addition to class work. The school years should be shortened, education should be revolutionized, and the domination of our schools by bourgeois intellectuals should by no means be allowed to continue. (Mao, 1966, "notes on the report")

Where in the early Revolutionary period Mao was concerned with the reduction of all forms of study including politics, comments of this kind set the stage for the all-consuming political struggle of the Cultural Revolution, a movement that saw the virtual closing-off of standard educational practice for two years and its general interruption for nearly ten years.

As discussed above, the early-revolutionary period was marked by a concern with a more balanced education and moves to deemphasize political study following the Revolutionary war. The focus of education shifted to the development of basic knowledge and skills required by socialist reconstruction and a praxis grounded in manual labour. The Great Proletarian Cultural Revolution, by contrast, rebalanced educational work in favour of political activism, a radical egalitarian vision of education, and the notion that political work was a necessary first step toward correctly solving the practical problems of socialist development. In terms of entry to higher education, this meant not only the reversal of privileges in favour of workers, peasants, and soldiers, but also the radicalization of the idea of balance by extending to "intellectuals" the requirement to engage in physical labour (Löfstedt, 1980, p. 126). In this context, *jianfu* referred to the re-focusing of the educational efforts on political labour in aid of class struggle and manual labour. More radical still was the notion of "de-schooling" in the first two years of the GPCR, "the

Table 2.2. Order of worth of the cultural revolution

Reference to	Descriptors
Common good	• Development as transformation of mode of production via ideational transformation, i.e., transformation of the material realm could not be achieved strictly through material means • pragmatism oriented toward radical egalitarianism
Persons and relations between persons	• youth • radical, exclusive valorization of workers, peasants, soldiers • more red rather than expert (Kent, 1981) • denunciation of intellectuals (e.g., teachers)
Knowledge	• new over old • radical valorization of "correct" political understanding • denunciation of excessive academic school work
Teaching/learning styles	• learning from the People • learning from practice • self-examination, self-criticism, self-rectification

ultimate goal...[of which] was to break all institutional barriers between school and society" (Cheng & Manning, 2003, p. 360). This revised mode of revolution was to be "broader and deeper" and was wholly dedicated "to [creating] public opinion, to [doing] work in the ideological sphere" (CPP, 1966, "A New Stage"). It was, in other words, an explicitly moral war that sought to overthrow an old order that had proved unable to bring about socialist development. While it did seek destruction of the old, it also presented a positive program, at the centre of which was a new portrait of the new socialist man, how such men were to relate to one another, and the kinds of knowledge and pedagogical relations should be put in place to advance socialist development.

During the Cultural Revolution, a different set of evaluative precepts emerged. Whereas in the early-Revolutionary period people were seen to be more or less meritorious based on their *demonstrable* commitment to the revolution – that is, through the activities they engaged in in support of social reconstruction – the Cultural Revolution doubled-down on the familiar test of class background, a decisive criteria that could be used to judge the commitment of individuals to the Revolution. One's historical membership in a desirable class came before tests of ability, though the latter continued to be important. New models of good people proliferated as the GPCR gathered speed. Red Guards represented an ideal of devotion to Chairman Mao. Studious in all things Mao and eager to display the fruits of their political labour, they were leaders of the common people, despite their youth. They initiated readings and praise of Mao and were resolute as though they were "steeling themselves in the fire of struggle" and determined to "wash away all the dirt left over from the old society" (Red Guards, 1967, p. 43). They struggled "to spread with fervour the invincible thinking of Mao Tse-tung" (p. 43),

CHAPTER 2

taking the initiative in one case to fasten red flags to the front of Beijing's buses and trollies. Special physical capacities accrued to these devoted pupils of Mao. Limited food and long hours did not discourage them in their missions, despite the fact that some were "barely 10 years old" (p. 43). They were a "shock force…performing immortal deeds to eradicate what is bourgeois and foster what is proletarian" (Pien, 1967, p. 6). Stories of the Red Guards often included examples of how parents used these models to guide their children, indicating that depictions of models were meant to provide guidance not only to children, but also to adults in terms of how to evaluate and relate to their new socialist children. Indeed, people in general were schooled in how to receive tales of the quotidian exploits of models. Red Guards, these reports tell us, were "praised…as excellent" by "China's workers, peasants and soldiers and other revolutionary masses, and the revolutionary people of the world" (p. 6).

Figure 2.4. Criticize the old world and build a new world with Mao Zedong Thought as a weapon (Propaganda Poster Group Shanghai, 1966). Retrieved from http://chineseposters.net/posters/e15-699.php, IISH/Stefan R. Landsberger collections. Reprinted with permission

THE HEAVY BURDEN OF REVOLUTION

Such portraits of the ideal Red Guard suggest that good people during the GPCR were governed by an ethic of self-sacrifice whose normative locus was the collective nation rather than the family. Consider the troop of Red Guards from Dalian who, taking the Red Army's Long March as a model, march from Dalian to Beijing rather than take a free train ride: "we want to temper and steel ourselves in the revolutionary movement" (A Long March, 1967, p. 11). Another such person is presented in the tale of Chang Yung-ching, who "dashed into the sea of fire" to open a valve in order to let off building pressure (Liu, 1967, pp. 26–31). In this story of the importance of "self-sacrifice for the people," Chang gave his life "heroically before he had time to carry out his aim" (p. 29). Even before his fiery apotheosis, he knew what to do as a result of his devotion to "creative study and application of Chairman Mao's works" (p. 29). He knew that such devotion could give him the power to overcome all kinds of obstacles, including poor health: "Comrade Chang was in poor health with a severe stomach ailment, but he worked tirelessly no matter how he felt" (p. 29). Collective obstacles could be overcome in much the same way, as demonstrated

Figure 2.5. New socialist things are good (anon, 1965). Retrieved from http://chineseposters.net/themes/new-socialist-things.php, IISH/Stefan R. Landsberger collections. Reprinted with permission

37

CHAPTER 2

by the Tachai production brigade's winning of a bumper harvest through assiduous application of Mao's core teachings (Chen, 1967).

It was specifically *political* study that allowed Chang to do the right thing, demonstrating that study itself was not an abstract value. Rather, it was study of *the right kind* of knowledge that could lead one to salvation. Returning to the *jianfu*, in the GPCR what needed to be reduced was not "education" or "study" *per se*, but, rather, learning or schooling of a particular kind. The GPCR held up different forms of knowledge and different modes of learning for emulation. Indeed, the body of knowledge represented in Mao Zedong Thought was the key to the accomplishment of all important tasks. It allowed devoted revolutionaries to "bend nature to [their] will" (Li, 1967, pp. 36–39). At the same time, heavy critiques of valued knowledges of the past were issued, the most famous target of which was "the poisonous influence" of Confucius (Chang, 1967; see also Soong, 1975 [1937]). The "Gang of Four's" Jiang Qing – who enjoyed high-status as a model of Cultural Revolutionary virtues – was in the vanguard of those aggressively pursuing the movement to "weed through the old to let the new emerge" (Chiang, 1967, p. 5).

The four posters included in this section (Figures 2.4 to 2.7) illustrate some of the precepts and propositions of the order of worth of the Cultural Revolution. Figure 2.4 represents a call to unrestrained critique of the past, a critique based solely on the word of Mao as contained in the little red book. In the upper right, the viewer is reminded of Mao's (1957) famous exhortation to be on guard against the spread of

Figure 2.6. Educated youth must go to the countryside to receive re-education from the poor and lower-middle peasants! (Revolutionary Committee of Sichuan Art Academy, 1969). Retrieved from http://chineseposters.net/posters/e15-35.php, IISH/Stefan R. Landsberger collections. Reprinted with permission

THE HEAVY BURDEN OF REVOLUTION

dangerous, counter-revolutionary ideas: "All erroneous ideas, all poisonous weeds, all ghosts and monsters, must be subjected to criticism; in no circumstances should they be allowed to spread freely." In the second, Figure 2.5, joy and confidence adorn the faces of idealized revolutionary citizens whose virtue is signaled by the co-presence of any number of good socialist things – a little red book, *yangbanxi* (样板戏 – eight model plays promoted by Jiang Qing), barefoot doctors, *geming weiyuanhui* (革命委员会 – Revolutionary Committees), and others (chineseposters.net, 2013). A third, Figure 2.6, portrays what is arguably the best known feature of the GPCR's movements – the forced migration of educated urban youth to the countryside. These youth, like the new socialist things of Figure 2.5, find joy in their submission to the truth of Mao Zedong Thought inspired labour in the countryside. What might otherwise be a humiliating experience is merely humbling, the impact lessened by the knowledge of one's virtuous service to a nation progressively illuminated by the brilliant red sun of Communism rising in the east. The fourth and final poster in this section, Figure 2.7, encapsulates the spirit of the most radical of all aspects of the Cultural Revolution, extending explicit permission – indeed, exhortation – to eternal rebellion against all mistaken ideas of the past, present, and future.

Figure 2.7. Hold high the great red banner of Mao Zedong to wage the great proletarian cultural revolution to the end – revolution is no crime, to rebel is justified (Revolutionary rebel command of the Shanghai publishing system, 1966). Retrieved from http://chineseposters.net/posters/e13-764.php, IISH/Stefan R. Landsberger collections. Reprinted with permission

CHAPTER 2

Jianfu in the Cultural Revolution took aim at the subjects, relations, and modes of education of the early Revolutionary period. Indeed, the order of worth that emerged during the GPCR can be read as a radicalization of the revolutionary precepts and propositions of the Revolution's early days. Where youth was elevated in the previous period, it was positively fetishized in the GPCR as children came to represent political purity and the possibility of a better collective future. The same can be said of the status progression of previously despised classes of people such as peasants and industrial workers. Not all members of these groups experienced the same fate as the work of classifying of people was also ramped up. Documents of the previous period tended to use broadly defined categories (e.g., worker, peasant, soldier, capitalist). In the GPCR, there was a proliferation of groupings, as much importance was ascribed to inherited "redness." At the same time, the virtuous person could become so by pursuing a narrowly defined political knowledge, which was equal to or more important than technical expertise. Indeed, the former was seen to be a precondition for the development of the latter in an era of radical idealism. It is this inversion of value that explains the plight of intellectuals in the GPCR. They were seen, quite simply, to possess the wrong kind of knowledge about inappropriate subjects and to use the wrong methods to gain and pass it on. Vessels of a cargo they could never unload and replaced by youth, peasants, workers, and soldiers as the preferred teachers of the nation, they came to be seen as oppressors, models par excellence of that which prevented socialist development.

Even before the fall of the Gang of Four, the radical volume of the GPCR had been dialed down. By late 1975, new models of political/practical work balance were being put forward. Out of Shanghai came indications that the GPCR, in its criticism of "the revisionist line that divorced school from proletarian politics, real life and work" (China Reconstructs Correspondents, 1975, p. 42), might have gone too far in its denigration of expertise and education. Presumably crises of production, education, and social order had drawn into question the notion that political study ought to take the lead in the search for the proper balance between work and study. New models began to emerge, such as "College" Wang, whose nickname was a badge of respect rewarded for his success as a learner of non-doctrinal knowledge (Yung, 1975). Indeed, reminders of Mao's comments on the need to balance "proletarian politics" and "productive labour" began to appear frequently, signaling a renewed commitment to the moral, intellectual, and physical development of citizens (p. 3). Images of hyper-revolutionary young Red Guards faded to the background in favour of a more representative depictions of good persons comprising the old, middle-aged and young alike (Han, 1975, pp. 2–5). Calls to re-balance types of knowledge and modes of learning became prominent at this time as students were called upon to combine the lessons of the early revolution and the GPCR "through combining study, productive labor and scientific experimentation" (Staff Reporter, 1975, p. 2).

This early rhetoric of re-balance, however, was only a prelude to the more thoroughgoing transformation that would mark the period following the death of

Mao and the return to prominence of Deng Xiaoping. In the next chapter, I turn my attention to this period, using *jianfu* as an object of analysis to open a window on the educational culture of contemporary China.

NOTES

1. Most commonly rendered *Kuomintang*.
2. Also *Chungking*.
3. Macfarquhar and Schoenhals (2006) recent account of *Mao's Last Revolution* is perhaps the most exhaustive account of the political maneuverings that led to and continued to fuel the chaos of the Cultural Revolution for more than ten years.

CHAPTER 3

THE "REFORM" ERA & THE EMERGENCE OF THE ASPIRATIONAL CITÉ

In accordance with the strategic arrangement of the 17th Communist Party of China National Congress to[, the plan aims to] "give priority to education and turn China into a country rich in human resources."
(Ministry of Education, 2010)

But this moral obligation, which was and remains vulnerable to the enormous pressures an authoritarian state can exert on critical inquiry, is now further complicated by the sheer motility of Chinese intellectual life itself, which has experienced a rapid change of habitus and attendant demands from the 1990s to the present.
(Davies, 2007)

Becoming and learning to be a parent has, at times, made the writing of this document easier and, at others, infinitely more troublesome. Ease and trouble clashed when I read Amy Chua's (2011) controversial *Battle Hymn of the Tiger Mother*. For some, Chua's aggressive, interventionist approach to parenting – and here one must pause to say that Chua seems to equate "parenting" with "educating," "educating" with "schooling," and both "educating" and "schooling" with ensuring that her children are better than everyone else – is a reminder of the lengths to which some will go will go to defeat "the competition." For others, her vision of the parent-child relationship appears as an abusive horror show. If many of the latter group have missed, as Chua and her daughters claim (Chua-Rubenfeld, 2011; Cochran, 2011), the irony that is responsible for fascination, horror, and page-turning quality alike, most have also missed the sociological insight most useful to understanding Chua's would-be guidebook for the hyper-competitive.

Whatever its strengths and weaknesses, Chua's book was quickly translated into Chinese and took its place among the much consumed and discussed treatises on model parenting that have exploded as part and parcel of the marketization of the mainland publishing industry (Kong, 2005; also see Kuan, 2008, for an excellent discussion of such books). The most famous of these, like Chua, take Anglo-American upper middle-class norms as their models, underscoring the "cultural politics of class rarely discussed in popular discourse" (p. 46). The notion that hers is a particularly "Chinese" method of parenting ought to be aggressively disputed, for while some parents who participated in this study expressed admiration for Chua's

CHAPTER 3

successes and some sheepishly admitted to having employed similar tactics at times, few held that her image of the "Chinese parent" could be taken to represent the norm in contemporary Chinese society. On the whole, they recognized the dedication and persistence, qualities they hoped to foster in themselves, but not the brutality and acquisitiveness, save for offering up negative evaluations of others who exhibit such behaviours.

It is this response from Chinese parents that highlights a significant flaw in Chua's claims to special knowledge of Chinese educational culture. Her "Tiger Mother" is a cartoonish figure drawn from a Chinese culture frozen in time, at best partial due to its failure to take into account countervailing tendencies and desires that characterize Chinese educational culture. Specifically, Chua's "Chinese mother" fails to take into account a long-standing preoccupation of both parents and policy makers in the birthplace of this supposed unchanging tradition – precisely the desire to overcome the kind of obsessive and often destructive tactics championed by Chua. The purpose of this chapter is to draw attention to this countercurrent, which might, superficially, be seen to contradict the spectacle of educational desire. The demands imposed on parents under the logic of scarcity and social competition rest uneasily alongside more moderate, gentle parental instincts, meaning that parents harbour feelings of guilt at constantly putting their children to the test (Kuan, 2008, 2011). An almost Quixotic impulse to ease the pressure that haunts the lives of parents and their children can be discerned in both the every day talk of parents and in the continual return to the policies oriented around the idea of *jianfu*.

THE EMERGENCE OF THE ASPIRATIONAL CITÉ

By 1994, more than fifteen years into the reform and opening-up that began with Mao's passing in 1976 and Deng's rise two years later, *jianfu* had taken on a new inflection. In a news release, the National Education Commission announced its plan to alleviate the heavy burden of primary and middle school students' lessons (CERNET, 2001). Schools were directed to work toward change in an "examination-oriented education system," to tighten control over class schedules (eliminate the practice of excessive lessons outside the curriculum guidelines), and reduce the dominance (frequency) of examinations (2001). Reference to political education and class struggle are notable mainly in their relative absence from educational documents of the 1990s. Education had been thoroughly renovated as a pragmatic exercise supportive of Deng's four modernizations and economic development (Deng, 1987 [1978]). By implication, *pingheng fazhan* no longer referred to work-life balance or to political correctitude but, rather, to a contemporary notion of child development as both individualistic, i.e., focused on the learner's individual development rather than an exercise in conformity meant to adapt the child to traditional norms of valued knowledge, and as an act of developing creativity and independent thought. Exams were no longer seen as a desirable way to make distinctions between students; rather, they were seen as an impediment to balanced development and, by implication, the kind of *suzhi* necessary under "socialism with Chinese characteristics" (see Wang, 1998). This declaration should also be understood in light of the fear of declining quality in the system as a whole following a long period of rapid popularization (Bakken, 1988).

To be sure, there have been many important changes in China in the past two decades, not least of which is the ascent of three new leader leadership groups for whom the Dengist vision is unassailable. We have seen the decline of the household responsibility system and the destruction of much of the state owned sector, not to mention the rise of what some see as a corruption of a golden decade (i.e., the 1980s) in the rise of a less generous or more rapacious capitalism (see especially Huang, 2008). The latter seems to have been confirmed in the early 2000s with the official recognition of Jiang Zemin's *san ge daibiao* (三个代表 – "Three Represents"), broadly seen as the intellectual and political justification for the entry of capitalist entrepreneurs into the Communist Party of China (CCP).[1] Furthermore, into its third decade of double-digit growth, the time has perhaps come for new models to replace those which still position China as a "developing" country. What can be said for certain is that in large segments of urban China, educational development is no longer focused on popularization but, rather, once again on quality, especially under the auspices of *suzhi jiaoyu*, a notion closely tied to processes of differentiation (competition and choice), privatization/marketization (Chan & Mok, 2001), and, according to a diverse group of writers, the bodily transfer of surplus value from the *nongmingong* (农民工 – peasant labourers) to the nascent "middle-class" (Anagnost, 2004; Fong, 2007; Murphy, 2004; Wang, 1998). In this context, *jianfu* once again calls for the reduction of students' school-related workload in order to encourage the *pingheng fazhan* of China's young people (Chen, 2000; Law, 2007).

The *Outline of China's National Plan for Medium and Long-Term Education Reform and Development (2010–2020)* (Ministry of Education, 2010) is the culmination of a long process during which the most current order of worth has come into being. As the quotation above from the document suggests, the overriding aim of pedagoic action in the coming decade is the production of a population with the knowledge, skills, and attitudes needed to excel in the economy of the future. This order of worth has at its core a heavy critique of past educational practice, in particular the lack of creativity produced by the system, said to be the result of *yingshi jiaoyu* (应试教育 – exam-oriented education), excessive indulgence of parents in their children, and excessive pressure placed on children by parents. The overall diagnosis claims that China's education system fails to produce top-notch talent, that Chinese students are "scoring machines," rather than "earnest [applicant]s in their chosen fields" (H. Zhang, 2010, p. 49). It is these qualities of China's educational system and culture that are the target of the most recent manifestation of *jianfu*. This iteration is articulated less often as a specific call to *jianfu* and more in the overwhelming weight of a normative vision for what the system and culture ought to be. The weight of this vision amounts to a *culture* of *jianfu*, a discursive

CHAPTER 3

Table 3.1. Order of worth of the present, the aspiration cité

Reference to	Descriptors
Common good	• maximizing personal potential, charity, volunteerism, compassion
Persons and relations between persons	• desire, curiosity, creativity, love of learning, optimism, autonomy, generosity, volunteership, dedication, all around development, special talents, environmentally conscious • filial piety, codependent learners
Knowledge	• Science, technology, creativity, world education, non-utilitarian, human resource development
Teaching/learning styles	• learning through practice, teacher as guide and mentor and co-learner

regime that uneasily reconciles desires for educational attainment with anxiety over excessive pressure, for the development of the nation with intensification.

China, and indeed the rest of the world, needs intelligent, inspired and creative people focusing on some of the biggest issues facing humanity. (O'Mahony & Bravery, 2011, p. 41)

Most recently, the provision of common good has added elements of charity and volunteerism. While the economic development is still the central focus of policy, the acceptance of inequality and even poverty as a consequence of market-oriented development has led to the promotion of an ethic of concern for the less fortunate. People are encouraged to volunteer to help when they see appalling situations and to give voluntarily to charitable causes. Failing to do so has consequences for everyone in the form of a weaker educational attainment for less fortunate children. Conditions of injustice and poverty lead to problems such as unsociability, irritability, and children who are "loathe to study" (Zhang, 2012, p. 27). At present there are strong movements to normalize disability and remove longstanding prejudices against the disabled. Models of acceptance and charity such as Xie Yun are held up as exemplars. Following a meeting with a disabled father, the elderly woman "steeled her resolve to devote her retirement to helping children in need" (p. 27). The call to be compassionate toward those in need goes out regularly to the public at large, reaching its zenith in Olympic promotions highlighting slogans such as "respecting every life, the world will become a better place" (Zhao, 2011, p. 55), in *Project Hope* (http://www.china.org.cn/english/features/poverty/95783.htm), and in Sichuan earthquake relief efforts.

What ought to replace the educational modes of the past is one grounded in qualities that define a good person in the early decades of the twenty-first century. Desire, curiosity, creativity, love of learning, optimism, autonomy, generosity, dedication, filial piety – all of these come together in descriptions of ideally "balanced" students, parents, teachers, and workers. Each of these categories of good people seek out opportunities for learning in a wide range of venues, including through self-study.

They love reading and self-cultivation like Xu Yuhua, one model this kind of person, who participates in learning sessions at the public library to "enlarge [her] mind" (Zhao, 2010, p. 51). This kind of learning, we are told, is better than playing mahjong or relaxing at home. After all, *good* learning is something to be spontaneously and freely shared with others. But learning is not all that good people do; they also desire to be together with their families. Families ought not to be overbearing; students ought to be allowed to and able to choose their own educational path and to express themselves freely in their studies. The education system itself should mirror this freedom and be freed from central control. Education ought to favour skill over knowledge memorization and move away from strictly teacher-directed content. This free atmosphere will allow students to "cultivate a rounded personality and strong and upright character" (p. 50). Institutional autonomy, academic freedom, and democratic movement are seen as crucial to the needs of the nation. "habits," "hobbies," "reactions to setbacks," "and ability to communicate and cooperate" account for differences in achievement (Zeng, 2008). Good people are able to support themselves, appreciate" the value of work, independence and help for others, building his confidence in his own ability to support himself like a man."

Other guidance in this order of worth targets specific groups. Migrants, for example, have the capacity to be good people, but they have a long way to travel in terms of self-improvement. Like other good people, they seek to enjoy life's riches and pursue their dreams. But they also seek self-development, learn skills, and desire urban life. They work to improve their diets, wardrobes, and lodgings, and they support the national economy through healthy consumption. They are conscious of their bad rural habits, and strive to become good at building respectful relationships in their new urban environments. One young woman, Zhang Qianru, embodies the difficulty of being a rural migrant living in Beijing: "as both ingénue and street-wise woman, [she] may be that odd combination that keeps a person afloat in the urban tides of Beijing" (p. 14). While striving to become good urbanites, they also remember where they came from, helping their families when they return to their hometowns, bringing goods to share and buying and building homes, and are glad to "serve the people" in this way (Hou, 2010). They miss their home towns, but are resolved to do well in the city.

> As a rising modern country with an ancient civilization, it is fitting for China to make a special effort to develop its higher education…and to in turn improve the quality of world education. The driving force for this stems from its tradition of reverence for education and its urgent need to cultivate its citizenry. (CWI, 2011, p. 4)

Similar qualities obtain in the figure of the good teacher. Good teachers are dedicated, intelligent, astute observers of children, and top-rated teachers are crucial to the success of China and its students. Good teachers promote, first of all, a sense of happiness and security in students, communicating passion for their work and optimism. They respect life, as does the model teacher, Zhuo Li, who exemplifies

CHAPTER 3

ideals of progressive education (Zeng, 2008). Zhuo is egalitarian in outlook, believing in the basic intellectual equality of the vast majority of students, and he disapproves of competition as a path to achievement, focusing instead on nurturing the good habits and skills of all students. The good teacher recognizes the dangers of heavy pressure and promotes moderation, believing in a high degree of latitude for children, room for play and experimentation. Another good teacher, Zhang Kailang, has a strong sense of obligation toward his students, feeling the need repay his advantages and pass on his interest in science. Zhang is a hands on scientist, working together with other scientists to pursue results and answer students' questions. The good teacher seeks to "kindle an interest in the natural sciences among students" (p. 47).

The good students such teachers seek to nurture are developed in an all around manner, including in hygiene, culture, and education. They are curious about the natural world, and pursue knowledge through scientific investigation. One such student is Zhang Hao, a grade six student who devised an experiment to test for

Figure 3.1. Respect yourself, love yourself, conduct yourself with dignity, improve yourself. (anon, 1987).Retrieved from http://chineseposters.net/themes/behavioral-standard.php, IISH/Stefan R. Landsberger collections. Reprinted with permission

48

THE "REFORM" ERA & THE EMERGENCE OF THE ASPIRATIONAL CITÉ

a whitening agent – and toxic chemical – in mushrooms (O'Mahony & Bravery, 2011). Good students like Zhang demonstrate "wild" curiousity about the natural world (Lu, 2010, p. 46), but are keenly aware of the connection of science and nation, aware of China's scientific pursuits. Good students have curious, creative minds and a "healthy and optimistic attitude toward life" (Zhang, 2012, p. 27). They carry themselves differently from the potentially unsuccessful. Wang Jingyun, for example, "walks out of a classroom beaming with a confidence and pride rarely seen in a three-year-old" (Hou, 2008, p. 31). Among other pursuits, those who seek education overseas are praised, especially those *haigui* (海归) who return to China. For all *haigui*, Deng Xiaoping is a the model par excellence, demonstrating the kind of fortitude, leadership, and, especially new skills and knowledge that can come from overseas study (Grossman, 2010). All overseas study is valued but the most desired *haigui* are those who hold master's and Ph.D. degrees in management,

*Figure 3.2. I want to be an amazing Chinese
(anon, 1996). Retrieved from http://chineseposters.net/themes/
amazing.php, IISH/Stefan R. Landsberger collections. Reprinted with permission*

CHAPTER 3

science, and technology. Good students work to expand their social circles, to "activate the positive side of their mind[s]" (Lu, 2009b, p. 56), and to study eagerly and pursue self-improvement. The virtuous student desires to "[return] home" and has "a deep passion and ambition to serve [his] country using…newly acquired… skills" (Jiang & Feng, 2009, p. 25). The intellectual does not dwell on past personal tragedies such as those suffered in the Cultural Revolution, but is, rather, grateful and future oriented. Like all good people, the student-intellectual puts his heart and soul into the job and is, above all, not conservative, while maintaining a simplicity of life, even to the extent of riding his bike to high level meetings (Jiang & Feng, 2009). Chinese students work hard, are well-behaved, value education, and aim high. In terms of their modes of study, good students are "active learners…capable of independent study and making [their] own decisions" (Ling, 2011, p. 26). Many students, like Zhang Jin, study English out of interest; others, such as Li Qiang, do it to ensure success (Lu, 2006b). Good students may love learning, but they are not

*Figure 3.3. Show concern for others
(anon, 1996). Retrieved from http://chineseposters.net/themes/educational-series-1996.php, IISH/Stefan R. Landsberger collections. Reprinted with permission*

naive about the material benefits that accrue to those who study well. Education is also an instrumental pursuit, so good students are willing to spend their own money to go abroad. One thing that good students are not motivated by is good marks, which ought to take a back seat to the pursuit of knowledge for self-development, the development of the nation, and the material well-being of one's own family.

There is a way, superficially at least, in which these new aims are pursued by familiar means. For example, the development of good students begins in the home, so these materials offer special guidance on how to be a good parent. It is not easy being a good parent in this new society, but what a good parent can and does do is pursue his or her own education. As a result, *jiating jiaoyu* (家庭教育 – family education) consultancies are becoming a popular way for parents to overcome their own perceived deficiencies as parents. These businesses help parents to see how they can raise the kind of children the country needs by teaching them that communication with their child, who ought to be spoken to as a person rather than as a child, is crucial. Above all, good parents avoid a sole focus on formal education and the pursuit of superior childhood "CVs" by way of entering the best schools (Lu, 2009a). Good parents offer help, patience, and comfort, enjoy the happiness and success of their children, and a feeling of intimacy with the child. A good mother pursues education to improve her parenting skills. Good parents understand the value of education and, in seeming violation of the model for good teachers above, competitiveness: "they do not want their children to lose out at the starting line" (Hou, 2008, p. 30). Children receive early education in order to avoid overindulgence. Still, the goal of good parents is the all around development of their child, often pursued through the spending of large amounts of money at companies such as Gymboree. Here, both child and parent are positioned as learners, the child, through "games, music and arts" develops his/her "coordination, communication skills and personalities, and are expected to become self-confident and sociable" (p. 31). As with good students, parents use such methods to pursue their dreams for their children. They are dedicated to the education of their children, desiring happiness and health for their children, and freedom from the excessive burden of repetitive and pointless homework.

As suggested above, relations between parents and children, teachers and students ought to be reconfigured in a manner no less radical than they were in the early-revolutionary period and the Cultural Revolution. Unlike the early-revolution, however, class is not a fundamental line of demarcation. And unlike the GPCR, respectful, relatively apolitical relations are to be the norm. Still, these new relations are neither traditional nor Confucian. Children are not positioned as servants of their parents and mere passive vessels to their teachers. Good relations between mothers and children, for example, are fostered as the mother remains close to the child. Tight early relations between parent and child are vital to the child's success throughout life. Equality in the home – as opposed a relation of governor-governed – is proposed as a new path to harmony and virtue. Likewise, close, respectful, equal relations between students and teachers set the stage for happiness and success.

CHAPTER 3

The new educational culture should value respect for children and an allowance for mistakes. Students should reciprocate, as demonstrated in accounts of graduation ceremonies where teachers were carried in sedan chairs.

Discussions of what are and are not good jobs are ubiquitous and these provide some insight in the kinds of knowledge valued in today's China. One such list focuses on the most highly desired post-graduation jobs, that is, "international investment banks, consultancy firms and transnational companies" (Lu, 2006a, p. 41). Such desire does not present itself in the absence of notions of academic balance; preferred fields of overseas study are diverse, if also practical if understood in terms of the demands of maintaining social harmony: "energy, resources, the environment, agriculture, manufacturing, information technology, space science, oceanography, nanometer technology, as well as humanities and applied social sciences" (CWI, 2008, p. 8). Notably, excellent students are still evaluated according to test results. But the privileging of practical subject areas is clear, with science and technology leading the way. International competition for "the cream" of the student crop is seen as ultimately productive of higher quality educational institutions on the mainland. High value is still placed on "learning through practice" (Lu, 2010, p. 29) rather than by classroom learning alone.

Still, the rhetoric of the present is replete with the kinds of talk heard from governments around the world. Knowledge and education are inextricably linked to "human resource" development, and efforts are made to link creativity to conceptions of good students. Indeed, the development of "creative talent" is often seen to of paramount concern (p. 29). Such balanced people are good stewards of the environment, as caring for the natural world is one of the "fundamental values and concepts required by every citizen" (Lu, 2009a, p. 57). Good knowledge is not necessarily utilitarian, but should be pursued for its own sake, and much effort is put forth to promote music, art, and literature as worthy pursuits.

JIANFU: A FLEXIBLE POLICY

A single policy expression; apparently diverse socio-economic contexts – how might sense be made of the shifting content of *jianfu*? In laying out the three distinct orders of worth above, I have attempted to lay a foundation for both answering this question and for the discussion of the contemporary educational culture of Shijiazhuang city that follows. What makes *jianfu* a compelling object of analysis is the fact that, while it has received much attention from both politicians and members of the public at large in recent years (see Chen, 2000; China Daily, 2007; Xinhua, 2004a), it cannot be understood as a fresh reaction to a newly perceived problem. It is not, for example, a unique response to the anomie engendered by the rapidly changing economic conditions of the post-Mao era. Indeed, as already discussed above, the notion of and perceived need to *jianfu* raised a stir at the highest levels on at least three occasions in 20th century China (CERNET, 2001). For this reason, that is, because the idea of *jianfu* appears repeatedly over time post-1950, it provided an object through which I was able to trace the shifting patterns of justification in mainland China's education system. As each call to *jianfu* reached its crescendo, so too did references to *pingheng fazhan* (平衡发展 – balanced development) and, more recently, *suzhi* (素质 – quality), though changing social-economic conditions and political exigencies of the day ensure that the meanings of these terms and the implications for practice do not remain static (CERNET, 2001).

In all periods, the "common good" includes some reference the nation as the bearer of what is good for all. Whatever the particular expression of common good, the nation takes on the paternalistic role as guarantor of that good; one need only align oneself with the dominant notion and work toward the good of the nation in order to be fulfill the requirements of good citizenship. From the perspective of the economic, revolutionary China has never ceased to pursue, by one means or another, a path of development through industrialization and modernization. Indeed, while popular understandings tend to draw sharp lines between, for example, the communist/socialist period and post-Mao China, they do so only by ignoring continuity in the modernizing aspirations of leaders from Mao to Zhou Enlai to Deng (Henze, 1987; Sautman, 1991; Shen, 1994). Yet highlighting such continuity does not account for discontinuity in the ways in which these general aims have been pursued. Put another way, if modernization has been the goal of China's pantheon of reformers and revolutionaries from Sun Yatsen to Chiang Kaishek to Mao Zedong to Deng Xiaoping, how is it that the radically different programs of change espoused by each could, to a greater or lesser degree, sustain their claims to legitimacy? In the case of public education, the same problematic appears. The will to construct a universal, high quality, basic education system has been a century-long project, a national mission whose realization has been pursued through various means (Cleverly, 1991). Yet, as described above, at least one desire has remained constant: the will to *jianfu*.

At present there are, of course, voices critical of the direction taken in pursuit of *suzhi jiaoyu* (education for quality). Such assessments provide ample evidence that *jianfu* need not be imprisoned by elements ultimately seeking to justify educational reform. They might, in fact, be seen as a revival of critique in the mold of the earlier Mao, that is, as genuine indignation at the hierarchies of worth endemic in feudal China; indeed, the rhetoric of today's critical voices recalls in detail Mao's egalitarian critiques of the 1940s and 50s (see, for example, Yang, 2006). Put another way, while the official call to *jianfu* clearly reflects a desire to develop a social body responsive to the requirements of an expanding capitalist economy, the viability of *jianfu* in general suggests that critical, outside voices are still able to exert some influence, thus forcing the dominant discourse of *suzhi jiaoyu* to incorporate elements of *jianfu*.

I have already suggested that, at least in the hands of the powerful, the call to *jianfu* at any given historical moment has little to do with an appeal for quantifiable reduction in a manifestly excessive workload. Rather, it is a critique of an objectionable or inadequate present and, at the same time, an endorsement of a more desirable configuration of the various components comprising students'

CHAPTER 3

burden. Following Boltanski and Chiapello (2007 [1999]), I argue that oppositional discourses like *jianfu* contain not only a critical assessment of the educational regime that is its target, but also the resources needed to revitalize the education system in terms of its ability to maintain the support of society as a whole. Each of the policy periods identified above represents a new arrangement of the norms by which people and things are valued in Chinese society, a renovation in that period's "economy of worth"[2] (Boltanski & Thévenot, 2006 [1991]). Policy is grounded in a distinctive normative framework by which people and things are evaluated as more or less worthy (p. 1), arrived at in part through an assimilation of the critiques and resolutions offered by *jianfu* (Boltanski & Chiapello, 2007 [1999]). Thus, an adequate interpretation of education policy entails attention to the economy of worth germane to a particular historical period and the critiques – in the guise of *jianfu* – that acted to spur this order of worth into being.

Whether conceived as a tool of critique wielded by the powerful or by everyday folk, I want to suggest that the order of worth that seeks hegemony in contemporary urban China is usefully understood as one in which *aspiration* takes centre stage. In order to draw attention to the fundamental character of this order, from here onward I will refer to it as the *aspirational cité*. What makes this order of worth aspirational at its core is that it is both *individualizing* and *future oriented*. Here it is useful to think in terms of Lin's (2000) and Kipnis's (2012) discernment of individualization at the level of the family. Where the orders of worth of earlier revolutionary periods re-balanced (Early Revolution) and usurped (GPCR) the role of the family and the power of parents, the aspirational cité is very much about returning responsibility to the family. Whether or not the withdrawal of state provision of social services amounts to a net gain in power for families is debatable, and the discussion of cultural capital accumulation in Chapter 6 indicates that even if it does, it appears that the gains of some are not those of all.

In terms of future orientation, the criteria listed in Table 3.1 that describe persons and relations between persons are suffused with notions of investment in the future. Note the future gaze implied in terms such as *desire, curiousity, optimism, love of learning,* and others. In the coming chapters, such an orientation manifests itself in material forms and practices that aim to create the kinds of places and conditions within which people of such aspirational character can be best fostered and thrive. Later, in Chapters 6 and 7, the nature and content of these aspirations come into to focus as I explore the beliefs, ambitions, and activities of parents with respect to their children's futures. Whether these are expressed as the desire to live "a somewhat better life," "a more relaxed life," or as desire for distinction from others, each can be understood in terms of the precepts, prescriptions, and propositions of the aspirational cité.

In Chapters 2 and 3 my aim has been to establish the shape and nature of the precepts, prescriptions, and propositions that seek to govern the thoughts, beliefs, and activities of contemporary Chinese parents as they go about educating and getting an education for their children. By considering the connection of *jianfu* to the structural and cultural contexts in which the policy was championed by leaders at the highest levels, I aimed to point out continuities and ruptures in the order of worth that oriented leaders and everyday folk at a particular moment in time. In describing the order of worth that prevails in the present, I aimed to show how the educational culture that has emerged since the turn of the century urges the people of contemporary China toward constant self-examination, achievement, and the pursuit of prosperity. This new order of worth, I suggest, is at its core aspirational, and its dominance helps us to understand much about the spectacles of urban renovation and educational desire.

Having examined the educational cultural system in at the level of "pure" ideas, in the next chapter, my aim is to show how these ideas take material form. Also, rather than taking the entire culture of contemporary China as an object, I consider how this aspirational cité is taking shape in the rapidly transforming spaces and places within which the parents of one city, Shijiazhuang, go about their lives.

NOTES

[1] Jiang's "three represents" were adopted as part of the CCP's official ideology in 2000. Seemingly innocuous and considered pedantic by many observers, they were meant to delineate the most current focus of the Party, specifically to represent "the development trend of advanced productive forces"; "the orientation of advanced culture"; and "the fundamental interests of the overwhelming majority of the people of China" (Xinhua, 2001).

[2] At the same time, I am not prepared to deny the possibility that *jianfu* is also an expression by the powerful (or the *would be* powerful) of solidarity with those for whom the lived-experience of the education process is less pleasant and/or rewarding than the promise of modernization has been able to deliver.

CHAPTER 4

BUILDING AN ASPIRATIONAL CITY

> In order to accelerate the process of urbanization with the consequence of building a moderately prosperous [*xiaokang* – 小康] society in our province as a whole in the long-term, we must continuously emancipate our mind and develop innovative new ideas, initiatives, and leadership.
>
> (Hebei People's Government, 2007, "Promote Urbanization and Institutional Renovation")

One year, following a company Spring Festival celebration in Shijiazhuang, I joined a number of colleagues for a late night karaoke session. The event was one of those jarring mixes of classy and tawdry that one sometimes finds at such gatherings. The venue was clean and brightly lit, the furniture comfortable, and the attendees drawn from the upper ranks of management and their courtiers. Both male and female managers and their clients were there, but it struck me as strange that so too were three karaoke hostesses whose job it is to dress and act beautifully, not to mention to pour drinks for, sing with, and generally fawn over the men in attendance. At the time, one could not switch channels, never mind round a curve in the road, without being aurally assaulted by the Beijing Olympic anthem *beijing huan ying nin* (北京欢迎您！ – Welcome to Beijing/Beijing Welcomes You!). To my ears, the song had become quite tiresome, so, when it inevitably came over the speakers that night, I thought that some creativity was in order. Taking my turn at the microphone, I ad-libbed alternative lyrics to the song, inserting "Shi-jia-zhuang in place of "Bei-jing," and encouraging my karao-lleagues to join in as I attempted to localize the song. One of them took up the task with aplomb, but only after insisting that we substitute "*Shi-men*" (石门 – former name of the city and one of many former villages that now constitute the city) for "Shi-jia-zhuang," at once more ably serving the rhythmic requirements of the song and invoking an oft-suggested fix for outsiders' negative perceptions of the city, that is, the rural backwardness implied in the word *zhuang* (庄 – village). To date, city leaders have not seen fit to make a name change but, as the following discussion shows, their utopian dreams are not limited by such small ideas. If the previous chapter demonstrated the capacity of the party-state to dream an aspirational body politic (cf. Harvey, 2003), the local effects of the recent provincial policy of *san nian da bianyang* (三年大变样) demonstrate the audacity of Hebei Province's leaders' hope to construct material manifestations of those dreams – cityscapes capable of nurturing the kind of citizenry imagined in the aspirational cité.

CHAPTER 4

In this chapter I explore links between the ontologically distinct entities that I have been calling "the aspirational cité" and "the aspirational city." I structure the chapter by pursuing two tasks concurrently. First, I draw connections between these distinctive elements of the cultural system and by showing how precepts, prescriptions, and propositions of the aspirational cité take material form as they are inscribed upon the landscape of Shijiazhuang and the surrounding countryside that it is slowly but surely consuming. Second, I demonstrate how the built city acts a component at the level of Archer's cultural system, that is, as a repository of intelligibilia "read to" and intended for the consumption of Shijiazhuang's residents – how the city itself is a collection of spaces of diffuse pedagogic action (Bourdieu & Passeron, 1990). Doing so has been no small chore. As David Harvey (2003) points out in his discussion of the plight of the artist as social commentator in Haussmann's Paris, a city as an object of analysis is far from transparent and never fixed: "the rapid and seemingly chaotic growth of Paris in the early nineteenth century rendered city life difficult to decipher, decode, and represent" (p. 24). Here Harvey is concerned with the degree to which authors who wrote works and set them in that time were able to penetrate the discursive effects of the emerging material forms of the city. These same conditions obtain with respect to both the viewpoint of the cultural outsider and the formalized social scientific gaze, and most certainly clouded my eyes in the eleven years during which I lived in and observed life in

Figure 4.1. Shijiazhuang's new railway station and the underground line that leads to it are a spectacular product of san nian da bianyang

BUILDING AN ASPIRATIONAL CITY

Shijiazhuang. The spectacle of growth and change in this city confused and fascinated me from the outset, but these processes accelerated and reached a crescendo in the years following the advent of a provincial policy known as *san nian da bianyang* (三年大变样 – three years complete change).

THE UTOPIAN SCHEME¹ OF SAN NIAN DA BIANYANG

Shijiazhuang (石家庄) is the capital city of Hebei (河北) Province. It is a comparatively new city sometimes said to be an *yimin chengshi* (移民城市 – immigrant city) because it has grown to its present size through an enormous influx of people from both the surrounding countryside and, as living in the city and interacting with its residents makes apparent, from all parts of China. This growth is only partly the result of recent urbanization and migration trends. Shijiazhuang began its rise to prominence with the arrival of both north-south and east-west railway lines in the early 20th century. The city is also located near Xibaipo (西柏坡) which, along with Zunyi (遵义) and Yan'an (延安), is one of the venerated bases of the War of Liberation. Shijiazhuang is a new city relative to any number of older and more famous nearby places, among them Hebei cities Zhengding (正定, which has now been annexed into Shijiazhuang), Baoding (保定, a former capital city, and Handan (邯郸, capital of Zhao during the Warring States period). As the provincial capital, though, it enjoys a range of infrastructure and services unrivalled in the province's other prefecture level cities. It houses a broad range of government agencies and is the centre of provincial

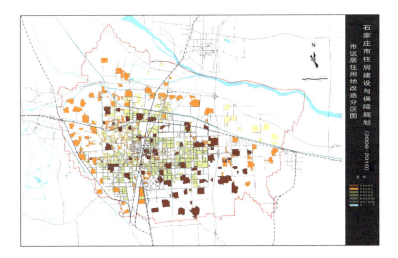

Figure 4.2. Shijiazhuang city residential land use renewal map 2008–2010 (shijiazhuang shi zhufang jianshe yu baozhang guihua; shiqu juzhu yongdi gaizao fen qu tu). The areas marked red and orange indicate, respectively, land to be redeveloped immediately and that to be developed over a longer period (Image credit: Retrieved from http://www.yzhbw.net/news/zt/sndby/ghimg/0001.jpg)

CHAPTER 4

healthcare provision. A sizeable People's Liberation Army garrison that provides protection to nearby Beijing is also located here. Shijiazhuang is an outward looking city. By this, I mean to suggest a number of things about the dominant orientation of Shijiazhuang's residents. First, identifying as a migrant to Shijiazhuang might mean only that one's *laojia* (老家 – hometown of one's father/ancestors) is elsewhere. One could be born and raised in Shijiazhuang and still identify another place as *laojia*. Second, for most of Shijiazhuang's youth, growing up in Shijiazhuang means dreaming about going elsewhere – to university, to larger, more cosmopolitan cities, or overseas. Finally, and perhaps most importantly for the purposes of this study, the normative locus of Shijiazhuang's residents is located outside of the city itself. Its shopping, housing, environment, recreational facilities, and job and educational opportunities are considered second rate. Indeed, Shijiazhuang's image in the rest of China is poor to say the least, and the city is all but unknown to the outside world.

Due in no small part to an ever-present layer of smog, Shijiazhuang is not a beautiful city. Indeed, it suffers from some of the worst air pollution in China, if not the world (Channel 4 News, 2013). But in recent years, it has sought to develop a new image manifested in the massive, indeed, near total demolition and reconstruction of the city space. I first became aware of this new direction as new roofs were added to the city's then ubiquitous six-floor walkup apartment buildings. Curiously, such attention to the city's image came at the expense of thousands of the solar water heaters that are a salient feature of the city skyline, but there was no denying the positive impression made by the brilliant red roofs and new coats of paint splashed on the apartment buildings lining the city's main thoroughfares. A high percentage of street-side small businesses and vendors disappeared, fences and green walls appeared in place of the still ubiquitous brick walls, and many of the city's decrepit, but nonetheless vital, markets were closed or relocated. Some of the former occupants gave way to massive new high-rise apartment complexes, others to persistent voids. In my own neighbourhood, for example, a popular plant and pet market closed, leaving a walled lot that still sits empty after close to ten years. The street fronting this and other markets was torn up and widened; torn up and its sewer and water lines expanded; torn up and widened again, this time at the expense of one of its two rows of shade-giving trees; and, finally but no doubt temporarily, adorned with periodic traffic lights that handle a traffic mix made all the more complex by the addition of private vehicles to the existing bicycle chaos. Banners and advertisements announcing a new program called *san nian da bianyang*[2] were hung here and there, including on the brick walls surrounding the hundreds of construction sites that rapidly sprung up all over the city. Governed ideologically and practically by *san nian da bianyang*, the effects of this renovation have been remarkable in scale.

Later that year, *san nian da bianyang* became a topic of discussion amongst a group of friends who had gathered for dinner at a small Korean-style restaurant on Shijiazhuang's recently renovated Yuhua Road. At that time, the government's new urban renewal program was making its presence felt mainly by its absence; changes were mostly superficial and more annoying than transformative. That night at dinner, its pending

BUILDING AN ASPIRATIONAL CITY

*Figure 4.3. The process of Shijiazhuang's urban redevelopment.
The buildings in the background are being constructed on top
of what was once an urban village*

effects were on my friend Xiao Lu's mind because plans had just been announced that Yuhua Road would again been torn up and widened. Along with the demolition of the restaurant in which we were eating and numerous other such establishments, recently planted rows of trees would be removed and replaced by additional traffic lanes and greenery. "*Da bianyang*," she said, "is more of a *da bian shi* (大便事)" – what city leaders envisioned as a "big shift" was initially received by many as a "big shit." Still, none of us had an inkling of the scale and scope of the renovation to come. At the height of the citywide demolition, city residents began to compare the destruction to that of Wenchuan's (汶川) 2008 earthquake. A joke that circulated concerning the extent of the change went like this: while returning home from surveying the earthquake zone from the air, Premier Wen Jiabao was astonished at the extent of the damage, only to learn that the plane was passing over Shijiazhuang, some 1600 km from Wenchuan.[3] While only a joke, it drew attention to the scale and rapidity of changes under *san nian da bianyang* and the deep impression that the demolition of 7.8 million square meters of residential real estate left on Shijiazhuang residents.

San nian da bianyang began as a policy of the Hebei Provincial government that aimed to respond to and promote rapid urbanization and economic growth by upgrading the province's cities. As the capital city – one with a rather dowdy reputation – Shijiazhuang was singled out for special improvements. The provincial government aimed for a capital city on the level of "advanced capital cities," with improved traffic infrastructure, a high quality environment, "improved cultural quality, and a high-end industrial structure," and to enhance its capacity to provide

CHAPTER 4

provincial level services to the south central region of the province (Hebei Province People's Government, 2007). As with all cities, Shijiazhuang was to be improved in terms of the "taste" of its urban construction, and the city was to be designed and built in a manner reflecting careful planning and ingenuity (ido.3mt.com.cn, 2009). Clear preference was given to high rise residential structures organized according to principles of "scientific planning." Public buildings were to pursue high cultural design principles so as to realize a city with a rich urban culture appropriate to the spirit of the times. Such a city ought also to be environmentally sound and pleasing to the eye, a principle that led to the creation of urban parks and a massive greenbelt around the city. Residents of the city were also made an explicit target of *san nian da bianyang*. Indeed, raising their *suzhi* was to be part and product of the program. *Da zi bao* around the city did more than announce the coming of *san nian bianyang* and projects related to it; they also broadcast messages urging citizens to self-renovation using such phrases as *jiefang sixiang* (解放思想 – liberate thinking) in an aggressive campaign of diffuse pedagogic action (Bourdieu & Passeron, 1990).

> Each landscape, green belt, and even street and neighbourhood – each should project 'ingenuity' so as to become a work of art. (ido.3mt.com.cn, 2009)

San nian da bianyang is in one sense a straightforward instance of spatio-temporal fixing (Harvey, 2005) deemed necessary in the wake of the 2008 global financial crisis. The collapse of international markets for Chinese-made goods meant that something had to be done to absorb the subsequent surpluses of capital and laid-off labour. Many world governments responded with a neo-Keynesian fix, but none did so with the vigour and on the scale of the Chinese government. It responded with a massive capital injection amounting to 4 trillion yuan (approximately $586 Billion US), much of which went into infrastructure such as a new high speed intercity rail system (Barboza, 2008). Government also progressively eased interest rates, provided capital through banks, and governments at various levels implemented a basket of policy measures to encourage new commercial and residential construction, including tax relief for households that purchased additional apartments and granting land transfer rights to peasants (Reuters, 2008). The last of these measures has been particularly important to the enormous spectacle of *san nian da bianyang*. Hebei Province as a whole and Shijiazhuang in particular have taken advantage of the credit made available through state owned banks, money that has gone toward both massive and numerous public infrastructure projects and private land development, the scale of which is apparent in the 2008–2010 municipal redevelopment plan. The city's 2008 redevelopment plan marked a large number of *cheng zhong cun* (城中村 – urban villages) and *penghu qu* (棚户区 – shantytowns) for demolition and redevelopment. Massive new housing projects now dominate long-established areas of the city and stretch to the horizon on repurposed agricultural land on the city's margins opened up by new high speed expressways. Public and private developments go hand in hand, as public projects spur the development of surrounding lands (see http://www.zhijia.com/zt/20111027_sjzhcz/ for example).

Figure 4.4. High rise apartments rise from the rubble of dozens of urban villages demolished under san nian da bianyang. The mountains to the west of the city are visible on a rare smog-free day

No doubt residents have welcomed many of the changes brought by *san nian da bianyang*, representing as they do tangible improvements in cleanliness and order, not to mention a sense of progress and the possibility of better private living conditions. Along with the mom and pop convenience stores and restaurants, many streets have been swept clean of a former commercial staple – the numerous karaoke, massage/bathhouses, and red light storefronts eliminated in favour of wider streets and sidewalks. Relief, however, is partial. Enormous versions of these have reappeared elsewhere, just as large supermarket chains have taken over from the mom and pops. Furthermore, while spatio-temporal fixing (Harvey, 2005) does partially explain *san nian da bianyang*, it is when one couples this concept with another of Harvey's (2005) work, "accumulation by dispossession," that the social effects of Shijiazhuang's urban redevelopment come into focus. Present-day urbanization, especially of the spectacular kind represented by *san nian da bianyang*, is in part a result of a progressive recognition and protection of private property in the PRC (Zhu, 2011). As L. Zhang (2010) points out about similar re-development processes in Kunming, the demolition of urban villages and decrepit housing by necessity involves the transfer of land and other state assets to individuals and groups that stand to profit from the process.

While accumulation by dispossession is convincing as a framework to explain the redevelopment of Chinese cities, what concerns me most in this study is the specific material and cultural effects of *san nian da bianyang*, especially those of significance in the lives of the parents interviewed and observed in this study.

CHAPTER 4

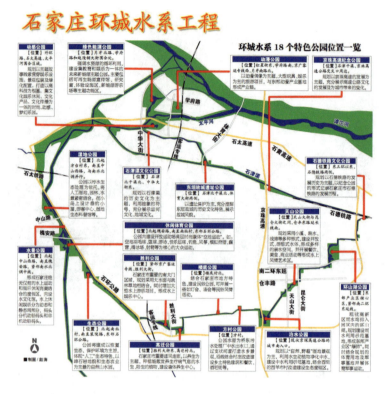

Figure 4.5. Shijiazhuang's huancheng shuixi (环城水系) will see the city encircled with a water drainage system and a series of eighteen parks. (Image credit: xici.net, 2011). Retrieved from http://www.xici.net/d147152753.htm

TANGIBLE EFFECTS OF RENOVATION

Apart from the discursive formation constituted by *san nian da bianyang*, the program has had a number of tangible material and cultural effects. The explosion of new housing construction and the general upgrading of the living conditions of many of Shijiazhuang's residents masks the more fine-grained process of social reorganization that took place under the aegis of *san nian da bianyang*. I highlight a number of these changes below.

The Decline of the Danwei System

In the National Film Board of Canada documentary *North China Factory* (Ianzelo & Richardson, 1980), viewers are introduced to the socialist utopia of Shijiazhuang's #2 Cotton Mill. Narrated by Donald Sutherland, the film covers all aspects of life in this late 70s *danwei*, which, to say the least, exists as a well-rounded community providing work, sustenance, education, and childcare for those in its permanent employ. During this period, to be *in the employ* of a *danwei* was to be a recipient of what was famously known as the *tie fan wan* (铁饭碗 – iron rice bowl). From child care centre and school to shop floor to wedding ceremony, the film shows how – in an exemplary instance, no doubt – the *danwei* both supplied the material goods needed by the society and provided for the material and social welfare of those under its care. Still, comprehensive social provision in this form should not be taken as evidence that an egalitarian utopia prevailed. As L. Zhang (2010) points out, inequality was a salient feature of the *danwei* system. A modified form of the *danwei* remains important today, especially in sectors where state owned entities such as universities and key commodity enterprises actively subsidize housing for employees. Despite this, the role of the *danwei* in production and the organization of social life began to wane in the period soon after this film was shot, and accelerated in the 1990s (Yusuf & Nabeshima, 2008). Concerns over productivity and non-performing loans led to reform of the SOE sector (Broadman, 2001), much of which was enabled through the new contract labour law in 1994 (Warner, 1996). This new law legitimated and furthered a process that was already well underway and which saw, by the early 1990s, one in five workers in SOEs working under limited term contracts (Warner, 1996). Along with the 1994 labour law, the sale, closure, or rationalization of SOEs has meant the dismantling of these staples of urban socialist life. While SOEs are still a vital component of the Chinese economy, they exist today as pared down – rationalized – versions of the total social institutions they once were.

Housing stock once held by the *danwei* have been privatized, sold outright to existing employee-tenants or demolished and replaced by upgraded, private living

Figure 4.6. Another demolished village makes way for high density apartment buildings

quarters. Interestingly, reformed SOEs do still provide subsidized housing for their most advantaged employees, as did the company I worked for in Shijiazhuang. These employees, mostly higher level management, pay for these upgraded apartments, but prices are much lower than the market might otherwise support. Indeed, the gap between the subsidized price and the market value of these apartments is an important source of the growing rural-urban wealth gap, as most rural residents have not been the recipients of the financial rewards made available to those advantageously positioned to gain from the dispersal of *danwei* assets (Khan & Riskin, 1998; Sutherland & Yao, 2011). Most importantly, the withdrawal of provision of housing from the majority of employees has made purchases in the enormous new housing market created by *san nian da bianyang* increasingly attractive for those able to afford them. Educational services (i.e., early child care and schooling) once provided within the *danwei* have not ceased to exist, but these too have been either brought under the aegis of the public school system or *shehuihua* (社会化 – "socialized," i.e., "pushed out into society" or marketized). Private provision plays an important role in this sector, especially as it caters to market segments comprising those unable to access increasingly strained subsidized state sector services, as well as people of means willing and able to pay more for preferential access and/or those who seek social distinction through the choices they make in the market.

The dismantling or reconfiguring of the *danwei* system has affected each of the families observed in this study. Those older than forty years (Xiao Jiao, Xiao Du, Lao Zhang/Xiao Li) began their careers at the tail end of the era in which the *danwei* still provided housing as a benefit to its employees, an arrangement that allowed them to save more of their incomes than otherwise possible. As these homes were offered to them for purchase, they saw their personal wealth established through the sub-market redistribution of an increasingly valuable asset.

As these families purchased second and third homes, *danwei* homes all but gifted to them have come to buttress their incomes as rental properties, a privatization movement that helps explain the growth of rural-urban wealth/income inequality

Figure 4.7. Traditional markets on the way out under san nan da bianyang. Markets like these were once dominant players on the Shijiazhuang food scene. Such goods are now more typically slaughtered before sale and plastic wrapped in the city's ubiquitous supermarkets

Figure 4.8. High cultural facilities and high rise buildings embody the spirit of san nian da bianyang. The Hebei Provincial Library (above) backs the newly expanded Hebei provincial museum (left)

in recent years (Li & Zhao, 2011). The study's younger subjects, those who began their careers later, have not benefited in the same way; indeed, many have had to endure increased job insecurity under reformed labour laws, unless they were lucky or well-connected enough to be granted a permanent job and consequent access to subsidized pricing. Still, most have managed to buy modest properties at reasonable prices and now enjoy the security provided by the rapidly increasing value of their homes.

De-Ruralization

A key component of *san nian da bianyang* was the removal of urban villages from Shijiazhuang. Indeed, Hebei Province's lagging urbanization was a key motivator behind the program as a whole. What's more, the province's new leadership believed that relatively low urbanization and the poor quality of its cities were a prime reason for Hebei's poor overall economic performance compared to advanced provinces (ido.3mt.com.cn, 2009). Over the past thirty years these neighbourhoods – literally villages – have been surrounded and incorporated into the city. During that time, some of the their land was taken over for other uses, such as office buildings and modern collections of walk-up apartments and associated services. But the pace of their conversion was slow prior to *san nian da bianyang*. With its introduction, the repurposing of these lands became an overriding principle that led to the rapid elimination of the last of these rural communities in favour of dense new urban neighbourhoods. In accordance with Hebei Province's *san gai* (三改 – three reforms)

CHAPTER 4

Figure 4.9. Office/hotel towers over the Hebei provincial museum and its renovated north plaza

project that aimed to eliminate urban shantytowns and villages, *san nian da bianyang* called for the demolition of the city's forty two remaining urban villages. These have been replaced by high rise communities (the two-tone brown buildings on the left in Figure 4.4 are typical) in most cases, and commercial developments in others (see the development in the centre background of Figure 4.3).

The legalized ability to "privatize" – or, more accurately, to reassign – rural lands is a crucial driver of both de-ruralization and wealth redistribution, as the fate of land redistributed to peasants in the Revolution and of those who once relied on them for their well-being, is more uncertain today than ever before. The consequences for urban village residents now being incorporated as proper urban citizens is even less so. Many villages demolished under *san nian da bianyang* have been turned over to private developers; others have been developed in whole or in part by the villages themselves under the aegis of pseudo-private village corporations. In the latter cases, Harvey has pointed out the class transformative implications of a peasant class acting as landlords (Harvey, 2005; see also Harvey in Harvey, Arrighi, & Andreas, 2008). Several parents I interviewed for this research told stories of this newly monied class of former village residents, insisting that most, as newly minted landlords, have no need or desire to work, choosing to live off income generated by their rental properties and playing mahjong and drinking night and day instead. The veracity of such tales of drunken peasant-landlord debauchery is questionable, and I have casually tried to verify them occasionally quizzing villagers in the vicinity of the new projects about how their lives have changed. My investigations haven't been fruitful, but regardless, the fact that this image of the lazy villager has become so widespread speaks volumes about the changing understandings of urban residents of the socio-cultural spaces they inhabit. This "final" campaign of de-ruralization is significant both for the cultural upgrading that rural elimination represents – i.e., the purging of the last vestiges of rurality within the city proper – and for the timely provision of the land required for the spatio-temporal fix that is central to both national level stimulus and *san nian da bianyang*. De-ruralization amounts not only to the elimination of village forms of organization from the city, but also the removal, so to speak, of the village from the villager, including the conversion of rural to urban *hukou* (户口 – household registration) and the provision of social services and training for new urbanites (Hebei People's Government, 2007).

For the study's respondents – especially Xiao Lu and Xiao Zhao – de-ruralization cannot happen soon enough. Both are highly committed to the improvement of both themselves and their children, a commitment that has been tangible over the period of my observations. The desire for self-improvement is perhaps most visible in the change in these young women's choice in restaurants, gyms, and shopping destinations. Where they once preferred restaurants with well-prepared, tasty dishes, they now seek eateries whose decor and corresponding prices reflect a sense of their rising status. De-ruralization under *san nian da bianyang* has accelerated the creation of an atmosphere more conducive to a *pinzhi shenghuo* (品质生活 – quality life); being faced less often with material reminders of Shijiazhuang's latent rurality, Xiao Zhao reports, allows her to feel better about the place in which she lives. Recently she and her husband bought an apartment in a new neighbourhood, a move directly related to the hyper-production of new residential neighbourhoods literally on top of the rubble of demolished urban villages. For Xiao Zhao, de-ruralization means that, despite the frenetic activity of ensuring the proper education of her daughter, she and her family live – to the extent possible in this crowded, bustling city – the "slow life" promised in the slogans and images that adorn Shijiazhuang's heavily marketed new neighbourhoods (see Figure 4.13, for example).

CHAPTER 4

Figure 4.10. Shijiazhuang's scenic shui shang gong yuan (水上公园). *Xiao Jiao and her family relocated to a new apartment nearby. Shijiazhuang has an air pollution problem whose severity is not apparent in this photo*

Cleaning up Streets and Markets

With the elimination of the urban villages has come the drastic reduction of urban produce markets in favour of "big box" supermarkets. Such conversions are not an unintended consequence of *san nian da bianyang*, but, rather, the result of an explicit policy designed to clean up Hebei's cities. Under *san nian da bianyang*, illegal buildings and street side operations were targeted for removal. According to Hebei People's Government (2007), cities were required to, within two years, "clean up street markets, severely crack down on illegal street side businesses and squatters' stalls, regulate night markets and breakfast stalls…and to plan and construct…convenience markets" (part 16; see also Figure 4.7). Marked for extinction, such operations nonetheless persist, though they have been banished from Shijiazhuang's high profile intersections, and the "convenience markets" referred to above have progressively taken over the provision of basic daily goods in Shijiazhuang. One no longer finds late night food stands at the city's most prominent downtown locations, but they still play a role in the commercial nightlife of common neighbourhoods new and old. Similarly, farmers' markets still play an important role in the provision of basic foods, but they are fewer in number and hidden from view inside neighbourhoods and away from major roads.

All the parents I interviewed in the study were supportive of the idea of cleaning up the city. For them, Shijiazhuang's dirty air and dusty streets were a source of concern, frustration, and embarrassment. Nearly all of them described how their practice of "family education" included instilling in their child a desire for a clean urban environment. Each had some version of a story in which they worked with their child to break the all too common habit of littering. Xiao Liu, for example, had this to say about teaching environmental awareness:

> I taught my child, when he finishes something to just keep the garbage and take it home to throw out. So now he remembers 'Don't throw it on the ground, mama! Take it home for me and throw it in the garbage!' (Xiao Liu, Interview)

Family vacation destinations were chosen in part based on the value of the place for helping their child see what a clean, natural environment could be like. As a group, they were more ambivalent about the shift away from smaller free markets. For those born and raised in the city, supermarkets, for example, were seen as a welcome change, representing as they do a more modern way of life, not to mention more confidence in the safety of their foods. Those who grew up in the country side, on the other hand, appreciated the potential for a safer food supply, but resented the inflationary effects associated with this new mode of grocery distribution, preferring to shop for vegetables in farmers' markets near their homes. The same can be said of their response to the arrival of foreign restaurants such as Starbucks and Pizza Hut. While all were quick to express their disdain for the mundane offerings of these chains, they were equally willing to indicate their positive impressions of the decor and cleanliness.

Beautification, Culturalization, and Spiritual Uplift

Museums, libraries, and beautified public spaces provide an environment that nurtures the residents of the aspirational city. Figure 4.8 shows the newly renovated north plaza of the Hebei Provincial Museum. In the past, the plaza hosted an endless stream of trade shows, the presence of which created constant coming and going, but also a sense of crowding in a city already under heavy pressure due to its overall population density. At the northwest corner of the plaza stood the entrance to an underground bar and karaoke club known to be a bastion of the local prostitution trade. Under *san nian da bianyang*, the plaza has been renovated and returned to its original purpose as a space of cultural uplift. The museum itself has been renovated and more than doubled in size. A new provincial library sits across the street (see Figure 4.8). Perhaps the most aggressive of all of these beautification plans is the now partially constructed *huancheng shuixi* (环城水系 – ring waterway/drainage system) that will eventually encircle the entire city with a ring of waterways and eighteen public parks. Such public places are conceived as spaces to promote both environmental stewardship and spiritual uplift.

Parents in this study saw the development of such facilities as positive. They appeared to offer high quality opportunities for the betterment of their children's overall development, though I observed little to indicate that they took advantage of them. To be fair, some of these projects, such as the museum and library, were only recently completed. The *huancheng shuixi* is not yet completed, but was specifically cited by Lao Wang as an important and unique feature of the new Shijiazhuang. On one memorable trip to Lao Wang and Xiao Lu's country villa, a number of us drove to a newly constructed beach park designed to offer the city's residents a rare opportunity to swim in parched central Hebei. The group clearly relished swimming here, but were less impressed with nearby mountains of rubble shipped out from the centre of the city and piled high for mile upon mile. The stark juxtaposition of old and new, polluted and pristine was a reminder of both the kind of place Shijiazhuang is and that which it hopes to become. As Lao Dong put it, "I don't really believe that Shijiazhuang will ever change. There is a lot of money being spent and there are a lot of new things, but it is obviously still Shijiazhuang."

CHAPTER 4

Mobilization

The aspirational city would be a failure absent a transportation network capable of moving goods and people around the city. The aspirational cité, after all, implies constant movement and growth, and requires freedom of movement for parents pursuing the development of their child through a myriad of educational activities. All of these are enabled, if imperfectly, by the explosion of private cars in Shijiazhuang, which provides both impetus and justification for expansion of the city's road network. Expansion of existing roads and construction of new thoroughfares is constant. On the relatively circumscribed two kilometre east-west avenue, Lianmeng Road, by which I access my apartment, three new north-south access roads have been added in the last ten years, and the street is bounded on each side by newly built high-speed elevated expressways. The avenue itself has been widened three times during my time in the city, each time consuming dozens of small, family owned street-side shops and restaurants that once did lively trade on the bicycle swamped street. Lianmeng Road was torn up a fourth time to install upgraded sewer lines to accommodate the dozen or so high rise apartment blocks that now cast long shadows over the trees lining the street. Despite these renovations, the street remains crowded due in large part to the increased presence of private cars. De-ruralization has reduced one form of traffic on the street – the noisy and once ubiquitous three-wheeled delivery carts that once flew through the neighbourhood in a cacophony of one-cylindered diesel combustion.

Figure 4.11. Shijiazhuang's new metro system eases intra-urban travel

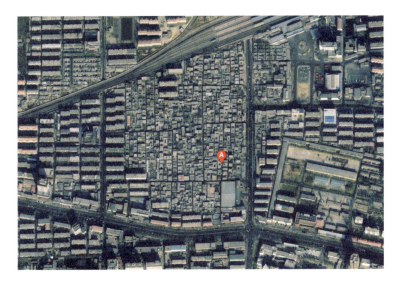

Figure 4.12. Beijiao Cun (centre) in 2010 prior to demolition (Image credit: Baidu.com) Retrieved from http://j.map.baidu.com/cV93i

Five hundred meters to the north of Lianmeng Road is a third expressway, this one the city's second ring road, a high speed link to each of the ten or so other freeways that divide the city into districts by a practical logic, funnelling traffic efficiently to this or that newly built high density neighbourhood. Bicycles were once the dominant mode of transport for commuters and are still an important means of transport for those of modest means or those who cleave to what remains a practical and inexpensive way to commute. They are also a cherished memory of what was, at the height of the socialist era, a rationed good, not to mention an important indicator of prosperity in the 1980s (Allaire, 2007). But the city's new middle-class travels in private cars that both reflect and engender a sense of autonomy.

Elevated freeways rapidly constructed under *san nian da bianyang* enable residents of new suburbs to commute previously unheard of distances to work or school. It is not uncommon to find every spare inch of bare ground in Shijiazhuang's neighbourhoods repurposed as parking lots, a problem that grows more serious by the month despite planners' efforts to curb sales and restricting the availability of licence plates by various means. The explosion in car ownership may render air pollution control initiatives, such as the reduction and banning of coal burning within the city and the relocation of the worst of industrial polluters to the countryside, moot.

Pollution effects aside, greater mobility has enabled a wider choice for some of the city's parents. For Xiao Lu and Xiao Wang, a move near SFLS was necessary to register their daughter in the school. This accomplished, they quickly bought a new, larger apartment near the city centre, a move that, in the past, would have made attending SFLS impossible. Now the daily commute to deliver and collect their daughter is, if not convenient, plausible and even preferable given the better living conditions of their new home. Similarly, Lao Zhang and Xiao Li's move to an apartment far from their places of work and near SFLS was enabled by constant improvements to the city's road network.

Both parents drive private vehicles, meaning that the burden of commuting can be shifted away from their daughter, freeing for the girl valuable time for study and rest. Situations like these were related by many of the parents in the study, although some suggested that, while they knew such movement about the city to be a possibility, they preferred to send their children to a school near home. For some, however, commitment to the local school was honoured in the breach. When the time came for Xiao Ren to send her son to *youeryuan* and an opportunity presented itself, she too registered him at the distant SFLS.

But the implication of freedom through travel in the aspirational city also implies liberation *from* restrictions of the horizon of possibilities that life in Shijiazhuang – no matter how well it comes to facilitate freedom or self-improvement – imposes. Intercity travel by private car is increasingly convenient. Two high quality toll highways connect the city to Beijing, others to destinations in the east, west, and south. Shijiazhuang's Zhengding airport is undergoing a massive expansion, and the recently established Hebei Air means the middle-class is better connected to national and international destinations by a high quality airline. More significantly, aggressive investments in intercity mobility in the form of a new integrated railway station (1.84B yuan – see Figure 4.1) and a six kilometre north-south tunnel to speed the passage of *hexie hao* (和谐号/CRH – "harmony express"/China Rail Highspeed) trains in and out of the city.

These massive public works broaden the life prospects of the middle-class by reducing travel time to Beijing to one hour, meaning that frequent trips to and from China's educational and cultural capital are less expensive and more convenient. Improved transportation thus allows for increased investments in curiosity, creativity, and love of learning. Rail travel, of course, remains stratified, and has become more so with the addition of dedicated, luxurious high speed trains and lines. While the ultra-high speed CRH system whisks Shijiazhuang's middle-class and elite residents between linked cities, lower grade – and much more crowded, dirty, and slow – options are offered to those travelling to less important destinations, or to those unwilling or unable to pay the higher fares.

The expansion of national and international transportation links is experienced as a great boon by Shijiazhuang's middle-class residents. For example, it has made Xiao Zhao and her husband's living arrangements more viable than ever as she and her daughter can now fly to visit him directly from Shijiazhuang rather than travelling to Beijing. Their Shijiazhuang apartment is near the city's new train station, which offers underground parking, direct airline check-in, and high speed transportation to the airport. The airport also has direct flights to many of China's most desirable destinations, opening the door for Xiao Zhao, Xiao Lu, Lao Zhang's family, and others to participate in travel activities they deem crucial to broadening their children's horizons (see Chapter 5).

New Neighbourhoods for the Aspirational City

The affective core of Chinese life is the family home, an understanding of which helps to explain, along with Harvey's concepts of spatio-temporal fixing and capital over-accumulation (Harvey, 2005), the central role of residential construction in Shijiazhuang's urban renovation. The desire to improve the domestic living conditions of one's family and to provide a better future to subsequent generations drives family members to seek, as Lao Dong said in an interview, a *hao yi xie de shenghuo* (好一些的生活 – literally, a slightly better life). China's policy makers are highly sensitive to the economic potential of this desire to improve living conditions. At times they work to incite and exploit the desire for familial improvement as an engine of economic growth, at others to restrain it to protect the economy from bubble formation (Zhang, 2013). Beyond direct economic implications, they are highly sensitive to the negative effects of an overheated real estate market on the daily lives of the less well-off and poor, and the potential of inflation in the housing market to stymie their familial aspirations. A population with an excessively large group of impoverished, "homeless," and stymied citizens is a potentially unstable one, and there are no principles more central to the governing philosophy of post-Mao China than those of stability and harmony.

Figure 4.13. Fields of flowers

Understanding the hand in glove relationship of familial aspiration and broader economic policy and practice is crucial to decoding the ways in which Shijiazhuang's urban renovation has unfolded. As discussed above, *san nian da bianyang* kicked off an explosion of new housing, much of it infill/densification units. The spectacle of this massive, citywide residential renovation overwhelms the eye, but it is the construction

CHAPTER 4

Figure 4.14. Shaded Forest Kingdom

Figure 4.15. Spring returns. The poetry of Laozi is appropriated to sell Linyuan Dayuan to passersby

and promotion of entirely new neighbourhoods on the clean slate of demolished *cheng zhong cun* that provides the most compelling object of analysis for my purposes. Such projects are enormous in scale and totalizing in their capacity to create and will to promote themselves as carriers of entirely new and, of course, superior ways of life.

One such "clean slate" neighbourhood is the 500,000 m² *linyin dayuan* (林荫大院/ Park County) (http://684505.soufun.com) only now rising from the rubble of Beijiao Cun (北焦村). The project has only recently started construction, but its sales centre and the walls surrounding the demolition-construction site have been in place for more than two years. Objectively, the development will represent a massive increase in population density on this piece of land and a correspondingly large profit for its developer, Guangsha Real Estate Development Company Ltd. (http://newhouse.sjz. soufun.com/company/1310684505_20120418151024.htm). The overarching slogan for the project, *fengjing yuanluo de gushi* (风景院落的故事 – a courtyard landscape story), appeals to familial aspirations to live the kind of good life imagined to be the norm in foreign countries. These understandings of the good life are cited and incited by ads papering the walls that surround the site (Figures 4.13, 4.14, 4.15), and

BUILDING AN ASPIRATIONAL CITY

in the promotional images featured in the sales centre and circulated on the internet. In one ad, an image depicting a child bathed in filtered sunlight is coupled with the project tag line (see Figures 4.13 and 4.14) to promise the opportunity of a "life story" composed in the "scenic courtyards" of this "500,000 square meter shady forest kingdom" (Figure 4.14). In another, a similarly bucolic image works in tandem with a slogan that alludes to the poetry of Laozi to discursively link the emergence of an improved Shijiazhuang and the reemergence on the world scene of China as whole (Figure 4.15). Buying a home in Park County, these ads promise, is just the first step of many toward a happy and prosperous life.

Figure 4.16. Front gate of SFLS. Motorists and cyclist compete for space on the crowded street outside the front gate of Shijiazhuang's Foreign Language School. The school has become a destination of choice for many of the city's upwardly mobile parents

EDUCATIONAL INSTITUTIONS FOR THE ASPIRATIONAL CITY

Growth, redevelopment, and renovation as a whole is mirrored in the realm of education and schooling. When the Hebei People's Government (2007) announced *san nian da bianyang*, it made the *jiefang sixiang* (解放思想 – emancipation of the mind) a condition of possibility of the rapid realization of a new urbanity for Shijiazhuang. The previous sections of this chapter address the extent to which the aspirational cité is increasingly embodied in the new material forms and spatial relations of Shijiazhuang. I have suggested that these forms and relations, not to mention direct invasive messaging, represent an attempt to create a city within which the kinds of people envisioned in the

77

CHAPTER 4

aspirational cité can be nurtured. Taken generally, this project can be seen as relying on a "pedagogy of everyday life" where the lessons of progress, modernity, and success are relayed to the population at large as they go about their daily routines. In what follows, I consider how this process of translation – from order of worth to material form – is accomplished in the domain of schooling.

As the residents of Shijiazhuang grow in number, become more mobile, and re-imagine the process of educating their children, public and private educational institutions alike are positioning themselves as "good" providers of the services demanded by both "society" and individual families. Below I introduce two such schools, one a public-private middle school, the other a private parent-child education centre.

Shijiazhuang Foreign Language School (SFLS)

The architecture, curriculum, teaching staff, and even the parents of SFLS all reflect a concern with constructing a school sensitive to the guidance of the aspirational cité. Established in 1994 as a provincial key middle school, SFLS has grown to include a *youeryuan* (幼儿园 – preschool/kindergarten for 3 to 5-year-olds), primary school, and both junior and senior middle schools (SFLEG, 2013d). It has been recognized by the China Ministry of Education as one of the best fifteen schools of its kind. Such lofty recognition implies both first-rate facilities and attention to image, and the school claims to "spare nothing to cultivate fine qualities in our students," qualities closely linked to those promoted in the aspirational cité: "we set it as our goal to educate our students to be qualified personnel who are patriotic, sociable,

*Figure 4.17. SFLS fosters an international perspective in its students.
A globe rests inside the school's front gate*

cooperative, polite, healthy and creative and who can meet the global challenges of the world" (SFLEG, 2013d). Doric columns and a stylized globe greet visitors and students to SFLS, along with its commitment to foreign language education, the most obvious indication that the school has adopted the global/international perspective recommended by the aspirational cité (Figure 4.17). Visual elements like these are important, but so too are excellent facilities in general. Above all, SFLS is a clean, well-appointed facility whose students' uniforms and overall aspect foster an image of uprightness and cleanliness. Indeed, SFLS comprises a set of facilities that embody the pedagogical precepts of the aspirational cité, as the school, unlike most in the city, houses a swimming pool, table-tennis centre, gymnastics hall and gymnasium, and an outstanding track and field facility. In other words, at SFLS, all-around development – training of mind, body, and spirit – is taken seriously.

Moral education is a core element of SFLS's mission and its particular vision of the moral student is an object worthy of analysis. The school undertakes dozens of activities each year under the aegis of the Moral Education Committee, promoting personal and collective pursuit of qualities central to the aspirational cité. Activities intended to bolster the moral quality of students are frequent, amongst these *shehui shijian dongtai* (社会实践动态 – social practice activities) that inculcate through practical action the values of, *inter alia*, volunteerism and charity, of patriotism and care for the elderly (SFLEG, 2013a). In one activity, students visit a nearby community, sweep its streets, and listen respectfully to an elderly veteran of the Anti-Japanese War. In another, they leaflet in a nearby park to advocate for environmental stewardship (SFLEG, 2013b). These voluntary, student-organized activities typify the ways in which the school encourages particular qualities in its students, as does reportage of it. Though the weather is cold, the students remain dedicated. They are thirsty, but they are not deterred from their mission to promote environmental consciousness. Such qualities in the service of advocacy is central to not only the moral fibre of the contemporary citizen, but also the key to a brighter, cleaner future: "Parents, friends, teachers, we have such a good boy, and I believe that our skies will be bluer, our water clearer, and the sun more bright" (2013b, "A parent's impressions"). As in the first example above, the school's moral education volunteer corps is active in showing respect for teachers, rushing to retrieve and clean teachers' bicycles (SFLEGc, 2013).

Like its developing students, SFLS's teachers embody the aspirational cité's prescriptions for both good people and good teachers. Teachers are introduced with photos, listings of hobbies, life maxims, and classroom management, along with a personal statement about teaching. One elementary school *banzhuren* (班主任 – homeroom teacher) enjoys calligraphy, painting, reading, travelling, and working out. Such pursuits are notable more for their breadth than for the uniqueness of any particular pursuit, for they paint a portrait of a teacher of broad and balanced interests. This idealized image of the balanced teacher is typical of those represented on the

CHAPTER 4

school's website. SLFS, it seems, is staffed by a team of teachers who, like those of any school heavily influenced by liberal/progressive educational ideas, approach students with an attitude of positivity and tolerance, love and compassion, and who take teaching to be a student centered practice. Such qualities are consistent with notions of teacher as guide or mentor, and with model teachers like those described in Chapter 3. Teachers also describe their teaching as a constant effort at self-development through practical experimentation and reflection. Their efforts in this regard are supported administratively under the guidance of the school's *jiaoyu keyan weiyuanhui* (教育科研委员会 – Educational Research Committee) and *jiaoshi zhuanye fazhan weiyuanhui* (教师专业发展委员会 – Teacher Expertise/Professional Development Committee), both of which figure prominently in the school's promotional materials.

Students are not the only target of SFLS's educational efforts. Responding to the insight that parental involvement and skill are a key predictor of success, the school works to involve, inform, and educate parents through its *xuesheng jiazhang weiyuanhui* (学生家长委员会 – Parent Teacher Association/Committee). It also engages in a mission that works through the reinvention of the notion of *jiating jiaoyu* (家庭教育 – family education), co-opting a term that conventionally refers to education (of children) in the home and investing it with a new meaning – education (of parents) *for* the home. The committee works to create a collaborative relationship between home and school, sharing the collective burden of raising excellent citizens, and instilling in parents an understanding of a balanced approach to their child's education. The tasks of nurturing children in body, mind, and spirit leads the committee to offer training to parents in each of these aspects. A cooking class for parents, a class from which parents are meant to learn not only a basic parenting skill, but also to absorb a more general life's lesson – that the result is less important than process when it comes to raising a healthy happy child (SFLEG, 2012a). Other activities include educating parents on both basic and specific concepts of developmental psychology (Ying, 2012), such as how to deal with childhood rebellion (SFLEG, 2012b), fundamental educational concepts (SFLEG, 2012c), the "art of criticism" (SFLEG, 2012d), and learning from successful model parents (SFLEG, 2012e). Notably, reportage on these events consistently contains guidance in terms of the way good parents respond to the information offered. Parents are excited to attend, contributing to a bustling atmosphere that indicates their wholehearted participation and fundamental dedication to the cause of their child's education (SFLEG, 2012c). They respond positively to what they learn, recognize their own faults, and resolve to correct their ways (SFLEG, 2012d). The good parent, in other words, is an eager consumer of parenting knowledge, a lifelong learner curious about the nature of children, and dedicated to the all-around development of his child.

Jinbaobei – Gymboree

Jinbaobei occupies space on the fifth floor of *Xiantianxia* (先天下 – Future Mall), a luxury goods shopping mall featuring spectacular finishings, products, and prices.

BUILDING AN ASPIRATIONAL CITY

Jinbaobei presents a different face to the public in China than in its North American outlets. Housed in *Xiantianxia*, a mall and high rise development constructed on land cleared for redevelopment under *san nian da bian yang*, *Jinbaobei* is spotlessly clean and, thus, an example par excellence of one of the primary criteria of distinction in a city that struggles – as the principles of *san nian da bianyang* make clear – to create and maintain a clean environment.

The Chinese Gymboree is, like *Xiantianxia*, elaborately finished, brightly coloured, adorned with photos of joyous foreign children, and festooned with inspirational English expressions. It promises happiness and cross-generational learning through art and play. Above all it is *clean*, a first impression not diminished when one enters and is immediately asked by an eager young greeter to don shoe coverings most commonly found in doctor's offices and surgical suites. Custodial staff in clean, coordinated uniforms are a constant presence, unobtrusively cleaning the floors with gleaming white dust mops, dusting shelves sparsely decorated with expensive and shiny toys the equal of their sparkling surrounds. Other, equally well-dressed young female staff greet visitors with smiling faces and eagerly offer tours of the centre and explanations of the educational programs on offer. What separates *Jinbaobei* and its imitators from other tutoring and training centres is that it focusses not only on early learning for children, but also on training for parents on how to work with their children to create independent, creative young learners. It also offers art and music

Figure 4.18. Central dome of Xiantianxia. Home of Jinbaobei, luxury goods mall Xiantianxia aggressively projects the kind of pinzhi shenghuo declared in da bian yang documents (Photo credit: w88880000 Retrieved from http://dcbbs.zol.com.cn/1/34002_7279.html)

81

CHAPTER 4

based international and multicultural learning experience for both parent and child. On a more practical level, *Jinbaobei* offers training in a range of *xuexiao jineng* (学校技能 – school skills) such as small group skills and general social skills. In all of these ways, *Jinbaobei*, like SFLS, exemplifies the core principles of the aspirational cité.

Jinbaobei, with its clean, gleaming surfaces, its references to a wider world beyond the boundaries of Shijiazhuang and China, and its promises of high quality, advanced educational opportunities, embodies the prescriptions and precepts of the aspirational cité. It offers to parents like Xiao Lu and Xiao Zhao the kind of distinguished and distinguishing training they desire. More than this, it offers explicit training for both parent and child, meaning that whatever they may lack as parents due to their having been nurtured in an earlier, now defunct order of worth, will not be passed on to the child, thus harming their chance of becoming good people in the mould of the aspirational cité. As Xiao Lu makes clear (see also Chapter 5), she trusts Jinbaobei, and the ideas and behaviours she has learned through its offerings inform her daily interactions with her children. Her identification with these ways of parenting also inform her selection of friends. In one conversation, for example, she identified other "good" parents in part by noting that they took part in the same activities as her, including taking their children to Jinbaobei.

NOTES

[1] Harvey (2003) uses the term "utopian schemes" to describe the " the romanticism and socialist utopianism that flourished so wildly in the 1830s and 1840s in France" (p. 58).

[2] This program was presumably inspired by a similar one that transformed Shanghai in the previous decade, a program Pan (2011) has translated as "a new image every year, and every three years, a completely different image" (p. 153).

[3] The Chinese blogosphere is replete with this kind of talk, as here: http://blog.sina.com.cn/s/blog_3fce69bc01009mmc.html

CHAPTER 5

EDUCATING CHILDREN IN THE ASPIRATIONAL CITY

From the earliest days of my expatriate life in China, the depth of detail of "education talk" amongst Chinese parents struck me as unique. Which school to send their (future) sons and daughters to; how much and what kinds of additional study to impose, not to mention the manner of such imposition; which extracurricular learning activities might best elevate the "quality" of their children, ensure their advancement to the best middle schools and universities, and, thus, propel them to lifelong success; whose influence to seek in pursuing these projects; how to *get ahead of others* – to that point in time, my own experience as a young adult contained no conversations of this kind. Even now, the way that my spouse combs internet forums dedicated to discussing, questioning, and chronicling in endless detail the efforts of Chinese parents to educate their children, strikes me as both remarkable and as so much unnecessary fretting. Her childhood friends send frequent reports on their children's progress through formal schooling, their success – or lack of – in gaining admission to the best middle schools, and their summer camp trips to the U.S. or U.K. That the dinner party described in Chapter 1 involved people who were not yet parents only served to underscore this impression.

Since then, my life has changed radically. Becoming a father – and son-in-law – in a family whose norms are very much embedded in and infused with these perspectives has meant that I have had to make adjustments in the way I orient myself to them. I, too, have begun to think about such questions, and not only because it is "natural" to do so, or that, as an educated parent, I am expected and driven to do so. Rather, it is also because the "Chinese" side of the hybrid cultural milieu within which I am embedded is steeped in the very educational desire that provided the impetus for this research. My integration into this culture of educational aspiration and worry has not always been, I should add, voluntary. A few years ago following the birth of my son, my father-in-law announced that he would be taking both my spouse and I aside for a week of "lessons" in traditional Chinese culture. My spouse was able to resist, but as an outsider and newcomer, I was an easier target, and was treated in isolation to ten or more hours a day of tutelage on the ancient teachings and contemporary practices of Chinese culture. Fortuitously, these lessons included guidance on the proper role of parents in family education and, thus, provided me with a range of paths to explore in my interviews with Shijiazhuang's parents. Less happily, it provided him an opportunity to lay out in excruciating detail all the ways in which I had failed to do the things that a good son-in-law should.

CHAPTER 5

Equally importantly, my part-time life in China in the family of which I am now a part immerses me in the high-speed urban transformation that has become an inescapable feature of contemporary life. We watch the value of the family's Beijing apartments rise and wonder when the time might be right to sell one or both of them. We watch the street outside torn up time and again to make way for new internet cabling or flower beds. From our kitchen window we look onto the courtyard of the local "experimental" elementary school. Watching its students doing morning exercises, we wonder if this is the best place to send our son when the time comes. Or are there other, better schools nearby, and how will we know the right thing to do? The kitchen window also offers a view of the university's new hotel and conference centre, the gleaming entrance plaza of which has recently become a battleground upon which hovering grandparents seeking play space protect the right of their grandchildren to play – and pee – despite the protests of hotel security and management.

In many ways, these experiences of integration – save for the initiation lessons of my father-in-law – have been taking place under structural and cultural conditions similar to those of parents I interviewed and observed in this study. The remainder of this chapter is dedicated to weaving together the perspectives of these parents with my observations of their activities as they go about educating and getting an education for their children. Returning to Archer's analytical framework, the object of this chapter is the realm of socio-cultural interaction, that is, the space in which "parts" (elements comprising the cultural system) and "people" (parents) come together. Before describing in detail the thoughts and activities of the parent-informants as a whole, I describe the process of data analysis. I then present a series of portraits of a week in the educational lives of four of these parent-child pairs. Taken together, these profiles and descriptions paint a portrait of parents who by turns "navigate" and "negotiate" the cultural environment within which they are immersed.

THE PARENTS

Before going on to a thematic discussion of parents' beliefs and activities, I first present brief descriptions of a week in the educational lives of four of the parents who took part in the study. These I present not so much for their unique characteristics or because they represent particularly acute cases of high intensity parenting. Indeed, people familiar with the day to day reality of Chinese education will likely see these stories as typical. Nevertheless, they will provide the reader with a better sense of a week in the life of a typical middle-class urban parent and child. The four examples, taken together, also serve to give a sense of the overall shape of a child's educational career, which, under present material and cultural conditions, are usefully framed by Bourdieu and Passeron's (1990) typology of "pedagogic action" (see Table 1.1). Of special note, these portraits and the analysis they engendered correspond to the period of most intense formal field work. It goes without saying that these portraits represent a moment in time. Three to four years have since passed; changes in the lives of these families are discussed below in Chapter 7.

Xiao Lu & Lao Wang's Family

Xiao Lu is a gregarious thirty-year-old woman and a native of Shijiazhuang. The daughter of a junior high school teacher and an SOE manager, she has been married for five years to Lao Wang. The couple has a four-year-old daughter and a newborn son, both of whom are cared for almost exclusively by Xiao Lu, though she does employ a nanny and is helped significantly by her mother. The couple's son was born overseas, as Xiao Lu and Lao Wang felt that a private hospital abroad was desirable given their dissatisfaction with hospitals and doctors closer to home. Xiao Lu's workplace skills serve her well in the after work world as well. An avid dancer and fitness buff, Xiao Lu worked for several years as an organizer in the party youth section of one of Shijiazhuang's colleges, but resigned this position to focus on having a healthy second child. Xiao Lu's abilities as a social organizer are near legendary among her friends, not to mention the relatively small group of young "foreign expert" teachers and business people who come and go from Shijiazhuang. She is constantly planning outings and deploying her *guanxi* network to help others. Indeed, one of my first acts when I returned to Shijiazhuang to begin the interview phase of this research was to contact Xiao Lu to help me arrange accommodation. She did so without hesitation, spending the better part of two days touring apartments before helping me settle on one and negotiate lease terms. Such activities, she reports, are as important to her as her work and family duties, though she says she finds it difficult to maintain the frenetic pace of her social life since the arrival of her son. Where she once seemed uncomfortable being forced into the role of *quan zhi mama* (全职妈妈 – full time mother), by outward appearances and by her own account, she has now embraced the role.

On the surface, Xiao Lu's husband Lao Wang is a well-dressed, successful man about town. He has a well-established career in the property development sector and a rapidly expanding set of investments in a variety of small enterprises. Lao Wang's role sees him spend much of his time wining and dining the partners and clients upon whom the company's success relies. He drives around Shijiazhuang in expensive vehicles and fosters an image he deems appropriate to the life he aspires to. As he often says, "when you go for a bank loan, you can't arrive on a bicycle." Like many men of his generation, there is more to Lao Wang than meets the eye. Like many Shijiazhuang-*ren* (石家庄人 – Shijiazhuang person), he hails from elsewhere, in his case, a nearby county attached to Baoding City, but his family has a long history in Shijiazhuang. His mother moved to the city in the 1960s to start a rooming house in what is now the city's largest and most anarchic wholesale market. The family's business interests morphed with the changing political times, adapting to policy shifts, but always remaining fundamentally entrepreneurial. Given Xiao Lu's recent resignation from her college position, Lao Wang is now the sole income earner in this

85

CHAPTER 5

family, and the nature of his work places the family squarely within a social class with "control over property" (see Table 2.1). His company has now built several substantial residential communities, properties that it also manages on an ongoing basis.

Xiao Lu, once highly resistant to the strictures of Lao Wang's more traditional understanding of a woman's place in the family, recently gave up her job to focus full time on raising the couple's two young children. Indeed, it would be fair to describe her approach to being a *quan zhi mama* (全职妈妈 – full time mother) as robust and all-consuming. Her week begins as she rises early in the morning with six-year old Xiao Ai, working together with the family's live-in *ayi* (阿姨 – nanny) to prepare breakfast for the family. Xiao Ai attends *youeryuan* from early morning (8 a.m.) to late afternoon (5 p.m.) at SFLS, and having a full-time nanny to care for their eight-month Xiao Yi eases the pressure on Xiao Lu. She drives Xiao Ai to school. From Monday to Friday the daytime child-rearing routine is much the same, but evening involves a flurry of activity that changes day to day. Xiao Ai has a piano lesson with a private tutor on Monday after dinner. On Tuesday in place of her piano lesson, she goes to an art class. Wednesday is for dance lessons and, depending on the time of year, whatever other activity Xiao Lu deems appropriate. On days when Xiao Ai has no piano lesson, Xiao Lu sits beside her on the piano bench counting measures for thirty to forty-five minutes as the young girl practices that week's pieces. Afterward, Xiao Ai heads to a shopping mall with her grandfather to practice ice skating, or to the nearby city park where she joins a group of same-aged children for inline skating lessons. On weekends, Xiao Ai usually spends a few hours ice skating, or playing with friends in the park. She occasionally takes part in a variety of sporting competitions on the weekend, including inline skating races. There is also more time available for formal lessons. The weekend is capped by two hours of English lessons each day at a nearby English school that promotes "English Language Arts" learning, the latest trend in the vibrant private educational market.

Xiao Zhao's Family

Xiao Zhao lives most of the year on her own with her primary school daughter while her husband works in the southern business centre of Shenzhen. She was introduced to me by Xiao Lu and is, by her own description, a *quanzhi mama* (全职妈妈 – full time or stay-at-home mother), a woman who focusses all of her efforts on raising her daughter as she and her husband see fit. Xiao Zhao has a modest level of education, having completed a diploma at a local college, but nonetheless exudes a self-confidence that belies her past as a salesperson in a local department store. Being a *quanzhi mama* is made possible by her husband's high salary, although the family is also engaged in another business that she prefers not to reveal. As her husband works as an enterprise manager, the family is firmly entrenched in the "control over organizations" class (see Table 2.1). Like others in her social group, Xiao Zhao lives in a new and well-appointed apartment building and drives a mid-sized SUV. She has learned to enjoy red wine, and is always near the top of Xiao Lu's guest list when social events are arranged. For a family of their means, their current living arrangement is not unusual. Xiao Zhao says she and her husband continue to live apart because Shenzhen is expensive and she believes she would feel isolated there. The relatively affordable cost of living and the presence of family members and other social connections that allow her to accomplish the project of educating her daughter are compelling reasons to live in this manner. Having said this, her husband's substantial salary and direct air connections between Shijiazhuang and Shenzhen allow him to visit home frequently.

In Xiao Zhao's case, taking up the role of *quanzhi mama* was an outcome of objective processes endemic to life in a city and culture in which the prospects for career advancement favour men over women. Her fate in this respect is similar to Xiao Lu's, although Xiao Zhao makes no claim to having resisted the end of her career outside the home. When pressed on the question of her marginalization as a contributor to her family's financial well-being, she expresses no regret. Indeed, where Xiao Lu's desire to stay involved in activities outside of her regular job met with Lao Wang's hostility and led to frequent conflict in their home, Xiao Zhao embraced her role in the home from the outset.

When I first interviewed Xiao Zhao, her daughter Xiao Shu was still a *youeryuan* student, and the pair maintained a weekly itinerary that looked very much like Xiao Lu and Xiao Ai's. Indeed, in many ways it still does, except that, as a grade three student, time for play has been scaled back as that spent on formal studies has increased. The biggest difference between Xiao Shu's and Xiao Ai's schedules is the time dedicated to homework on weeknights. Specifically, Xiao Zhao is particularly concerned with English language learning, so Xiao Shu attends a *ke wai* (课外 – after school) class two nights during the week. Because of Xiao Zhao's focus, doing well requires that significant time be spent on homework in the form of lesson review (*fuxi* – 复习) and/or preview (*lianxi* – 练习). Whether the task is review or preview, the routine in their home each evening is much the same – after supper Xiao Zhao sits together with Xiao Shu for as long as one hour, or until the necessary work is complete. Other weekday activities include piano and dance lessons, and Xiao Zhao plans to add additional one on one English tutoring. Weekend activities include a third set of lessons at the English school, the same one that Xiao Ai attends, as well as ice skating and art and music appreciation classes.

Lao Dong's Family

Lao Dong works as an assistant bank manager. A friend of Xiao Lu and Lao Wang, he leads an active social life and is well-liked for his fun-loving attitude and tendency to use clever turns of phrase to make the group laugh. During the period of the study, he and I became friends, joined the same gym, and often shared meals. Lao Dong also helped me to get around the city to take photographs, suggesting locations to take interesting photos, and clarifying my understanding of the financing arrangements of *san nian da bianyang*. Born at the height of

CHAPTER 5

the Cultural Revolution, he is the only male child in a family of five siblings and likes to attribute his well above average height (he stands about 6'2") to his family having owned a goat that provided him with extra milk to drink during childhood. He and his wife, an accountant, have a daughter. During most of the period of this study, the family lived in housing connected to her workplace, but they recently bought an apartment in one of Shijiazhuang's sprawling new southern suburbs. Their daughter's place in Shijiazhuang's most desired school, Shijiazhuang Foreign Language School (SFLS), however, is guaranteed by the location of the older residence, which now also provides significant rental income due to its location near SFLS.

Lao Dong's daughter Xiao Yi is four and six years older than Xiao Shu and Xiao Ai respectively and now a *chuzhong* (初中 – middle/junior high school) student. As such, the unique educational tasks that comprise a week in her educational life tend to conceal that which their lives hold in common – a very intense week of pedagogic action. Monday after school, Xiao Yi has a violin lesson. Tuesday evening she attends math *buxi* (补习课 – remedial, supplemental, or "cram") lessons arranged by her school. Thursday after school she plays ping pong, and on Friday she has a *ke wai* Chinese lesson. Saturday's supplementary class is English, and on Sunday, she practices with her school's orchestra. Every night of the week she has two to three hours of homework, and although Xiao Yi has two activities, ping pong and orchestra, built into her schedule for enjoyment, Lao Dong feels that school-life balance is a problem. Even the "fun" activities require a high degree of discipline and practice, and Lao Dong worries that Xiao Yi doesn't get enough exercise. Still, he feels that there is little choice but to engage Xiao Yi in this tight, high pressure schedule, lest she fall behind in her grades and class ranking. Sadly, a small group of peers that Lao Dong and other parents organized for their children three years ago (see below) no longer meets to relax and play, as each went to a different school or was placed in a different class at the start of junior high school. More importantly, each of them is now pursuing an educational itinerary like Xiao Yi's and has little time to maintain a social life outside of the strictures seen to be imposed by the logic of social competition and *yingshi jiaoyu* (应试教育 – exam focused education).

Xiao Jiao's Family

Xiao Jiao's family lives a comfortable middle-class lifestyle. She is a section head in a state owned enterprise (SOE) I came to know through our common work with teachers. She graduated with a bachelor's degree in chemistry, leaving her first job in a chemical factory to start her tenure at her current job, and has now spent more than a decade in that job. She now seems happy to remain in this position despite an earlier restless period when she openly speculated about the wisdom of *xia hai* (下海 – going into business). Her husband occupies a similar middle-rung position as an accountant in another state owned firm. Like many of Shijiazhuang's educated residents, they come from elsewhere, Xiao Jiao from a nearby county, her husband from a village likely to be consumed by the city in the next decade or so. Xiao Jiao is thoughtful and modest, and has succeeded to the degree she has by being a go-to person in her company. When something absolutely must be done and be done competently, her company's higher ups often seek her out.

In the past three years, she and her family have twice moved to new homes. The first move was long-planned for and took the family to a newly constructed apartment building near both her workplace and the high school the family anticipated sending their son to upon completion of junior high school. This second home is in a new high rise building constructed by a village corporation on former village lands. The building itself is unspectacular, but conveniently located near one of the city's few urban parks. The apartment is not large, but is well appointed, featuring wood floors and other features one expects in newly constructed apartments in China. This move completed, their son Xiao Lei tested above expectations on his high school entrance examinations, gaining admission to one of the city's top high schools. His earliest days there meant two hours of commuting each day, so the family quickly bought another smaller apartment near the school to ease the burden of a long commute to school every day. Xiao Jiao and her husband now take turns returning home from work to prepare the boy's lunch, a heavy burden for them to be sure, but one they deem worthwhile given the potential their son has shown on successive rounds of examinations.

When I first interviewed Xiao Jiao, her son had recently started high school. Having unexpectedly scored highly on the *zhong kao* (中考 – junior high graduation/ high school entrance examination), he found himself in a higher pressure situation than expected at one of the top high school's in the city. Most of the stories of this transition were more humorous than heartbreaking as both mother and son struggled to get up to speed with the school's rigid regimen. At this level, the institutionalized pedagogic action is highly coercive and at the peak of its powers to push aside alternative or oppositional beliefs parents might otherwise assert more strongly. Compared with the educational lives of Xiao Ai, Xiao Shu, and Xiao Yi, Xiao Lei's is comparatively bitter, dedicated almost entirely to formal study, although Xiao Lei did once confide that he spends too much time chatting with friends during study time. Despite these moments of relief, little is heard of balanced development or happiness, except to occasionally lament the dearth of both in the present circumstances; such aims are overwhelmed by the potential rewards and penalties of a *gao kao* well or poorly written.

Xiao Du's Family

Xiao Du is younger than me, but has earned the respectful appellation *jie* (姐 – Older Sister) by virtue of her maternal, helpful aspect. She was also introduced to me by Xiao Lu, and was once a constant presence in Xiao Lu's social circle. Capable and eager amateur chefs, at one time, Xiao Du and her husband were the go-to cooks for

CHAPTER 5

parties at Xiao Lu and Lao Wang's country bungalow. These parties have continued in recent years, but without the presence of Xiao Du's family. It seems that Xiao Du was shunned by Xiao Lu following a disagreement over her role in renovations to Xiao Lu and Lao Wang's new apartment. In some ways this split seemed inevitable given Xiao Lu and Xiao Du's diverging social trajectories. Whatever the content of the precipitating disagreement, Xiao Lu reasoned that the *faux pas* committed was the result of some qualities innate to those of Xiao Du's social ranking. As discussed later in this chapter, Xiao Lu strongly believes that *suzhi* (素质 – "quality") is largely *tiansheng* (天生 – innate or natural).

Xiao Du works at an electrical generating company, a job that is the main source of the family's financial security, and has done so since graduating from college. She also operates a small business out of one of the innumerable business apartments in the city centre, bringing the family's total monthly income to about 5000rmb, only 1800 of which comes from her regular job. When asked what kind of business she does, she replies vaguely that she buys and sells things, but reports that it doesn't bring her much extra income. A junior middle school graduate, her husband of fifteen years has become a jack of all trades since retiring from the PLA (People's Liberation Army) and leaving his subsequent job at the same state owned enterprise (SOE) as Xiao Du. For a time he was a taxi driver, but didn't enjoy the pressures of driving, and found the demands of making a living at that job detracted too much from family life. Now he does *ziyou zhiye* (自由职业 – freelance work), working at anything that comes along, meaning that his financial contributions are inconsistent. Xiao Du assesses her work situation as not very good, that is, her salary is too low for her ability and responsibilities. She feels that this standard of living places the family "somewhere near the middle" in terms of standard of living in Shijiazhuang, but that this means they are in the lower middle class in relation to China as a whole.

Family life for Xiao Du is of paramount importance. The daily routine in their household centres on making a good home for their junior high school son. The boy was thirteen years old during the period in which I observed the family, and attended a typical Shijiazhuang middle school. He is a noticeably portly boy, as are Xiao Du and her husband, reflecting a lifestyle focussed on the pleasures of cooking and eating – far from unusual amongst Chinese families. They often invited me and other friends to their home for generous, multi-course meals, one of which was attended by my mother, who was astonished by the amount of food placed on the table. Memorably, I once met Xiao Du and her husband for lunch near Bobby's school. The meal ended with a comical struggle between father and son, who insisted the boy cap his meal with a number of chocolate treats despite the boy's protests.

Xiao Liu's, Xiao Ren's, and Xiao Hua's Families

These three young women were introduced to me as a group by a colleague in the company in which I worked. I introduce them collectively because of their common characteristics. All are now in their early thirties, have advanced university degrees, and are married to men with similar levels of education. Each has a background in teaching, but now works in a lower level position. Their husbands have achieved somewhat higher positions in their various companies, two acting as head teachers in colleges, one a middle-manager in a large provincial level SOE. All have young children who are now about four-years-old. Among the families observed in the study, these three stood out because each lived together with their parents, mainly for the purpose of providing valued childcare to the family. Such a living arrangement is not uncommon, although it seems to be less so amongst middle-class families. Amongst the families observed, however, only these three lived this way, an arrangement likely explained by the fact all are educational migrants to Shijiazhuang from smaller cities in Hebei, places where their parents maintain residences or rent them out. Grandparents in each of the other families have their own homes in Shijiazhuang and, while they do provide childcare, they do so only occasionally to supplement other arrangements. It was these three mothers who in the midst of my observations asked me to start a short-lived English class.

Lao Zhang & Xiao Li's Family

Of the families interviewed and observed for the study, it was that of Lao Zhang and Xiao Li that more than others seemed to embody the standards and promises of life under the aspirational cité. I became acquainted with Lao Zhang through a common contact. He is an upper level manager in the SOE that he has worked in since graduating from university with a degree in Chinese art and literature. The family is firmly entrenched in a class characterized by its members' "control of organizations" (see Table 2.1). Xiao Li, a member of the "skilled and semiskilled labour class," has been a music teacher in the same school her entire working life. Their home was unlike any other I visited in Shijiazhuang. While others gesture toward an interest in art and literature, placing books here and there in an effort to appear "learned," the Zhang's seem to have come by their taste for objects of art and the artistic life by virtue of being born into it. Xiao Li's father is a well-known artist whose works are chronicled in any number of professionally published texts displayed on the bookshelves of the apartment, not to mention in numerous original clay and stone sculptures. Lao Zhang's photos of his daughter and famous natural sites around the country adorn the walls of the family's atypically decorated loft apartment. Unlike most homes, theirs is dimly lit and finished in dark woods, exposed wood beams, and floor to ceiling bookshelves. When I visited their home to conduct interviews, Lao Zhang served tea *gongfu* style (功夫茶 – hand steeped tea in an elaborate, if informal "ceremony") from a lacquered tree root tea table. His office is in the loft of the apartment, which opens on to a roof top patio-garden overlooking one of Shijiazhuang's large public parks. His is a life of artistic masculinity (cf. Kipnis' (2011) literary masculinity), but with an incongruous twist – like many of those who

CHAPTER 5

live such a life in today's China, Mr. Zhang gets around the city and countryside in an enormous 4 × 4 SUV.

BELIEFS AND ACTIVITIES OF MIDDLE-CLASS URBAN PARENTS

Parents tend to follow trends blindly and to believe most of what they hear. (Chang, 2008, p. 82)

In contrast to previous generations, China's young university aspirants – and their parents – are pragmatic, individualistic, even self-centred in their values and strategies. (Rosen, 2004)

For intellectuals and everyday Chinese folk alike, "worrying about China" (Davies, 2007) is an obsession. The moral decline of contemporary society is a common topic of meal time conversations, including those prompted to the latest stories of crime and corruption relayed by the daily national newscast that is a dinner time staple in the home of my Chinese family. Indeed, my father-in-law's lessons were in part his attempt to cure the cultural amnesia that is, in his view, the primary cause of the ills of Chinese society. High on the list of these perceived and real ills is the apparent acquisitiveness of parents, a problem that tends to be interpreted by commentators like my father-in-law as morally vacant or, like Chang and Rosen in the quotations above, as blindly selfish mob behaviour. For Chang (2008), parents run from one fruitless pursuit to another, rarely stopping to consider the utility or costs of the pressure they place on their children. Likewise, Rosen (2004) holds that these activities indicate the triumph of pragmatism and materialism in a society with increasingly stark class divisions. But in focusing on the spectacle of educational desire – the hustle and bustle – and conflating the apparently aggressive educational pursuits of parents with a-reflexivity, moral depravity, or cultural decline, these authors miss an opportunity to understand why Chinese parents join in such apparently absurd and hard to defend behaviours.

In the following sections I challenge this vision of Chinese parents as blind and acquisitive cultural dopes by detailing how they conceive of "education" and how they live out these conceptions as they go about the task of "educating" their children. By paying attention to both talk and action, I gain insight into a number of aspects of contemporary urban educational culture. What meanings and purposes do parents attach to the word "education?" What kinds of people do they want their children to become and how should they treat others? What modes of teaching and learning do they value? What kinds of knowledge and skills do they wish their children to obtain and develop? What criteria guide their choices of schools? What activities do they engage in outside of school? Such questions provide a means to consider parents' socio-cultural entrainment (Willis & Trondman, 2000), that is, the ways in which their conscious beliefs about education align with and/or defy elements of the aspirational cité discussed in Chapter 3. Inevitably, this process has led me to consider "critical operations" – the ways in which parents accept, reject, and/or modify not only the normative prescriptions that necessarily orient them, but also the new ways of living and moving on offer in the aspirational city that Shijiazhuang's political and business leaders are attempting to construct. As I detail and emplace (Kipnis, 2011) the thoughts and activities of these middle-class parents, I highlight the active and contingent nature of their engagement with the socio-cultural environment, interaction which, when considered separately from the cultural system that was the subject of Chapters 2 and 3, reveals the realm of sociocultural interaction to be one of deliberation and critique rather than passive consumption.

Education as a Zonghe De Pursuit

In formal interviews, my questions about the meaning and purpose of education were initially understood to indicate my interest in the process of schooling. Parents responded in a more or less uniform manner, agreeing that the fundamental purpose of education (as schooling) is the transmission of basic knowledge and life skills. Lao Dong, for example, said that "the goal of education is…I suppose it allows people to gain knowledge and skills…some survival skills, techniques." When I clarified that that I was interested in a broader conception of education, interviewees responded by saying that education and *educating* their children ought to be about more than the narrow aims typically associated with schooling. Without exception, these parents held that education ought to be a *zhonghe de* (综合的 – comprehensive) pursuit, a kind of education they saw to be entirely contrary to *yingshi jiaoyu* (应试教育 – exam-focussed education) that stresses the accumulation of knowledge through rote memorization. They spoke of education as a process that also fosters a particular character or set of characteristics. Lao Dong said that education should produce *zhen zheng de ren* (真正的人 – a fully developed person in all aspects). Similarly, Xiao Lu used the term *duli de ren* (独立的人 – independent person) to describe the outcome of an education properly conceived and accomplished. These and other such terms indicated how education is closely connected to conceptions of morals and/or morality. As Xiao Liu said, "people don't care so much whether you are clever or not. But whatever you do, first you'd better be moral, be good. You can't have a lot of bad ways of thinking." This perspective was echoed in Xiao Lu's thoughts on the word *jiaoyu* (教育 – education), which she sees as closely connected to the inculcation of morality. Doing a good job as a parent – the ultimate indication of moral parenting – is that one has raised a *you jiazhi de ren* (有价值的人 – a person with value), by which she means that such a person is needed by others or offers a *teshu rencai* (特殊人才 – special talent) to society.

In the case of Xiao Jiao, personal qualities are expressed through hard work rather than special talent. That she holds this view is not surprising given her own impressive work habits and extraordinary dedication to the task at hand. The purpose of education, she told me, is to develop just such habits and dedication. An urbanized native of a nearby county city, Xiao Jiao works hard and assiduously avoids controversy, although it should also be said that her competence and hard

CHAPTER 5

work has earned her the ear of her company's leaders, so she is better positioned than most to advocate for her co-workers. Her outlook is also shaped by childhood experiences in a family targeted during the Cultural Revolution for its undesirable class background as *funong* (富农 – rich peasants), but also importantly influenced by the reform and opening up period, during which hard work and dedication have brought significant rewards to people like her who have managed to take advantage of new opportunities in education and employment. Xiao Jiao approaches the task of educating her son with the same kind of dedication, making long trips home to serve him lunch and dinner, supervising his studies in the home, learning difficult curricula alongside him so that she can provide help, advocating for him when troubles occur at school, and attending parent education classes whenever offered by the school.

Themes of morality and hard work suggest that the children of these parents may be faced with a strict and traditional educational process. Conceiving of education as a comprehensive pursuit, however, means that notions of happiness and autonomy are equally prominent in informants' understandings of the purpose of education. For Lao Dong, part of living a *pusu de shenghuo* (朴素的生活 – a plain and simple life) is creating conditions for a more relaxed, less stressful, *wending de* (稳定的 – stable), and happy life. Lao Zhang and Xiao Li maintain that the ultimate goal of education is to produce a child with a general love for learning. Like Lao Dong, they believe that the best way to achieve this goal is to create an environment that fosters a sense of happiness and well-being in the child. Even high achievement in school (*chengji hao* – 成绩好) is subjugated to this aim, for achievement is a corollary of happiness, and certainly not the only measure of successful parenting or a life well lived. Indeed, Lao Zhang and Xiao Li identified happiness and satisfaction as the main aims of education, and toward this end, they endeavour to make their daughter's educational experiences stress-free and as positive as possible under the circumstances. Other informants agreed with this principle. Xiao Du believes that parents ought to act as guides to their children. She is more concerned with her son's inner qualities than his performance and sees it as her job to care for her son's physical and emotional needs until he can decide for himself what he wants to do in his adult life. It follows that her success as a mother will be measured by her son's future happiness and the extent to which he becomes an "accomplished person with a good job."

Liberal Talk, Illiberal Action

Xiao Du's invocation of "accomplishment" and good jobs serves as a reminder that, while parents attach conceptions of good persons and good education to notions of happiness and autonomy, there is a point at which reality bites, and the relationship of educational attainment, material security, and aspirations come to the fore. As Xiao Ren put it, "of course if his abilities are good, he will have a good future and career." At times parents express a feeling of helplessness with respect to the competitive nature of schooling and society (i.e., they don't like it but must join in). Performance in school, in other words, cannot be ignored entirely. For Xiao Liu, despite her commitment to her child's happiness and her attitude towards the practice of ranking students, it is not the case that any result will suffice: "If he can test in the better half, that is good enough for me. But if he brings home last place every day, trailing along in that way, that's no good." This bottom line is a common feature of parents' understandings of the balance that needs to be struck between happiness and the objective demands of contemporary society, and reveals a contradiction between the "liberal talk" of parents about education and schooling and "illiberal action." Like their middle-class counterparts in other parts of the world, these parents want their children to be happy, creative, and free, but often pursue these aims by exhortation and force.

Pursuing Mianzi

Social competition is a driving force behind illiberal action. Parents tend to pay careful attention to their child's relative merit and academic standing. As Xiao Lu explained, it is very natural for parents to feel proud if their child does well, though she also claims that others are more concerned with grades and achievements than she is. Competition of this kind is closely related to a (perceived) scarcity of high quality educational opportunities, but must also be understood through the concept of "face" (see Hu, 1944; Ho, 1976; King & Myers, 1977; Hwang, 1987, 2012). In some aspects, Xiao Lu readily admits to being a more "face loving" person ("*wo bijiao ai mianzi*" – 我比较爱面子) than others, that is, she is quite concerned with "exerting effort to obtain the attention or admiration of others" (Hwang, 2012, pp. 279–280). The desire for recognition applies in a wide range of domains, from the superficial – being seen wearing fashionable clothing, driving the right kind of car, living in the right kind of neighbourhood, eating in the right kind of restaurants – to the more substantive – being seen to be a moral and capable person. It also applies in the domains of child-rearing and schooling, but Xiao Lu makes a crucial distinction in terms of the specific criteria of educational distinction. Where most parents, in her view, would connect *zuo mianzi* (做面子 – making face) or *zheng mianzi* (整面子 – maintaining face) with the degree to which the children *chengji hao* (成绩好 – achieve high grades) and gain access to top schools, her criteria are closely aligned with the educational benchmarks established by the aspirational cité. For Xiao Lu, face will be gained insofar as her children exhibit qualities of well-rounded people or display a recognizable special talent. These, she believes, would reflect more positively her efforts as a mother and bring her great happiness. In terms of well-roundedness, a good child capable of accruing face for her parents will also display excellent interpersonal skills, good habits, and be warmhearted and happy every day. Compared to such qualities, the ability to score highly is less important.

Unlike Xiao Lu, Lao Dong claimed that he is not particularly concerned with this kind of face, although, like her, he does not compare his daughters performance with others. Xiao Zhao, on the other hand, thinks about face in much the same way

CHAPTER 5

as Xiao Liu. She believes that good people are those who exhibit a good outward image rather than those who score high grades in school. Education, then, is social in a crucial sense – it matters what others think of how a person's behaviour exhibits appropriate morality. This relates to the concept of *lian* (脸), which is, like *mianzi*, part of the concept of "face," but in this case is concerned with "public trust in the individual's morality" (Hwang, 2012, p. 268). Comprehensive or all-around development works both *from* and *toward* happiness, that is, as both a means and end. In other words, where one ought to have a set of qualities that gives *mianzi* and *lian*, these are mostly important because they are conditions of possibility of living a happy life.

Suzhi & Suzhi Jiaoyu

The kinds of qualities that bring public recognition to good persons and pride to parents are closely connected to the traits desired and pursued through comprehensive and all-around education. Along with the discourse of *zonghe*, informants commonly expressed their understandings of the meaning and purpose of education using the language of *suzhi*. Xiao Lu, for example, often invoked this word, saying that she thinks of *suzhi* as comprising a comprehensive set of qualities of concern to human development, including *de* (得 – morals), *zhi* (知 – knowledge), *ti* (体 – body/physical), *mei* (美 – beauty), and *lao* (劳 – work ethic). Similarly, Lao Dong defined *suzhi* as a comprehensive set of qualities including work ethic, temperament, knowledge. Notions of *suzhi* (素质 – "quality") and *suzhi education* (素质教育 – education for quality) are central to the discursive structure of the aspirational cité. That *suzhi* was on the minds of Shijiazhuang's parents was not surprising, for the concept of *suzhi* has, according to Kipnis (2007), become central to governance in post-Mao China. Generically, the word refers to the relative "quality" of individuals and groups and, at the same time, acts to justify their differential life conditions and prospects (Anagnost, 2004). *Suzhi* is a flexible concept capable of expressing both inter- and intra-group evaluations. For example, one might hear of the high *suzhi* of urbanites relative to their rural cousins, or of the low *suzhi* of one *minzu* (民族 – officially recognized minority nationality populations) compared to another. Within urban settings, low *suzhi* migrant construction workers might live alongside high *suzhi* urban elites. Indeed, situations where such labourers work to construct the very offices and homes that define the high quality urban lifestyle reveal the emergence of the differentiated class structure necessary for the extraction of surplus value from the former to the latter (Anagnost, 2004). *Suzhi* can also be seen as both means and end. Raising the *suzhi* of the rural peasant is crucial to rural development or, alternatively, rural development is the necessary if insufficient condition of high *suzhi* in China's rural residents.

Given the extent of its infusion into everyday life, my probes into the meaning of *suzhi* sometimes frustrated interviewees. After all, the meaning is obvious to those who have absorbed the concept practically from birth:

Why ask such obvious questions? Isn't it obvious? If his *suzhi* is high, he can have a good future. If his *suzhi* is high, his study skills will be strong, his social skills will be strong, he will look after others. He'll be a man of good character. (Xiao Du, Interview)

Interviewees dealt with this concept in terms of the question of whether *suzhi* is something a child is born with or something that is fostered is a difficult one. While parents disagree on this point and shift their own positions from time to time, most agree that *suzhi* is a comprehensive set of qualities, is mainly developed through family education and schooling, is vital to having a happy life, and that it is closely related to social class. On the whole, *suzhi* needs to be inculcated in children, and Xiao Lu believes that the process begins early on in the home with the development of *xingge* (性格 – dispositions) required to be successful in both school and society in general. Xiao Lu often stresses that her daughter should have a *duli jingshen* (独立精神 – independent spirit), and lists things such as dressing herself, climbing stairs by herself, and eating without assistance as ways to encourage this disposition. For example, she hopes her daughter will learn to love reading, that she will broaden her horizons through travel and other activities. She will study music as a way to raise *suzhi*, though the specific instrument is not as important as the act of pursuing personal interests.

Xiao Zhao, on the other hand, feels that there is something to the notion that *suzhi* is inborn. If this were not so, she suggests, how could we explain the different outcomes of schooling? Some children work very hard, but still cannot *chengji hao*. Or how can the example of Mao Zedong be explained? The reference to Mao is not meant as a political statement of her adherence to Maoist principles or of support of the CPP. Rather, she refers to Mao's early astuteness, the way that from a very young age he distinguished himself as intelligent despite being *sheng zai nongcun, guang pigu zhang da* (生在农村, 光屁股长大 – born and raised bare-bottomed in a village). "What education did he have?" she asks, to make clear that, to her, not everyone is born with an equal allotment of intellectual resources or work ethic. Furthermore, it is clear to her that any number of qualities apparent in an adult – whether excellent of not – are apparent at an early age. She offers up her own father as an example. He was seemingly born with a desire for education, and pursued it throughout his life. Considering her own daughter's natural orientation, she points out that a child's temperament seems to be inborn and not particularly amenable to modification. But it is also to be instilled in children. A child's outlook on life, for example, is something to be fostered in the home and school.

Cooperative/Collective Strategies

Not all the educational activities of parents can be critiqued as being entirely individualistic and/or illiberal. Lao Dong described how he, his wife, and a group of other parents plan weekly get togethers for their daughters in a *xiao zu* (小组 – small group) assembled in part to compensate for the absence of siblings. More than this,

CHAPTER 5

it acts as a support group comprising parents who think in similar ways about child-rearing and education. The group goes out to shopping malls, museums, or movies on weekends. Alternatively, they play together in parks or take classes together. This spontaneously organized group suggests a more cooperative approach to the task of child-rearing and education than is often portrayed in literature on Chinese educational culture. This small group of cooperating parents indicates forms of solidarity contrary to common depictions of the avaricious educating parent or complementary to those of the individualized family (Kipnis, 2012). Lao Dong indicates that members of the group help each other out by offering advice and mutual support in the absence of grandparents to help out or, equally important, because grandparents – steeped in the precepts of previous orders of worth – are ill-equipped to deal with the educational environment of the aspirational city.

Other parents also spoke of forming *xiao zu*, some with their child's classmates, others with same-aged children in the workplace or neighbourhood. For several weeks, a group of the parents asked me to teach English to their toddlers, an opportunity they could not pass up – and an appeal I could not refuse – given my request to interview and observe them. Given my lack of experience teaching young children, little came of these "classes," but they did provide a valuable opportunity to observe parents in action. Observing the four mothers who joined this short-lived *xiao zu* clarified the target of *Jinbaobei's* tutelage for parents. Three of the four, including Xiao Liu, were well-schooled in the precepts of modern pedagogy. Two in particular had worked for several years in a school curriculum reform project grounded in constructivist principles and were familiar with notions of child-centred learning, exploratory play, and positive reinforcement. Still, they tended to push for fixed curriculum and tangible outcomes, despite the fact that none of these children were three years old yet, and in clear violation of the precepts of the aspirational cité concerning preferred modes of learning and teaching. Despite their professions of adherence to new ways of educating their children, for these parents and in this particular situation, casting off traditional "'dictatorial' attitude[s]" (Zhu, 1999, p. 238) allowing their children to learn through exploration and play was not easy.

Family Education

Jiating jiaoyu (家庭教育 – family education or education in the family/home), is considered crucial, especially at younger ages. Indeed, informants universally agreed that the primary site of such moral education is the family, and its primary agents are the parents. Parents should teach the child a general orientation to life. The goal of *jiating jiaoyu* is to give the provision of a stable home, a good education, and, as a result, better opportunities that will lead to a more secure, better life. This form of education in the home is accomplished in the main through modeling; parents and grandparents are models for the child, or, as Lao Dong put it, "*haizi shi fu mu de jingzi* (孩子是父母的镜子 – *children are a reflection of the parents*). A common theme in interviews was that *jiating jiaoyu* is first and foremost concerned with the provision of life's basic needs.

But it is also about the inculcation of basic habits of thought, of how to tackle everyday problems, and to work diligently to solve them. Besides these aims, family education is about learning to live with and get along with others. *Jiating jiaoyu* is, in other words, about learning basic habits of thinking, learning, and relating to others.

Grandparents play an important role in *jiating jiaoyu*, especially the grandmother, whose special role is to ensure the health of the child by encouraging – indeed, at times forcing – the child to *chi bao le* (吃饱了 – eat until he/she is full). In contemporary urban China under the influence of the aspirational cité, however, many of the habits of the older generation (*e.g.*, spoon feeding, carrying the child up stairs, intervening in parental discipline) are viewed with suspicion and frustration. Parents in the study universally, if lightly, criticized their parents for faulty *jiating jiaoyu*, worrying that their parents' excessive care for the child would result in a *niai de* (溺爱的 – spoiled) child. Relatedly, most held that their parents have had or will have little role in determining their choice of schools and after-school activities. Grandparents, they said, tended to see such choices as unimportant, excessive, and/or expensive. In this regard, grandparents were seen to have little knowledge of contemporary schooling, and their input was not particularly valued. Nonetheless, the education of good persons begins in the home at the earliest ages with family education that is conducted in an immediate way by grandparents, especially grandmothers. As several informants confirmed, a good child is raised with responsibilities in and to the family, and fulfills these by being hardworking, enjoying studying, and studying useful knowledge. Developing good habits, such as a love for reading, are central to being a good person, and a disposition toward sitting and enjoying reading is one that ought to be developed early in a socially useful person. This focus on bodily habits indicates the relatively restricted role that parents see themselves in, particularly in the early years, for while they do see it as their role to transmit knowledge, in the long run, they tend to see themselves as most influential in the realm of family education. Others linked to diffuse and institutionalized forms of education – such as the school, social agencies, and media – join parents in this task, but parents are seen to have the ultimate responsibility for teaching children "what is right or wrong" (Xiao Ren, Interview).

Recently, family education has begun to take on a new meaning as schools have taken up task of "educating families." Most schools organize parent education classes, at minimum to orient new parents to the school and its expectations, but some offer ongoing sessions with specific age/grade-based topics on offer. Xiao Jiao, for example, told a humorous story about the first weeks of her son's enrollment at one of Shijiazhuang's top middle schools. Arriving late for a parent orientation session, she was singled out by the session's facilitator as a poor example of how parents should model habits for their children. This accusation was not entirely fair given the long distance she had had to travel, but it hit home as her son had been struggling to be on time and alert in the first weeks of school. Soon afterward, she and her husband bought a tiny apartment near the school to ease the boy's commute, but greatly exacerbating her own. Not all family education sessions of this kind are mandatory or of such a high stake. For example, Lao Dong takes advantage of

CHAPTER 5

the sessions offered to parents at SFLS (see Chapter 4) to learn about parent-child communication, child psychology, and child development. These sessions are not usually mandatory, but nonetheless have the effect of increasing pressure on parents to see themselves as integral to their child's success at school. Given the long history of educational desire in Chinese culture, it seems unlikely that such exhortations are necessary. Still, what is perhaps unique about such programs is that they encourage a "scientific" approach to child-rearing, and place at parents disposal up-to-date, research-based knowledge.

Cultivating an Aspirational Habitus

Beyond *jiating jiaoyu*, parents reported engaging in a bewildering array of extracurricular activities. Xiao Zhao, for example, registers her daughter in ballet, music appreciation, piano, and *guzheng* (古筝 – Chinese zither) lessons, and oral English. The primary intent of these activities instruction is not to develop skill in these areas or to prepare the ground for a future career in these areas. Rather, they are means of inculcating culture and discipline. At the same time, ballet and *guzheng* are seen as means to developing appropriately feminine *suzhi* and *qizhi* (气质 – literally "temperament" but conveys a sense of the intangible). Like other parents in the study, Xiao Zhao also believes strongly in taking her daughter outside of Shijiazhuang to see what the world outside is like and, thus, to expand her daughter's *yanjie* (眼界 – outlook) and *sixiang* (思想 – way of thinking/ideology). This is a topic about which she is passionate. After all, "If a child only lives and experiences her small neighbourhood life," she says, "how can they be prepared for the outside world? She must see different situations and things" in order to *kaikou yanjie* (开口眼界 – open/expand her horizons). Xiao Zhao is proud of the results of her pursuing such activities, noting that her daughter is quite brave when approaching me. Where many little girls might be shy when meeting a "strange looking foreigner," her daughter greets me eagerly.

Like Xiao Jiao, Lao Zhang and Xiao Li moved to a new home far from their places of work, but near to SFLS when their daughter was still young. According to their understanding, this school provides an atmosphere best aligned with their own aims, despite – or perhaps in virtue of – the fact that Xiao Li works in a school that would seem an equally likely and convenient choice. For her part, Xiao Li explains her choice of this alternative by noting that her school is a good one, but also that it is too exam focused and puts too much pressure on students. This focus would mean undue and undesired pressure on both her daughter and herself, given that the potential failure of her daughter to live up to these standards might also reflect poorly on her.

The couple's daughter is tall and considered beautiful by a narrow set of standards, and moves and speaks with a grace partly cultivated in the home – i.e., through the family education practices of her parents and grandparents – and partly through a series of extracurricular activities carefully arranged to inculcate an approach to life favoured by her parents. Music appreciation, ballet, and piano complement the usual supplementary classes in core subject areas fill her time when on weekends when school is out. Like Xiao Zhao, her parents occupy holiday times exposing her to life and nature far from Shijiazhuang. The apartment is lined with Lao Zhang's photographic portraits of *gucheng* (古城 – ancient/old towns/cities), and alpine and grassland vistas around the country. These photos are carefully composed, naturalistic portraits collectively depicting a growing young girl skilled at posing nonchalantly before this or that mountain, temple, or river, and thoughtfully considering the middle distance. When I complemented Lao Zhang on the beauty of both the photographs and his daughter, he smiled proudly and launched into descriptions of why he took this or that photo in such and such a manner. This topic, it turned out, was productive with respect to my interests. The photos provide concrete illustrations for Lao Zhang to elaborate his understanding of the purposes and aims of education. The family has travelled to China's cultural heritage sites like Pingyao (平遥) and Lijiang (丽江) to encourage a sense of respect for the vast history and cultural patrimony of the country. Trips to Jiuzhaigou (九寨沟) and the grasslands of northern Hebei were intended to not only instill an awareness of the environment, but also an appreciation for the beauty of nature. A trip to the Tibetan areas of China in Sichuan and Qinghai exposed the child to the value of an ascetic or spiritual approach to life, and to help her to appreciate that there are other ways of life far removed from her own – all of these were meant to open her eyes to beauty and difference in the world or, as Xiao Zhao put it, to open her eyes to the fact that there is a larger world out there. Like her father, the young Ms. Zhang is being encouraged to develop an aesthetic disposition, but in her case these take a specifically feminine form, what might be a called a life of 'aesthetic femininity' – the world is as much an object of aesthetic appreciation as one to be dealt with pragmatically or instrumentally.

Xiao Lu began taking her daughter to the Shijiazhuang outlet of the U.S. chain Jinbaobei (Gymboree, rendered 金宝贝 or "Golden Baby" in Putonghua) at a young age hoping to instill qualities of independence and creativity. I accompanied mother and daughter to one such session to observe a mother and toddler training session. At that time, Xiao Lu was still very much absorbed in learning how to *zuo hao mama* (做好妈妈 – be a good mother), a desire explicitly encouraged and exploited by Jinbaobei. On occasion, the young teacher/facilitator focused on how to play with toys and work with basic art supplies with small children. She modeled for parents how to build interest in the child; how to interfere less and encourage more; how, in short, to be more involved and more hands off. She chided the parents when they displayed the tendency to criticize imperfections in the child's play and art, when they became upset with the child making a mess, or when the child displayed a tendency to wander about aimlessly, reminding them that their main task was to help the child develop positive self-image, a willingness to try new things in new ways, and to explore the environment spontaneously. She provided explicit directions on how to work positively with the child: "You shouldn't always tell them 'bu dui!' It is better to ask the child, 'what did you draw?' or 'what can you do with this toy?'" In this example, it becomes clear that children are not the sole targets of improved

101

CHAPTER 5

suzhi. Indeed, Jinbaobei's classes are as much about challenging Shijiazhuang's mothers to critique and improve themselves as they are about training talented children, a challenge that Xiao Lu is aware of and has taken on with her typical verve. Indeed, Xiao Lu believes that Jinbaobei's educational ideas are better than most training centres in part because they focus on developing parents' ability to guide their children. Also, she places much stock in Jinbaobei's worldwide reputation; she trusts their experience, research, ideas and mature management. While she hadn't heard of it before it came to Shijiazhuang, she went on line to learn about it and found that its ratings from other parents were very high. As such, it is a primary agent of transmission of these precepts to willing middle-class parents like Xiao Lu.

As her daughter has grown older, Xiao Lu has added dance and skating lessons to her weekly routine, and hopes that the girl will eventually enroll in figure skating lessons. This, Xiao Lu says, is a way to cultivate a sporty, feminine *xingge* (性格 – nature/disposition). Xiao Lu's on line profile is a catalog of various activities designed to further this project. Photos of her daughter amount to a stream of representations of Xiao Lu's vision for the child she hopes to raise. In one, the girl stands clad in alpine ski gear at the top of a crowded Hebei mountain. In another she stares down the camera bravely as it captures her carving a tight circle on her recently mastered two wheeler. In numerous others she strikes ballet poses in a frilly pink tutu. At a precocious four-years old, the girl was already expert at striking appropriate poses – circumspect, chin bowed, eyes pointed upward, hands posed elegantly – while singing songs for gatherings of Xiao Lu's friends. Family travel to nearby countries such as Singapore and Indonesia – Xiao Lu hopes to go to Australia and Canada on future trips – are meant to give her daughter a broad outlook, and to open her eyes to the possibilities of a rich life. The girl is exposed to models for such a life in her own parents. Xiao Lu took up competitive dance in university, and now teaches classes in aerobics at a number of local clubs. Lao Wang is an avid participant in a variety action sports such as off-road car racing. Their daughter comes along to watch her parents do these things, and Xiao Lu is hopeful that from these experiences she will learn to think of life as something to be actively pursued rather than passively lived. "It is not enough," she says, to "work and eat."

In addition to the *xiao zu* activities mentioned above, Lao Dong's weekends are scheduled full of activities centered on his daughter's education. She attends dance classes, English lessons, and *yinyue xinshang* (音乐欣赏 – music appreciation) classes. The courses fulfill the mandate of balanced education, and are an important break from the grade/exam focussed study of the school week. Of course the academic extra-curricular activities support the school mission, but Lao Dong, like others, is careful to select courses that more closely aligned with the newly preferred modes of learning of the aspirational cité. English courses are chosen because they are focussed on oral skills or communication in general as opposed to memorization or recitation. Music appreciation is about inculcating a habit of disciplined study and habituation to an artistic mode of life rather than mastery of one instrument or another.

CHAPTER 6

MAKING ONE'S WAY THROUGH THE FIELD OF URBAN EDUCATIONAL CULTURE

It was the summer of 2012 when I first became aware of the extent to which I was immersed in the reality of life as a parent in an aspirational educational culture. True, three years earlier my spouse and I had signaled our awareness by jokingly posing our son for pictures while on a walk at nearby Tsinghua University. We waded through the scores of one-child parents who arrive daily to tour the grounds of China's most desired institution of higher learning (see Figure 6.1). In subsequent years my father-in-law began to plan regular trips to local tourist sites, particularly those that he associated with traditional – and, thus, desirable – Chinese culture. At the same time, he and my mother-in-law began to offer periodic evaluative interpretations of our growing son's behaviour. A range of toddler missteps – crying too often, being toilet trained too late, failure to wash hands, eating meals with insufficient dedication – were taken to indicate stunted moral development and, more disturbingly, inadequate parenting and/or family education. Other behaviours – asking to play with other children's toys, not responding immediately to the command to go in for dinner – added the humiliation of very public loss of face in front of other grandparents on the university campus where we lived.

In this chapter I continue to focus on the realm of socio-cultural interaction, but also work to fulfill the deeper promise of the research questions by explicating the ways in which parental beliefs and activities articulate with the cultural systemic entities of the aspirational cité and aspirational city. Where much of the previous chapter was descriptive, here the aims are more explicitly theoretical.

NEGOTIATING & NAVIGATING: THE LOGIC OF CHINA'S URBAN EDUCATIONAL CULTURE

In the remainder of this chapter my aim is to theorize how the cultural-systemic elements and practices of people discussed in previous chapters are bound together. I begin by revisiting Harvey's (2005) notion of "accumulation by dispossession" in order to develop a theory of urban educational culture sensitive to the ineluctable spatiality of social processes, and use this integrated notion to reconsider the parental accounts developed in the previous chapter. Bourdieu's (1986, 1990) concepts of capital, *habitus*, and field provide one means to indicate this relation, and I strive to link the cultural-systemic elements that comprise the aspirational cité/city with the beliefs and activities of parents. Following this, in Chapter 7 I return to Archer

CHAPTER 6

for a perspective that offers a more agentic, and, perhaps, optimistic view than that suggested by the Bourdieusian interpretation. While it is the case that most might consider Bourdieu and Archer incompatible (this conflict is usefully reviewed in Adams, 2006), from my perspective, the gulf separating the two is exaggerated, most often in Archer's (1985, 1993, 1996) unrequited critiques of Bourdieu (see Elder-Vass, 2007 for an attempted rapprochement). In considering each in turn, my aim is to produce a practical social theory of China's contemporary urban educational culture that recognizes both the familiar (the efforts of middle-class parents to maximize their own share of scarce resources) and the strange (the intensity of these practices and the spectacular scope and pace of material and cultural change). Such a theory ought, at minimum, to account for how parents orient themselves in relation to powerful educational ideas under conditions of rapid transformation of the urban spaces within which they live. It might, furthermore, provide some hints about the future Chinese educational culture as a whole.

Figure 6.1. Parents and their children pose for photos at the gates of Tsinghua University

The Spatiality of Social Processes

> Any overall strategy for dealing with urban systems must contain and reconcile policies designed to change the spatial form of the city...with policies concerned to affect the social processes which go on in the city. (Harvey, 1988, p. 50)

At a number of points in previous chapters I have suggested that urban renovation in Shijiazhuang is guided in part by principles, precepts, and propositions defined by the moral order of the aspiration cité. As Harvey puts it, such an overall strategy is rarely formulated, never mind achieved on the ground, and I do not mean to suggest here that there has been an active effort on the part of the formulators of *san nian da bianyang* to do so. What I do suggest is that a de facto strategy of this kind has brought about a shift in the terrain upon which urban China's educational culture plays out. Intentional or not, my interest in Shijiazhuang's renovation remains squarely on processes related to the production of inequality.

For Harvey (2005), spatio-social processes of the kind playing out in China's cities in general and in Shijiazhuang in particular can be understood as "accumulation by dispossession." Harvey draws on Marx's notion of "primitive accumulation," renaming it to take account of contemporary forms of dispossession in an era of advanced capitalism. Harvey (2001, 2005) describes accumulation by dispossession as a response to a "crisis of overaccumulation," a condition characterized by the existence of stocks of unproductive capital that, inevitably, seek productive outlets to restart the process of accumulation. Accumulation by dispossession comprises a collection of processes, some "cutting edge" (p. 147), and others, more useful for my purposes, familiar throughout the history of the capitalist order, specifically "the commodification and privatization of land and the forceful expulsion of peasant populations; the conversion of various forms of property rights…into exclusive private property rights (p. 145).

The role of the state is also crucial (p. 145), as is the process of proletarianization, by which whole classes of people are co-opted as wage-earners (p. 146). Accumulation by dispossession involves not only the enclosure of new physical spaces, but also the "appropriation and co-optation of preexisting cultural and social achievements as well as confrontation and supersession" (p. 146). In the case of contemporary China and other developmental states, it is the process by which "determined entrepreneurs and developmental states…'join the system' and seek the benefits of capital accumulation directly" (p. 153). Accumulation by dispossession, in this connexion, is "the necessary cost of making a successful breakthrough into capitalist development with the strong backing of state powers" (p. 154). The task of assessing the linkage of urban renovation to inequality in China is necessarily a matter of linking "the mechanisms which connect allocational decisions…on such things as transportation networks, industrial zoning, location of public facilities, location of households, and so on with their inevitable distributional effects upon the real income of different groups in the population" (Harvey, 1988, p. 51).

Judging these effects is one of the aims of Ren's (2013) work on the role of urban real estate development in the production of inequality in reform era China. One way to resolve the difficulty of evaluating these changes in terms of the lives of real people is to pay attention to the kinds of people that these new spatial forms are intended to serve, not to mention the kinds of people they actually benefit. By doing so, we move away from identifying specific extant groups and class fractions, and toward an assessment of the normative thrust of urban reform. In the case of Pan Shiyi and Zhang Xin, developers of Beijing's Jianwai SOHO business district, a particular set of skills – "sharp business acumen and entrepreneurial skills" (p. 147) – have led to rich rewards under reform era policies. Thus the dispositions – themselves in part

CHAPTER 6

native to existing class fractions and fostered through educational processes enabled by educational reform – of a group of people with access to capital, knowledge of the market, and social connections, are implicated in the spatial forms that emerge in particular places and times. Put simply, if we pay attention only to the spectacle of demolition and construction in China's cities, we may miss the fact that these spatial processes have real effects in terms of the material well-being of some relative to others. Jianwai SOHO, after all, rose from the ashes of bankrupt Beijing No. 1 Machine Factory (Ren, 2013), enriching its developers in the short term and creating a new spatial order specifically dedicated to the task of capital accumulation over the long run. In densely populated urban China, such redevelopment always involves the displacement of existing residents. Insofar as it enables a new urban elite "to get rich much faster than the rest" (Ren, 2013), it hides from view both a past city upon whose soil manual labourers that once earned their living and a present in which it is implicated in the production of social inequality.

Because of the scale and rapidity of change in Chinese cities, they provide examples par excellence of the ways in which the "transformation of geographical and social spaces…[changes] the nature of moral experiences and [reshapes] power relationships among individuals, institutions, and localities" (Pan, 2011, p. 154). The entire city of Shanghai and its program of rapid redevelopment, which served as the inspiration for Shijiazhuang's renovation more than a decade later, indicate the extent to which urban spaces have become tapestries upon which imagined cities of the future can be constructed. Transformation in that city has taken place both on the ground and in the minds of its residents. Once a bastion of Chinese industry, Shanghai has been rebuilt as a centre of international finance and exchange, its proletarian core transformed in short order into a highly stratified spatial order imagined to comprise three rings: a privileged "English speakers'" ring, a marginalized "Shanghainese speakers'" ring, and a middle ring occupied by migrant "Mandarin speakers" (Pan, 2011). Far from representing empirical reality, these social locations nonetheless correspond to "differing degrees of cultural and moral worth" (p. 155) with real consequences for inhabitants assumed to belong to them. In other words, these moral assessments map onto patterns of exploitation in the material realm. At the same time, the new Shanghai preserved many of the old identifications and prejudices associated with times past, a new social hierarchy mapped onto locational schemes – imperial, colonial, and socialist – long since expired.

The experience of Shijiazhuang's renovation is rather different. Because it is a relatively new city, the product of a fortuitous location along both north-south and east-west transportation corridors, the consumption of surrounding villages through progressive sprawl, and in-migration, the kinds of cultural and moral differentiations so clear in old cities like Beijing and Shanghai were nearly impossible to discern in the pre-*san nian da bianyang* order. Still, the capital intensive nature of the changes the city continues to undergo means that the city is subject to spatio-social transformations of a similar kind. A number of concrete observations can be made about Shijiazhuang based on the general effects of urban renovation identified in

Chapter 4, including the decline of danwei neighbourhoods; de-ruralization; the shift from "free" markets to supermarkets; beautification, culturalization, and spiritual uplift; and mobilization. I also dedicated a portion of that chapter to a description of two exemplars of Shijiazhuang's new institutional landscape in relation to the aspirational cité, one private, the other quasi-private.

First, a general movement of privatization of residential homes is facilitated by policy that enables the investment of large amounts of capital in new neighbourhoods. Many of these neighbourhoods are being constructed on the rubble of demolished *chengzhongcun* in a process that is most accurately described as accumulation by dispossession. Still, precisely who accumulates economic capital in this process is not as simple as it appears at first sight. It is clear, for example, that property developers are the immediate beneficiaries of redevelopment, and an ownership class of urban rich has emerged through this process, as has a supporting geography of luxury automobile retailers and shopping malls, five star hotels, and expensive restaurants, not to mention exclusive gated and guarded residential communities. At least one family described in this study belongs to precisely this class. But it is not only developers who benefit monetarily through the transfer and redevelopment of land in the city. The explosion of new residential housing stock would do little to benefit developers absent the people to purchase and live in the new neighbourhoods. Real estate holdings, whether gained in the *danwei* housing divestment process or through purchase of new housing stocks in the marketplace, are crucial repositories of economic capital for middle-class urbanites. Rapid inflation, particularly in the housing market, has multiplied the value of transferred wealth. Newly transferred and purchased apartments have become an important source of wealth for the urban residents of contemporary China, a factor that became apparent in interviews with Xiao Jiao. As her family deliberated where to send their son to university following his graduation from high school, one of the possibilities explored was overseas enrollment. Anticipating the expenditure of a large amount of money, they actively considered the sale of one of their three apartments as a way to finance the plan.

Capital flows have not moved exclusively in an upward direction. Given the structure of land-use rights in the still socialist state and the peculiar spatial organization of Shijiazhuang, some benefit has had to flow to the large number of residents of *chengzhongcun* in order to free up the land for redevelopment. The most common form that such compensation took was the granting of apartments in new developments to former residents, transfers that amount to a genuine gain of a fixed capital asset and an absolute upgrade in standard of living. These residences are used either as homes for grown children in the future or as rental properties and important sources of income for former villagers. The precise financial effects of such redistribution schemes are beyond the scope of this research, but informal inquiries with current and former villagers confirm that this is the most common result of redevelopment even though a significant number of settlements are perceived as unjust and that there is no shortage of cases of absolute dispossession without compensation. Despite the fact that most residents have apparently been compensated in the process of removal, the unequal proportioning of the proceeds of redevelopment nonetheless indicates a process of accumulation by dispossession. The investment of massive amounts of capital in this process underscores the extent to which the re-spatialization of the city is directly connected to the social re-classification of Shijiazhuang.

Second, the shift from "free" markets to supermarkets indicates another aspect of the spatiality of social processes. This process is more obviously linked to notions of cultural betterment and conceptions of the good life found in the aspirational cité. The removal and replacement of farmers' markets with supermarkets is not unrelated to the redevelopment of village lands, of course. Indeed, it is an integral part of the process as many of the new residential complexes are also commercial. Developers, to be sure, aim to benefit from all opportunities available to them. But accumulation and cultural uplift is achieved in a single stroke – villages and adjacent unsightly outdoor markets can be paved over and replaced by massive new residences and commercial complexes as two avenues of future accumulation are followed at once. At the same time, the proletarianization of village residents, already a decades-long process begun when the city physically surrounded the village, is taken to its logical conclusion as surplus farm labour is absorbed into the new commercial districts.

Third, and intimately related to this process of proletarianization, the re-designation of land for new purposes related to beautification, culturalization, and spiritual uplift demonstrates the integration of spatial and social processes. As discussed in Chapter 4, the construction of such spaces is an important aspect of *san nian da bianyang* and can be attributed to ways of thinking about modernity closely associated with the aspirational cité. For example, one of the major long term projects initiated under *san nian da bianyang* is the *huancheng shuixi*, a vast, city-encircling project that aims to solve the city's drainage problems and, at the same time, improve the quality of life of residents. In most cases, construction of this waterway will involve the reclassification of land previously set aside for food production. In others it will involve the demolition of villages that previously stood outside of Shijiazhuang proper. Other projects related to cultural uplift have required more traditional redevelopment in the centre of the city, including the removal of derelict housing and commercial space to make way for an expansion of the provincial museum and library (see Figures 4.8 and 4.9).

In some ways, each of these re-developments are counterintuitive from the perspective of capital accumulation. Each involves the dedication of enormous amounts of capital to the construction and ongoing operation of facilities that will be money losing ventures in the long run. Here, combining the notion of accumulation by dispossession with a related concept, spatio-temporal fixes (Harvey, 2001, 2005), helps to resolve this apparent contradiction. Recall that for Harvey, accumulation by dispossession is a response to a crisis of accumulation, a crisis resolved by the movement of capital into new spaces (spatial fixes) and into new fixed assets that enable future accumulation (temporal fixes). Accumulation by dispossession is, of course, most obviously a case of the former type of crisis resolution, as socialist housing stocks are brought into capital circuits through privatization, mainly of land resources. The array of beautification, culturalization, and spiritual uplift projects amount to another form of spatio-temporal fixing, one that aims through public pedagogy (cf. diffuse pedagogic action) to create new kinds of citizens (modeled on precepts, prescriptions, and propositions described in the aspirational cité) and, in the process, open up to exploitation a new class of workers once protected within work units and other forms of collectives, especially in the case of village-in-the-city residents. The creation of these new citizens through educational processes is a way to open up new "territory" for capital accumulation.

Finally, new patterns of mobility have been enabled through the construction of an advanced transportation system. The most obvious indications of this new system at present favour the shift from bicycle travel to private cars, although it should be noted that the bicycle remains a prominent mode of transportation. The development of a transportation network involves a finely textured array of changes. First, expansion and widening of the existing grid in the older parts of the city aims to make travel by private car more efficient, especially for traveling to and from the city's new commercial districts. Second, a series of freeways have been constructed to enable rapid transportation across medium distances. Third, more high speed freeways link old areas of the city to new residential districts that lie far from the city centre. Finally, long distance travel infrastructure connects Shijiazhuang to China and the outside world. A second phase of the upgrading of the transportation system is now underway as the city has invested a large amount of capital in the building of a subway system. From the perspective of accumulation by dispossession, the development of this new transportation network both enables and directly dispossesses. In terms of the former, new and far flung neighbourhoods, commercial districts, not to mention cultural and educational institutions, could not fulfill their promise as centres of capital accumulation if people could not practically live in them or travel to patronize them. With respect to the latter, vast new roadways require land, and former residents of the lands required have had to move to make way. Most importantly for my purposes, the development of an advanced transportation network is also very much about enabling the new classes of aspirational residents imagined in the aspirational cité. It is to this mode of enablement that I turn now turn my attention.

Cultural Capital Accumulation

Harvey's concepts of spatio-temporal fixes and accumulation by dispossession have helped to demystify the spectacle of urban renovation that so haunted my early experiences of Shijiazhuang. They have also played a role in clarifying the second – the spectacle of educational desire – by forging links to a range of concepts introduced and clarified in the empirical work of Pierre Bourdieu. Throughout this work I have deployed a series of Bourdieu's concepts associated with pedagogic action to recognize the different kinds of teaching and learning that go on in contemporary urban China. These concepts have allowed me to identify pedagogic action in the family education efforts of parents and/or grandparents as they teach their children to eat properly, to walk up the stairs by themselves, or to care for others by doing simple things like picking up litter in the neighbourhood. Similarly, parents subject their children to institutionalized pedagogic action by registering them in compulsory education and, at considerable expense, enrolling them in an array of extracurricular classes and activities. Finally, everyday life in Shijiazhuang is replete with a less obvious if equally intense diffuse pedagogic action under the tutelage of the spaces, places, and networks of the constantly changing city in which they live.

Capital, Habitus, Field

Still, viewing these activities, intentional and otherwise, as practices of teaching and learning that produce, with greater or lesser success, particular kinds of citizens, only partially explains the transformations of Chinese educational culture occurring at present. A second set of concepts of use in the present research are those of "capital," "habitus," and "field" (Bourdieu, 1986). For Bourdieu (1997), capital exists in three "fundamental guises" (p. 47). Economic capital is only one of these, though it is typically the most visible and, from the perspective "life chances" (Weber, 1999 [1922], p. 116), the most important. Indeed, growth in the income and wealth in Chinese society at large and of the informants at the centre of this study is essential to any explanation of the depth and breadth of educational activities that Chinese parents engage in both inside and outside of the family home. Having enough money is, to say the least, a condition of possibility of pursuit of the high *suzhi* promoted in the aspirational cité. It is also clear that all the informants in this study are – some more, some less, some directly, others less so – beneficiaries of the enormous quantities of economic capital released and generated through the process of urban renovation.

Money and property of various kinds, however, tell only one, albeit pivotal, part of the story. Also crucial and often misrecognized are concurrent processes of "social" and "cultural" capital conversion and accumulation, that is, the processes by which social connections and social status, esteem, and expressions of taste come into play to differentially position and reposition people over time. Today, social capital is most often associated with the work of Coleman (1988) and Putnam (2000) and diminished in its capacity for social critique as a consequence.[1] For my purposes, it is cultural capital that is of most concern as two of its three forms – "embodied," "objectified," or "institutionalized" states (Bourdieu, 1986, p. 47), are of special significance to my observations in this study. I am particularly concerned with the ways in which parents pursue particular forms of embodied and institutionalized cultural capital, for these practices can be seen as both objects and products of pedagogic action, whether diffuse, family, or institutional (refer again to Table 1.1). Bourdieu sees the embodied state as the fundamental form of cultural capital (p. 48) precisely because it is disproportionately acquired through bodily practices that begin very early on (Bourdieu, 1977; Eagleton & Bourdieu, 1992). In terms of the former, in the previous chapter, I hinted at the notion of embodied cultural capital most obviously when I described the parenting practices of Xiao Lu, Xiao Zhao, Lao Zhang, and Lao Li with respect to each of their daughters' educations. Pedagogic action, especially in the early years, is only tangentially knowledge-focussed and is explicitly concerned with cultivating habits of the body. Reading, for example, is not only about learning to read but also about learning the habit of sitting quietly and paying attention. Walking up the stairs is less about getting exercise or saving grandma's back than it is about developing the important habit of not relying on others and of working toward explicit goals. More subtly, the kinds of poses constantly encouraged, required, and practiced for photo taking indicate the ways in which the accumulation of valued cultural capital is encouraged. The myriad commonplace practices of *jiating jiaoyu* that amount to an effort to instill valued forms of embodied cultural capital – what Bourdieu more succinctly refers to as *habitus* – are supplemented by the direct pedagogic action described in the previous chapter.

Reinterpreting the precepts, prescriptions, and propositions of the aspirational cité through the concepts of cultural capital and *habitus* help to clarify the objects and aims of pedagogic action and the social economy of cultural forms and practices. Reference to another of Bourdieu's concepts, *field*, brings the importance of the aspirational city back into focus. In Bourdieu's social theory, *what* people think and do cannot be separated from *where* they do it. The parents whose lives informed this study live in a social geography of "intersecting fields" (Bellamy, 1994), each featuring a specific quantity and distinctive distribution of available capital resources. These fields are characterized by conditions of unequal power, scarcity, and competition, in Bourdieu's (1986) terms, "the unequal distribution of capital, is the source of the specific effects of capital, i.e., the appropriation of profits and the power to impose the laws of functioning of the field most favourable to capital and its reproduction" (p. 49). Those with the greatest quantity of the most valued forms of capital in a given field, in other words, also have the power to set and change the rules of the game within the field. It is obvious that one could identify a Chinese "educational field" and analyze it in precisely this way. While a heavy reliance on examinations gives the Chinese education system a sheen of meritocracy, widely varying conditions between regions, cities, and even within cities and individual schools engender heavy competition for educational placements deemed to be of the highest quality. This competition also brings economic capital into play within supposed public schools, as parents are often able to pay special fees to charter schools set up within the walls of otherwise publicly built and funded schools, of which SFLS in Shijiazhuang is only one.

My main aim in invoking the concept of field, however, is to use it to bring the pedagogic activities of parents like Xiao Zhao, Xiao Lu and others into relation with the conditions imposed by the physical, geographical field of contemporary Shijiazhuang. Attempts to measure up to the ideal through educative projects of one kind or another are enabled or constrained by the way that capital endowments position one within the moral and physical orders of the city. Economic capital endowments are particularly telling in the new Shijiazhuang, built as it is to foster differing scales of mobility in its citizens. Where roadways were once built to facilitate movement over relatively short distances, typically by bicycle or public bus, a second layer of higher speed traffic arteries has been added to enable longer commutes and shopping trips for those with the resources to buy private cars. It remains to be seen what lines of force the construction of a new subway system will introduce to the urban field of Shijiazhuang. Parents who in the past could realistically chose only between sending their child to a local school or relocating to a new district can more readily exercise choices in the educational marketplace so long as they have enough money, time, connections, and/or knowledge to do so. For parents endowed with such assets, Shijiazhuang is a field of educational opportunity that supports a vision of the "educating parent," one that is closely aligned with the precepts, prescriptions, and propositions of the aspirational cité. A birds eye view of the city emerging from the latest round of property investment reveals the scope of this expansionary project – a city that ten years ago could only be travelled across with great time and effort can now be circumnavigated in a fraction of the time, but only for those families with access to private transportation and whose homes lie in close proximity to these new transportation networks.

JIANFU RECONSIDERED

Xiao Lu and Lao Wang are parents in one such family. Despite their desire to send their children to school abroad, for Xiao Lu and Lao Wang, the Shijiazhuang reconstructed under *san nian da bianyang* has brought opportunity, nascent wealth, and a lifestyle attuned to and increasingly aligned with the precepts, prescriptions, and propositions of the aspirational cité. Social and economic capital have afforded them the mobility required to buy a home near the school to which they wished to send their daughter, and later near a central Shijiazhuang park in a home that provides efficient access to all areas of the city, not to mention the family's nanny. Family connections gave them access to a piece of land in the country side – both a "private paradise" (L. Zhang, 2010) and a place where the "slow life" is possible) – made accessible by roadways rapidly constructed under *da bianyang*. Improvements to these same roads have allowed them to move to a larger new apartment in the city centre overlooking the city's largest park, a home large enough to accommodate a second child and, on weekends, Xiao Lu's mother, who helps with the children more often now that she has retired.

Xiao Zhao's is another family similarly positioned. In my interviews and discussions with her, matters of class and status came up often. Xiao Zhao is not naive about the unequal capacity of families to realize a child of high quality/balanced development, and is especially aware that it is easier for people of higher social class to pursue kind of all-around development encouraged under the aspirational cité.

She maintains that, although it is possible for a child from a poor family to study well, ensuring that such children exhibit qualities of balanced development is not easy, that is, the *zonghe suzhi* of such children is not easily achieved. But for a family of means, if the child can study well, it is likely that the child will be well-developed in all respects. She holds that this is related to the family's capacity to provide the opportunities to broaden the child's horizons. It is obvious to Xiao Zhao, in other words, that a child from the village who has studied well and thus added to his or her stock of institutionalized cultural capital in the form of an educational credential, is very likely to be lacking in other areas considered crucial to the formation of a person of balanced education. In other words, as discussed above, such a child is likely to fall behind in terms of his or her stockpile of other forms of valued cultural capital, most importantly the kinds of embodied capital cultural that Xiao Zhao goes to great lengths to instill in her daughter.

For Xiao Zhao, a *quanzhi mama* in a family of significant means, *san nian da bianyang* has modified the city in ways more in line with the kind of life she aspires to and a life that her material circumstances make possible. The ability to easily move about the city by car enables the pursuit of her educational projects in ways impossible before *san nian da bianyang*. What's more, these social and economic conditions and her family's positioning within them that make it likely that her daughter will succeed in living up to the precepts of the aspirational cité. One aspect of their current life that works in favour of this eventuality is precisely the family separation that might otherwise be seen as a detriment. Xiao Zhao's husband works in Shenzhen, meaning that she and her daughter often go to that city to visit him. While there, they can also go to nearby Hong Kong, a more modern and advanced city than Shijiazhuang. They can visit Disneyland Hong Kong, which Xiao Zhao believes can work to broaden her daughter's horizons. Xiao Zhao knows that money matters, and compares the situation of her daughter favourably to that of one of her neighbours. The income of that family is very low by comparison, and this means that their daughter has never eaten at Pizza Hut before, and maybe even never at KFC, despite living near these places and McDonald's. Xiao Zhao emphasizes the significance of this comparative lack of experience by letting her letting her sentence trail off and emitting a sigh, finally concluding that the little girl nonetheless studies very well, ranking third in her class at school and being well-appreciated by her teachers. That girl's lack of broad experience, she believes, has direct educational consequences, and she imagines the difficulty that girl might have in completing diary writing assignments, something that her daughter, with her broad experiences, has no problem with.

San nian da bianyang has affirmed and accelerated processes already enabled to great extent by the privatization of housing. Lao Zhang and Xiao Li's family, already entitled to homes subsidized by each of their respective employers, the establishment of the semi-public-private SFLS opened a venue for the realization of their educational aspirations for the daughter. At the same time, *san nian da bianyang* has allowed that school to grow in size, to increase its intake of students, and to

CHAPTER 6

upgrade the quality of services and facilities it offers. It has also led to high density redevelopment of former village lands in close proximity to the school. Where six floor walkups and villages comprising single family dwellings occupied much of the surrounding lands, the school is now dwarfed by newly developed commercial and high rise residential developments. Their close proximity to SFLS means that such homes are in high demand for families like Lao Zhang and Xiao Li's whose desire for the offerings of SFLS is matched by the material means to realize the dream of providing the best schooling possible.

Successfully inculcating a socially useful *habitus* is an intensive and high stakes game in contemporary urban China, both from the perspective of academic success and in terms of the future social success. As I suggested earlier, the apparent ejection of Xiao Du from the larger social group to which she once made a vital contribution must be understood in part by recognizing the extent to which the aggregated capital resources of her family made them. From the perspective of economic capital, they simply can no longer afford to take part in the kinds of activities required to move with Xiao Lu's "in crowd." Economic capital is important, though not determinative in this respect, as a number of current members of Xiao Lu's social circle are of similarly modest means. Nor should objectified cultural capital be ignored, as it is obvious that much attention is paid in this group to famous brands and the possession of them. Driving a Range Rover rather than a far more modest Buick or, even further down the social value chain, a domestically produced Cherry, most assuredly grants a degree of access to the group. What finally separates these members from exiles like Xiao Du, however, is their ability to exhibit the kinds of embodied cultural capital that mark them as members of a common social group – working out at the right kind of gym; not just drinking red wine, but also being seen to *appreciate* it through a set of socially sanctioned and carefully monitored bodily gestures; seeking out opportunities to live an adventuresome and active life; responding eagerly (with a ready "absolutely!") to invitations to take part in adventurous activities; and crucially, demonstrating the frenetic activity associated with pursuing any and all means to achieve collectively desired *zonghe jiaoyu* outcomes for their children – their ability to exhibit, in short, an aspirational *habitus*.

When I returned to Shijiazhuang in the summer of 2013, the consequences of the logic of cultural capital accumulation for the prospect of *jianfu* were clarified by a fortuitous meeting with an old friend in the provincial education bureau. This chance meeting immediately led to a family luncheon date during which matters of education took centre stage. We chatted for some time of the difficulties facing the bureau, chief amongst them the ongoing battle against exam-focussed education, the intrusion of market-based selection of students, and the heavy pressure that parents and students alike are placed under in the current system. When I suggested that the way these problems were laid out suggested that *jianfu* remains a central concern, the acquaintance heartily agreed, saying that *jianfu* remains the fundamental task for all those charged with raising the quality of both life and education in China. The problem, however, is that efforts of centralized policy makers and administrators are seen to be scuttled by local officials and, in the final instance, by parents themselves. Even as higher-ups work toward *jianfu*, the end users of educational services, repositioned as educational "consumers" under the socialist market economy and eager to accumulate cultural capital as efficiently as possible, replace that which was cut with ever more enticing options.

When experts, commentators, and every day folk talk about the shortcomings of Chinese education, without exception they place at the top of their lists of complaints the overwhelming pressure generated in a formal education system that relies heavily on high stakes testing of a narrowly defined set of knowledge and exam-taking skills. This pressure is felt by all those with a stake in this system. From educational officials at various levels of the bureaucracy to headmasters, from subject heads and classroom teachers to students and their parents, all respond in earnest to the incentives produced in China's exam focussed system. Besides being comprehensive, *yingshi jiaoyu* is highly resilient. Working in the English education sector in China allowed me to experience firsthand how the best-intentions of reformers were often thwarted by rent-seeking school-level officials, by pressures exerted by parents seeking higher ranks of institutionalized cultural capital, or in the final instance as teachers found themselves largely unwilling or unable to adopt new teaching materials and methods designed to foster a more pedagogically balanced approach to English education (Yochim, 2006, 2012). Evangelists of curriculum and teaching reform were from the outset shouted down – most often metaphorically, but sometimes literally – by teachers who could not be blamed for hesitating to put their necks on the line in the name of the new, no matter how much they might have agreed with its general precepts. At the same time, those teachers inclined to take up reform initiatives tended to translate them at the classroom level into yet another high stakes exercise. For example, pushed to place more focus on listening and speaking skills, many teachers did so, but tended to demand the production of perfect English pronunciation and structure over effective communication. Where communication was the nominal focus of classroom activities, teachers typically reinforced student productions that followed the prescribed models, rather than promoting creative, flexible language use. In other words, reform of the English curriculum and teaching materials brought into being a more "balanced" pedagogy, but "balance" in this case should not be mistaken for a lessening of pressure. Rather, it is better understood as a lateral redistribution of pedagogical action across a broadened domain.

The same can be said of the child-rearing activities of parents. My conversations with Chinese parents along with my observations of them have led me to adopt a different outlook. Intense pedagogic action does not begin and end with a child's entry into formal schooling. Rather, whether parents act as they do as a result of ongoing pressure to help "save the nation" or do so as a way to accumulate cultural capital in response to pressures of scarcity and social competition, intense pedagogic action is exerted across all three domains of Bourdieu and Passeron's typology (see Table 1.1). Much of the pressure comes from an intensification of "educational"

CHAPTER 6

activities that aim at a nominally "balanced" conception of development, that is, where institutionalized education focusses pedagogical action on cognitive capacities, narrowly defined, other forms of pedagogic action apply pressure on the "whole person," often in ways that are very enjoyable to the object of action. Intensification of competition, that is, does not reflect a narrowing understanding of what it means "to educate." Rather, it occurs in concert with new discourses that focus on precisely the opposite of narrow conceptions of education. Competition for and accumulation of valuable cultural capital, in other words, focuses on being the *most* balanced person or raising the *most* balanced, *most* capable child in all respects.

NEGOTIATING & NAVIGATING EDUCATIONAL CULTURE

Given his theoretical and normative commitments, it is not surprising that Bourdieu is helpful in clarifying both the tendency for continuity in class alignments over time, and the links between the concurrent accumulation of different forms of capital. As others have noted, while the relative status of identifiable classes shifted with the coming of market socialism, conversion of social capital into new forms has meant that many powerful individuals and/or clans have managed to parlay valuable capital assets in such a way that their positions, atop the hierarchies has been more or less maintained (see, for example, Andreas, 2009). Where it is less helpful is in explaining the oppositional currents that come to the surface in parents' accounts of their beliefs and activities.

As I discussed with parents' their perspectives on the meaning, purpose, and aim of "education," it becomes clear that they at times align with and at others diverge from the precepts, prescriptions, and propositions of the aspirational cité. That many of them have done relatively well under present conditions does not prevent them from taking up positions of critique. At the same time, those who have seen their lives stagnate in a material sense are also represented here. Concerning the aspirational city – especially the ways in which schools are set up – the ambivalent level powerful critiques against the failure of these schools to work toward the common good. There is no guarantee, in other words, that any given person or family unit will align itself with the dominant or preferred order of worth. At the same time, it cannot be assumed that each is equally endowed with the capacity to align itself with a dominant or preferred order of worth. One might point to an elective affinity in Weber's sense, but it would make more sense to pay attention to the shifting prospects of those endowed with some combination of capital endowments – whether social-political, cultural-educational, or economic-rent – necessary to take advantage of the new normative and material landscape.

In the previous chapter, I chose examples of "a week in the life" to represent four different stages in the educational careers of Chinese children, and to highlight the ways in which the mode, as opposed to overall intensity, of pedagogic action changes over time. Middle-class parents, it seems, educate their children ever more intensively despite the demands of formal education. In some cases, they do so do so *to spite* the formal education system, as a manner of protesting the intensification of the narrow focus of institutionalized pedagogic action.

Still, given the way she has bought into the precepts of the aspirational cité, it is not surprising that Xiao Lu finds Shijiazhuang to be lacking. Xiao Lu feels that Shijiazhuang's schools don't live up to the promise of the aspirational cité because they are too narrowly focused on grades and exams. This is not helpful to raising the kind of person of balanced characteristics at the core of both the aspirational cité and to Xiao Lu's vision for her children. Furthermore, she believes that Shijiazhuang's schools as a whole are not set up to develop and recognize special talents and creativity. At present, SFLS is her first local choice, but she is ambivalent in her endorsement of the school. Instead, Xiao Lu hopes that her children will go abroad for school, preferably by the time they enter middle school. Doing so will allow them to learn in a low pressure environment, making school a happy experience without the excessive homework burden typical of China's schools. She has a ready stock of anecdotes she uses to affirm her beliefs about schooling abroad. She points to the positive experience of acquaintances who have sent their children to these schools, and the preponderance of evidence suggests that it is better to go earlier than later. Xiao Lu's own experience as a student informs these desires, and it is in relation to her bitter experiences as a middle school student that the power of the aspirational cité – as the foundation of a desire for educational culture and as a motivator for the withdrawal of those in the position to do so – can be seen. A promising primary school career did not translate into success in middle school or when it came time to go to university. Limited space meant that she had to study in a technical college instead. While this wasn't a bitter experience in the end, Xiao Lu still expresses a significant degree of desire for self-improvement through education, but much of this is now channeled into hoping for an overseas education for her children.

Lao Dong's evaluation of the present state of schools is similar in some respects to Xiao Lu's. He has complaints about *yingshi jiaoyu* (应试教育 – exam focussed education) and the ways in which this focus affects his ability to rear his daughter according to his own understandings of the meanings and purposes of education. In general, he says, the quality and *qualities* of schools does not measure up to the needs of society. This is particularly problematic because the school is as important as the home in child-rearing. He believes his daughter's current school, SFLS, is inadequate, but it does offer training to parents, and this is helpful. Still, there are ways in which the school is too *siban* (死板 – rigid), and this works against the accommodation of children from different backgrounds, a fact that means the school fails to educate properly according to the prescriptions of the aspirational cité. The school's uniforms for both boys and girls and, more specifically, hair styles for girls – each of these indicate a rigidity inconsistent with the kind of creativity and individuality encouraged in the aspirational cité (Lao Dong, Interview). Other incentives, such as the practice of *baosong* (保送 – recommendation to university without the need to score highly on the *gaokao*), also seem misplaced. While these

CHAPTER 6

do appear to reward special talent, they are one more way that marks/grades are too central to education. Thinking about the positioning of Shijiazhuang in the larger educational hierarchy of China, he believes that present state of things is not fair. Children from Hebei are disadvantaged compared to those registered in Beijing when it comes to admission to top universities, still another inequality engendered by over-reliance on high-stakes tests. It also exposes a fatal flaw in the fundamental structure of the aspirational cité, as do social conditions in general, which militates against fair access to quality schools. Also, a scarcity of quality along with income/wealth inequality means that while the aspirational cité demands recognition of good persons of morality, talent, etc., those with the economic capital to purchase homes near the best schools are disproportionately advantaged.

For someone who now enjoys many of the benefits that the new Shijiazhuang offers, Lao Dong has a surprisingly low opinion of the present state of life in the city and in China at large. Much of this dissatisfaction is attributable to his heightened sense of injustice due to the impact of deprivations suffered during the Cultural Revolution. Lao Dong related a particularly poignant story of loss from this time. During a time of heightened unrest, his younger sister fell ill with a fever. Because health clinic staff were engaged in a prolonged criticism session, the condition went untreated and permanent brain damage was the result. According to Lao Dong, his sister's current difficult life stems directly from this deprivation. Now in an abusive relationship with her husband, her problems often raise difficulties for Lao Dong and his other siblings. His memories of the deprivation of the GPCR allow him to maintain a high degree of empathy with those less fortunate than he might otherwise, and he has little difficulty linking corruption to deprivation. Indeed, he was once active as a critical blogger before his blog was shut down by his service provider. While he enjoys the benefits of the renovation of the city in favour of people who, like him, find themselves closely aligned with the aims of the aspirational city, he nonetheless is quick to condemn present arrangements as deeply unequal and unfair.

In the future, Xiao Zhao hopes that her daughter can go to university without experiencing the kind of exam-induced terror she herself lived through. She recalls meeting a mother in the women's clothing shop she opened when her daughter first went to kindergarten. That mother, she recalls, was very beautiful, but she was also emaciated. When Xiao Zhao asked why, the woman replied that her daughter was in the midst of her *gaokao* (高考 – high school exit/post-secondary entrance examinations) and that she wasn't sleeping or eating. Xiao Zhao doesn't want to be in the kind of circumstance in the future, or to pass on that kind of pressure to her daughter. In this respect, the aspirational cité and its requirement for balanced education promises a healthier future for parents and children in families who can gather and deploy the capital – both economic and cultural – to think and live differently. In pursuit of such a situation, Xiao Zhao imagines her daughter going to a school nearby home, rather than actively pursuing a far-flung school considered more desirable in terms of upping her daughter's narrowly measured performance. Still, she hopes that the school will be better than most as rated by other parents.

MAKING ONE'S WAY THROUGH THE FIELD OF URBAN EDUCATIONAL CULTURE

Most important is to find a good teacher, one who is "kind, but also not too soft. Most importantly, the teacher must let her daughter have some room to learn and be creative, to make her love learning." Later, when her daughter reaches middle school age, Xiao Zhao, like many other of Shijiazhuang's parents, including those followed in this study, aims to register her daughter in SFLS. She believes that this will offer her daughter the widest possible opportunities, including that of going overseas both while attending SFLS and afterwards. This particular school, in other words, offers the kind of opportunity to *kaikou yanjie* that Xiao Zhao pursues in out of school activities, and she is more than willing to pay money to afford her daughter this kind of experience. Her mother says that this overseas trip is a waste of money for so few days, but Xiao Zhao believes the experience gained is worth the money. Like Xiao Lu and Lao Wang, Xiao Zhao buys into the precepts and propositions of the aspirational cité, expressing little doubt about the promises of excitement and security it contains.

These people might be described as being fully invested in the aspirational city. Despite their concerns with aspects of the city they find to be lacking, they nonetheless judge it to be legible, empowering, and satisfying. For them, that the city fails to achieve the promise of the aspirational cité means only that they are more likely to exercise options available to those with the resources to live elsewhere and otherwise, that is, to abandon Shijiazhuang for greener pastures they believe to exist in other Chinese cities or abroad. They are, so to speak, fully invested in the *potential* of the aspirational city rather than its reality. For the most part, the precepts of the aspirational cité appeal to them, and they have incorporated its prescriptions in terms of the ways in which they conceive of good people; the kinds of knowledge and modes of education they support and pursue; and how they understand the contribution that living life according to these precepts and prescriptions to the good of society as a whole. It can also be said that these people have seen their lives improve in many ways under the market economy, and that this lends them a sense of satisfaction that they are doing the right thing. This is not to say that they have no critique of present circumstances. But their critique tends to be leveled against what they see as failures of the aspirational city to embody the promises of the aspirational cité. Also, as Xiao Zhao's discussion of her less fortunate neighbour attests, those who find the aspirational city legible and empowering are not blind to social inequality. They can easily find evidence of the uneven terrain of the aspirational city. Indeed, all are aware of the way that the city has worked against people they know. This result is most obvious in the case of Xiao Du and her family, for whom Shijiazhuang's new geography of aspiration promises much but delivers little. Their new neighbourhood in the city's high tech development district seems to rest in a permanently unfinished and disorderly state, and their move to that home came at the price of the loss of easy access to a quality high school. At the time I interviewed Xiao Du, her son Bobby had to commute more than one hour each way to and from school, two hours per day that might otherwise be dedicated to homework and other *suzhi*-heightening activities.

CHAPTER 6

THE ASPIRATIONAL FAMILY?

Through decades of challenges beginning, arguably, with the critiques of the republican movement, continuing with the modernizing efforts of the early Mao Zedong, and culminating in the full frontal assault of the Cultural Revolution, the Chinese family has proven resilient. Indeed, as a repository of resources – filial piety, ambition, security, farming and business know how – crucial to the success of reform and opening up, it might be argued that the family has been the institution most responsible for the economic successes of post-Mao China to date. Once seen as precisely the opposite – as one of any number of institutional barriers to "take off," perspectives seeking to explain what is lacking in Chinese families are now nowhere to found, barring those that lament the pressure cooker the contemporary family has become in its pursuit of success in the field of education. Indeed, when it comes to education, the opposite seems to be the case, where the interest of outsiders in model Asian students finds a ready explanation in the figures of "Tiger Mothers" and/or families with "high respect for education."

The family has proven resilient and crucial, but it would be wrong to say that it has not been subjected to forces that have changed its nature. In terms of the structure of the urban family, affluence, changing educational values, and opportunities presented in a robust employment and real estate development market have forced changes in the "traditional" stem family. In many, if not most, Chinese families, grandmothers are charged with providing a significant amount of care for grandchildren, particularly in the three years leading up to the child's entry into *youeryuan*. The demands of such care once meant that grandparents commonly lived together with their children and lived an essentially shared life. For the families in this research native to Shijiazhuang, however, this arrangement is no longer the norm. This is not to say that grandmothers are no longer involved, but in these families, the role of the grandparents is one that would be more familiar to Western eyes, one in which grandparents provide occasional babysitting and affective support. This is the case for Xiao Lu's and Lao Dong's families, and in both families, private car ownership in a city with an increasingly convenient road network facilitates an arrangement in which the nuclear family has more space to make independent decisions, but benefits from the close presence of elders. Xiao Zhao's situation is different, as her parents do not live nearby, meaning that it was practically necessary for her to leave her job to take on all childcare duties. For other families, however, the same affluence and opportunity has allowed them to effectively maintain the stem form by moving their parents from distant hometowns in the countryside. Xiao Ren, and Xiao Liu both live under such an arrangement, and the support of their parents is central to family life, not to mention crucial to their current economic condition. The presence of grandparents allowed them to return to work early and maintain their jobs more easily than might have been the case otherwise.

The structure of the family is relatively resilient, but the persistence of grandparents' role masks more crucial changes at the level of cultural system. Overall, the aspirational cité represents a reimagining of the precepts, prescriptions, and propositions that guide educational activities in the society as a whole even as it has reinvigorated the family as an institution of education. Where the core of traditional family values was mutual support and filial piety, the institution now works to forge individuals with attributes more appropriate to the current demands of a globalized market economy. The family is meant to encourage creativity rather than duplication, to value flexibility over constancy, to instill autonomy instead of dependency. This is not to say that these changes face no resistance. Indeed, in my own family, challenges to traditional forms and ideas is seen as so much more evidence of westernization, of negative individualization, as selfishness raised to the level of moral principle.

Still, for the culturally conservative, even the cities within which they live challenge tradition. The aspirational city, through the pathways it builds, through the market opportunities it creates, and through the educational activities it encourages, channels, funnels, and facilitates the efforts of families towards the means and ends defined in the aspirational cité. Those who seek support for old ways of educating children find themselves disappointment by the material embodiment of the aspirational cité in the newly built environments they find themselves living in. New cities like Shijiazhuang, while facilitating new models of relating and educating, appeal to other dearly held values, making it possible for families to pursue material well-being and the security of future generations. As described above, the purchase of additional homes is an important contributor to family wealth and, in some cases, to ongoing income from rental properties. At the same time, the renovating city is home to an explosion of private educational institutions, all positioning themselves to take advantage of the demands of family looking to educate their children in ways aligned with the demands of the aspirational cité.

In this chapter my aim has been to move beyond description and to finally bring into relation changes in the educational cultural system of China, the new spatial forms emerging in its cities, and the beliefs and activities of parents. I have strived to demonstrate that social processes are always also spatial processes, that while the former inaugurate the latter, the latter also importantly influences the content and the direction of the former. This is perhaps most obvious in the way that processes of economic capital accumulation occurring through the renovation of urban spaces are manifested as processes of cultural capital accumulation in the educational activities occurring in and through the family. The implication of the relatedness of these proposed is that they work hand in hand to co-constitute a new educational culture that aims to integrate new "human resources" into circuits of capital accumulation.

CHAPTER 6

NOTE

[1] In Coleman, *social capital* is conceptualized in a way that neutralizes and diminishes the critical capacity of the concept. Social capital is seen as something that is collected by all, though in differing amounts. What is missing is Bourdieu's understanding of dominance, legitimation, and exploitation, that is, the notion that not all social capital is created equally and that there is an economy which forms of social capital are unequally valued and traded. Putnam similarly misses the mark with his tendency to see social capital as something held in common by communities (or regions) rather than as held differentially by different social groups within a community.

CHAPTER 7

URBAN EDUCATIONAL CULTURE REVISITED

It has been fifteen years since I first set foot in Shijiazhuang. No longer a confused teacher trainer with negligible Chinese language skills, the decade and a half of Shijiazhuang's transformation has coincided with my personal transcultural journey. When I wrote the first version of this concluding chapter, I was sitting on an Air Canada wide body. The flight was sold out, packed full of tourists going to China or returning from Canada, students returning home from overseas study, business people on yet another excursion to the hottest economy and potentially largest market in the world. Since it was late May, many of the predominantly youthful crowd were no doubt university students returning home to visit their parents or spend the summer under their mothers' loving care, products of the kind of families discussed in Chapter 5, some of them from cities very much like the Shijiazhuang of Chapter 4. Save for the aura of foreboding engendered by the imminent completion of my doctoral studies and entry into an uncertain job market, that flight to Beijing was very much like any other I have boarded over the past fifteen years.

In other ways, however, that trip felt different. For much of the duration of this research project, my own son's entry into formal education had been but a distant worry. But as of the completion of this work drew near, the prospect of a return to China to live near my aging parents-in-law loomed. My spouse and I had long known that caring for her mother and father was an unavoidable obligation, and we had agreed long ago that we would return to Beijing when our son began grade one. In retrospect, our decision to return to China for a portion of his schooling was an easy one, but circumstances in Canada and the prospect of entering the hurly burly of Chinese education culture eventually scuttled those plans. When I first began to plan that trip, my spouse and I toyed with the idea of me bringing our son along to spend a few months in a Shijiazhuang *youeryuan*. We ultimately deemed the idea impractical. Given our lack of practical knowledge of registration requirements and procedures, the uncertainty of my work schedule, and the financial implications of maintaining child care in two countries, we decided to abandon the plan. Still, the anxiety engendered by difficulties of asking questions about registration and, above all, the realization that I trusted only those schools considered best by the parents in this study revealed the extent to which I had absorbed elements of the culture of educational desire and become subject to the precariousness of life in the would-be aspirational city of Shijiazhuang.

As I write the second version of this chapter, I have returned on my own to China, this time to take up a faculty position in a prominent university in the capital. An

© KONINKLIJKE BRILL NV, LEIDEN, 2019 | DOI:10.1163/9789004381261_007

CHAPTER 7

outsider might expect that the problems identified in the previous paragraph might have been resolved in a stroke when I signed my contract. They have not. The university provides no family package, and seems to lack the power to allow my son to register in its highly regarded schools, despite the fact that all other faculty are assured of having their children enrolled. Another previously unmentioned element of China's culture of educational desire has perhaps reared its ugly head. In Beijing's highly regarded universities, faculty and administration know the value of seats in nearby schools and have little interest in sharing their social advantage with outsiders from home or abroad.

Figure 7.1. The redevelopment of Dong San Zhuang

This circumstance demonstrates the degree to which, despite the not insignificant length of my experience in China, I remain a cultural outsider. Notwithstanding my efforts to adapt to an unfamiliar cultural world, I still experience many of the processes, procedures, and, in particular, expectations of Chinese educational culture rather jarring and, occasionally, downright offensive to my most cherished beliefs and instincts. At the same time, they serve as reminders of the "observations of spectacle" that first got me thinking about this project. The production of this book has unfolded as a process of seeking explanations for the educational desire I observed in Shijiazhuang, not to mention an immersion into the lives of the people I met at that long ago dinner party, the retelling of which kicked off this book. When I began to look for explanations for what I experienced at the time as curiously overwrought worrying and overbearing parenting, I implicitly sought explanations that centered on parents' understandings of their lives, and especially those *mistaken* perceptions upon which their beliefs and activities were founded. I was convinced that history, particularly revolutionary history in the form of officially sanctioned ideology, had an important influence on today's parents, despite the relatively hands-off role of the contemporary CPP under "socialism with Chinese characteristics." But only after significant periods of observation of these parents and personal immersion into local educational culture did it occur to me that insight into the spectacle of parental desire and anxiety might be enhanced by recognizing the significance of the constantly transforming urban landscapes through which each of us found ourselves "making our ways" (cf. Archer, 2007).

Of course, no collection of people gathered together in a circumscribed space can be viewed as each doing precisely what he or she feels or desires at any given moment. It is obvious, even upon the most cursory of examinations, that the lives of these people are somehow organized, however imperfectly, by external agents that enable many of them to lead their lives in ways quite similar to nearby others. One might point to any of a number of agents that perform this roll, such as economies, markets, societies, classes, families, or clubs, to name but a few. The external agent of primary concern to this research is what I have referred to throughout as "educational culture." It has not been my intent, however, to describe some comprehensive set of principles defining an all-encompassing Chinese Educational Culture that stands above people and governs their every thought and action. Instead, following Archer (1985, 1996), I have been working from the assumption that dividing educational culture into two components – "cultural system" and "socio-cultural interaction" – is an analytically productive way to deal with the observed phenomena that inspired this research. Adopting Archer's distinction allowed me to analyze objects that might otherwise be seen as incompatible and unrelated.

Figure 7.2. Time goes on in Shijiazhuang in the form of new slogans presented to patrons of Metro line 1

CHAPTER 7

The curious and persistent policy of *jianfu* and the myriad of materials produced, consumed, and reproduced in the various historical conjunctures at which it was proclaimed led to my discernment of the set of normative precepts, prescriptions, and propositions that I labelled the "aspirational cité." As a collection of resources intelligible (cf. Archer's "intelligibilia") to the "residents" of a particular educational culture, the aspirational cité stands firmly within Archer's conception of the cultural system. The material things and organizational patterns of the city, too, are a part of the educational cultural system of contemporary China, and are a particularly important component given the ongoing, massive changes wrought by a collection of governments' determined to actively shape China's urbanized future. Despite the apparent differences between the propagandistic materials that carry the messages in the guise of *jianfu* – these were texts that are "read" in the literal sense of the word – and the urban forms of the new Chinese city, the latter are nonetheless a collection of spaces that *read to* and are *read by* urban residents as they go about the mundane tasks of everyday life.

Having said this, there is an important sense in which this *reading* of the city should be taken literally, for modern cities are papered over with images and text whose raison d'être is to be read. This seems to be particularly so in China's cities, which, according to the author Yu Hua (2011), are now plastered with propaganda and advertising that put the excesses of Cultural Revolutionary *da zi bao* sloganeering to shame. Shijiazhuang is no different, as the small sampling of images in Figures 4.13 to 4.15 demonstrate. These two aspects of the urban landscape make the material objects and forms of the city – its spaces and places; its transportation networks; its institutions both private and public – crucial components of the Chinese educational cultural system.

But there is more to educational culture than a set of systemic elements that overwhelm its members. Indeed, it is these very members who are responsible for its production and reproduction, and for this reason it was important that I consider the beliefs and activities of Shijiazhuang's parents. As "objects" of analysis, both thoughts and activities depart radically from textual and material artefacts. "Thoughts" or "beliefs" are not "read" – that is, consciously, actively – in the same way as the textual remnants of propaganda. Nor are they semi-passively absorbed in the way that a city is by those who call its places, spaces, and networks home. Rather, beliefs and thoughts are probed in dialogue between researcher and researched in a process that mirrors the more mundane daily reflections, both internal and collaborative, that parents engage in every day as they struggle to know and do what is best for their children. Ideas, thoughts, beliefs, commitments – all are constantly reconsidered and sometimes modified.

As attention is drawn, through dialogue, to extant mainstream and marginal ideas about education and schooling, the positions of those engaged in the discussion are sometimes affirmed and occasionally modified. The same can be said of the activities engaged in by parents. Schools, evening and weekend *buxi* schools, ice and inline skating lessons, piano lessons, art classes, math and English competitions – the roiled spectacle of China's vibrant educational marketplace reveals much about the dynamics of the nation's urban educational culture. My concern, however, was to demonstrate the extent to which everyday life is not a realm of passive consumption of a dominant and dominating educational culture. Rather, it was to conceive of educational culture in everyday life as one of socio-cultural interaction, one in which the activities of parents are causally significant for the content and shape of the future cultural system.

Figure 7.3. "I'm elite!" Elite English (精英英语) offers more than just English education to its students

RENOVATION AND DESIRE IN 2017

Shijiazhuang remains unchanged with respect to the phenomena that defined the original problem space of this study. The hustle and bustle of educational desire persists; urban renovation and growth continue apace. Indeed, it might be argued that both have intensified, even as the peak of the first phase of urban renovation seems to have passed. When this study was just being completed, as many as five hundred construction cranes dotted the city skyline as more than two hundred large projects are underway (Lao Wang, Personal Communication, June 13, 2013). The city's road network was expanding with no end in sight. One transportation project was the construction a six kilometer elevated expressway to Shijiazhuang's Zhengding Xin Qu (正定新区 – Zhengding New District) which has since become home to, among other things, the relocated city government. Coincidentally, this road now runs directly over Xiao Lu and Lao Wang's since demolished villa, a village getaway that now sits in the shadow of a massive mountain of rubble formed from the detritus of Shijiazhuang's demolition frenzy. This isn't to say that growth of the city is a thing of the past. Indeed, village is rapidly becoming city, and construction of the city's first three subway lines, a project that has once again thrown most of the city's major roadways into a degree of chaos, is nearing completion.

The scale of *san nan da bianyang* makes imagining anything larger difficult to grasp, but now Shijiazhuang seems poised to join in a new utopian scheme of

CHAPTER 7

impossible proportion. Periodic news stories trumpet the creation of a new supercity – *Jing-Jin-Ji*[1] –with Beijing at its centre (Johnson, 2017). The precise shape of this city and the effect of its creation on Shijiazhuang, its residents, and the surrounding educational culture remains to be seen. It seems unlikely, however, that any changes will include better access to jobs and educational resources in Beijing itself. To the extent that the status quo remains, Shijiazhuang is likely to remain a marginal city in which parents look to Beijing and abroad to ensure the best educational outcomes for the children.

Revisiting Key Informants

In the four years since the formal period of this study drew to a close, the terrain of educational desire in Shijiazhuang has shifted. The path followed by Lao Wang and Xiao Lu has been particularly chaotic. As 2014 dawned, they no longer planned to keep their daughter at SLFS, and had chosen instead to join the ranks of China's upper middle class by sending her to an international school in Malaysia. When I visited their home to meet their newborn son for the first time, Xiao Lu cited the inadequacies of even the best regarded of Shijiazhuang's schools as justification for the decision to go overseas. Lao Wang agreed, but also expressed his disdain for the city's deteriorating environment and the general poor quality of life. His perspective on the city didn't strike me as new; his lamentations over crowding in the city have been a constant since I have known him, typically expressed with weary repetitions of the axiom *di shao ren duo* (地少人多 – too many people, too little land). Lao Dong seemed less hopeful about providing a more balanced and less stressful education for his daughter as the strictures and demands of her *zhong xue* (中学 – middle/junior and senior high school) years set in.

By 2015, however, things had changed again. Malaysia hadn't worked out, and the new destination was Singapore. As the year went on, a family financial crisis, related, it seems, to shady financial dealings of a since fallen Hebei Province official, led to Xiao Lu and Xiao Ai returning from abroad. Xiao Ai is now back at SFLS. I am not privy to the details, and can only speculate that the pressures of the aspirational life have had some effect, but by 2016, Xiao Lu and Lao Wang were divorced. Both work in Beijing Monday to Friday and return to Shijiazhuang on the weekend to spend time with their two children.

In the case of Lao Dong and his family, the shift from junior to senior high school saw them preparing for a number of possibilities. Recall that Xiao Yi had attended SFLS since kindergarten, and the hope was that she would continue there through high school. As 2016 approached, however, the family had to prepare for the possibility that her high school entrance grades wouldn't be high enough. To do so, they had purchased an apartment in Tianjin, a city whose residency restrictions are less strict that those of Beijing. Moving to Tianjin would allow Xiao Yi to attend a better school than would be otherwise possible. What's more, she would face less a stringent standard on the *gaokao*, meaning that university in Beijing would be a somewhat more realistic possibility. Failing this, Tianjin would offer a choice of stronger universities than those in Shijiazhuang or nearby Baoding, so not all would be lost. In the end, Xiao Yi came through with exam scores high enough to remain at SFLS, meaning that the family will be stay together through her high school years. On the downside, Xiao Yi will face heavy *gaokao* competition. She may yet see relief from the pressure cooker of schooling in China, but will likely have to wait, as her parents tend to see study abroad as a post-*gaokao* possibility rather than as a solution to the negatives of *yingshi jiaoyu*.

Xiao Zhao, too, doesn't talk so much about giving her daughter a less stressful education than she once did, although she has partially resolved this problem by reuniting her family by moving to Shenzhen in 2014. Her commitment to Xiao Shu's English education, however, may indicate a plan similar to Xiao Lu's, that is, to move Xiao Shu out of the regular public school system to one more in keeping with a family of means, and one that aligns more closely with her understandings of balanced education.

By early 2014, Xiao Lei was preparing to write and eventually completed the highest pressure examinations of his life to date. It was an anxious yet hopeful time for his parents, as his exam results at every level had surpassed expectations generated by his standing over the school term. Xiao Jiao was nervous, but outwardly calm, and continued her commitment to commuting to and from work twice a day to prepare the meals that keep the boy fuelled and ready to perform. In the several days it took to write the exams, she booked off from work to feed, accompany, and encourage her son.

When the *gaokao* results arrived, it was once again good news, though not on the scale of his achievements a few years earlier. Once the results arrived, Xiao Jiao immediately began the task of calling various universities around China to which Xiao Lei's exam scores might allow admission. Before watching Xiao Jiao go through this process, I had failed to appreciate just how complex a task this is, never mind how strategic the parent in charge had to be in collecting information on quotas from these schools. The family eventually settled on a second tier Beijing university. At that time, Xiao Jiao and I had a long discussion about Xiao Lei's future study prospects in China and/or overseas, or some combination of the two.

In 2018 Xiao Lei will complete his undergraduate degree, and as the time approaches, I receive frequent messages from Xiao Jiao asking for information on master's programs at various Canadian universities. No doubt she will soon know much more about these than me.

The thought processes of each of these parents concerning their child's future differ in their specifics, but nonetheless reveal the extent to which they live lives in which the future is less closed for their children than it once was for them. For each of them, the pressures of *yingshi jiaoyu* do not define permanently the horizon of possibilities for them or their children. Each is able to consider options that would see this pressure relieved, although each comes to a different decision based, in part, on economic realities and affective concerns. The same cannot

CHAPTER 7

be said for all of Shijiazhuang's residents, a fact revealed by the experience of Xiao Du, whose family, while nominally a member of the ranks of China's middle class, in reality lives a life at best on the lower rungs of this ill-defined social class. As a result, *yingshi jiaoyu*, however undesirable, provides the best hope for her family, and much more pressure is ultimately placed on her son's shoulders. Indeed, if this research has confirmed anything about the operations of capital, class, and educational beliefs and practices, it is that income and wealth are very much determinative of the degree of coercive power of institutionalized pedagogic action.

Figure 7.4. Tackle difficulties; pursue excellence (gongjian kenan, zhuiqiu zhuoyue)

Urban Educational Culture Revisited

The years following 1950 in Mainland China have been accurately and usefully described as a series of "eras" in which different leadership configurations have forwarded different versions of socialism and different paths of development for China as it seeks to become a modern, technologically advanced, harmonious, and prosperous society. The Chinese Communist Party would prefer to see this history of a succession of steps on the same more or less – with obvious, recognized exceptions – upward trajectory, culminating – though not permanently – in the present state of things. Writing in 1991 on education in the revolutionary state, Sautman characterized this period as one of swings from "politicization" (in the early

Revolutionary period, to "hyperpoliticization" (in the GPCR), to "depoliticization" following the death of Mao. There is a sense, however, in which the present period is the most radically politicized period of all, in part because a patina of apoliticality clings to the surface of a developmental path that, in reality, favours certain segments of the population over others. The task of this book has been to look below the surface of contemporary social life to reveal the scope and shape of this radical reorganization of the educational apparatuses – familial, diffuse, and institutional alike – of Chinese society.

The educational culture of contemporary Mainland Chinese society is one fundamentally characterized by the sound and the fury of Chinese parents striving for and with their children. According to some, all of this hustle and bustle indicates the rise of an ethic of acquisitiveness, evidence of a moral decline, and the final, best proof of the folly of the current direction in Chinese education. Contrary to this view, I have suggested that the present state of affairs in Chinese education ought to be seen to indicate the prominence of a reconstituted order of worth according to which people, knowledge, and schools/institutional arrangements can be evaluated. This order of worth is both a product of and productive of the new urban spaces rising from the rubble of demolished socialist era cities and through the depopulation/consumption of their rural hinterlands. New urban China is a place in which now well-entrenched conditions of material prosperity and inequality map onto patterns of spatial organization, one in which where one lives determines one's access to the good life. In terms of education, the new urbanity privileges those able to travel by private car to access the choicest and most expensive educational opportunities. Using their economic capital in an educational marketplace, the new urban middle-class are able through various means to buy access to the opportunities needed to ensure their children's happiness and prosperity.

Since the beginning of my engagement in China in 2002, it has become clear that, in expressing their commonsense views of China, outsiders – especially those who locate themselves in Anglo-American traditions – rarely go beyond readings based upon "fascination and fear" (Faure, 2008). Especially vexing is the tendency to reduce "China" to an "imagined totality" defined by proclamations of its ruling elite (Zhang, 2008). Central to such views are understandings – both commonsense and scientific – of self and other as inextricably attached to the interests of nation of origin and to a notion of the Chinese *other* as deeply alien. Yet, many in this "Western" world would find the trends of the past thirty years in Chinese education familiar indeed – constant reform (cf. "school improvement"); increasing pressure on students to compete (cf. standardized examinations); a retreat of the state from its role as guarantor of equal provision (cf. "schools of choice"). Much of this sense of serendipity is no doubt due to the global spread of the "new planetary vulgate" of neoliberalism (Bourdieu & Wacquant, 2001). But superficial resemblances and even substantive ideological affinities should not prevent us from deep inquiry into the specific and variegated conditions that exist despite such broader global and historical movements. Indeed, it is inquiry of this kind that is capable of revealing the

CHAPTER 7

power of neoliberalism as a transitory *modus operandi* of that larger, transhistorical movement – capitalism – of which it is a part, that is, its adaptability to local material and cultural conditions.

Fundamentally, then, one of my aims has been to challenge stereotypical notions of "China" and "the Chinese," and to assert from an admittedly Western perspective the common humanity of those typically considered alien. This should not be taken as a signal that I ascribe to the notion that "deep down" we have always been or, alternatively, are becoming, exactly the same. My conviction is that, if China is emerging as the most recent and perhaps ultimate power in East Asia's long half-century of "economic renaissance" (Arrighi, 2007), casting off preferred frameworks, (e.g., those that see in all cultural movements only "Westernization") in favour of more subtle deliberations on the social dynamics referred to above is critical to the project of building mutual understanding and cooperation. I tend to agree with Woodiwiss (2005), that a resurgent China is "a probable source of distinctive global social forces capable of changing the way in which life is lived in the West" (p. 4). In this sense, my research aims to contribute to greater intercultural understanding by working toward knowledge that rejects notions of east versus west in favour of a spirit in which "the farthest West is but the farthest East" (Smith, 2008).

NOTE

[1] This awkward appellation indicates the three jurisdictions the new city would encompass: *Jing* for Beijing, *Jin* for Tianjin, and *Ji* for Hebei Province. At present Beijing and Tianjin are cities positioned directly under the central government. Hebei is a province with its own capital. The creation of this supercity is intended to both enable the division of economic functions and limit the excessive growth of Beijing.

APPENDIX A

METHODOLOGICAL PRELIMINARIES AND SPECIFICATIONS

Naïveté may better explain my nostalgic take on schooling in small-town, working-class Alberta than does institutional reality. It may be said without controversy that school choice has little meaning where only one school exists or only one school is seen as an option, which isn't to say that geography and class are conditions that determine absolutely the agency of some and constrain that of others. Upon deeper reflection, I recall my mother's considerable ambivalence toward the values, content, and outcomes of the Alberta schools to which she delivered five of her seven children over the course of three decades. Indeed, the confluence of opposition and opportunity eventually led to her two youngest children joining the nascent home schooling movement. What's more, the intervening years have demonstrated how an encroaching neoliberal policy regime can bring a measure of "choice" to what had previously appeared as an intractable sectarian divide.[1] Personal reflection does not, of course, exhaust the range of experience in the social-historical-political context with which I have the most direct experience, that of post-1970 Alberta. Yet, for reasons that should become clearer in the discussion of methodology below, the inconsistent nature of my recollections seems highly relevant. Educational processes in my natal context have always been more complex than my common-sense understandings of them. Indeed, my struggle as a student of education has largely been a process of coming to grips with the personal effects of the *méconnaissance* (Bourdieu, 1990) so apparent in the statements above.

But these reflections on a taken-for-granted past do not erase the distinction upon which this research is founded. Nor have they closed the gap between the strange and the familiar such that it can now be said that little distinguishes the concerns of Canadian parents from those of China. The suspicion that all that seems strange is actually familiar reveals a habit of mind endemic to the dominant form of liberal education espoused in post-1970 Canada. After all, who would dare argue with the notion that Canadian and Chinese parents alike care about their children's education and act accordingly? To say so is to engage in a wholly warranted if symptomatic universalism. An alternative claim, more palatable to the contemporary academic ear, might go like this: globalization is bringing about convergence in the material and ideational conditions in which people find themselves, and this accounts for the convergence of strange and familiar. This, too, is partly true. Still, it does not follow that the beliefs, values, and concerns of various groups and individuals "making [their]

APPENDIX A

way through the world" (Archer, 2007) have come about as a result of precisely the same complex of structural-cultural conditions and processes, or will at some future point lead to a universal set of institutional circumstances, values, and behaviours. Indeed, a fundamental assumption of this research is that the content of Mainland Chinese parents' concerns and the socio-historical conditions under which these have come to be present features that are quantitatively and qualitatively distinct.

The movement described above parallels the emotional-intellectual journey of both the thoughtful tourist-traveler and the ethnographer. For a visitor to a strange socio-cultural environment, moving beyond initial impressions can be a challenge. Where fascination or fear tend to dominate, for the generous of mind, these responses to experience of the strange are most often resolved through appeal to a universalism, through recognition of that which makes the foreign other "just like us." For those disposed toward going beyond this humanistic impulse, experience of the strange can lead to heightened self-awareness, a recognition that what was previously known of the self was incorrect or at least less than clear-eyed self-awareness. These three steps – from strange to familiar to de-familiarization – model more or less precisely the process through which this study unfolded.

In the remainder of this chapter I describe this process in detail. I begin by defining a set of metatheoretical foundations for the study (see Morrow & Brown, 1994) based on the elements of research design suggested in Crotty (1998). Upon these, I propose a methodology capable of answering the questions posed in this chapter. Finally, I detail the specific methods and process used to collect data (Crotty, 1998).

METATHEORETICAL PRELIMINARIES

> The fundamental sources of any theory's pictorial power are the selective or filtering effects of its ontological assumptions concerning what it is being used to look at, and its epistemological assumptions concerning how to go about gaining knowledge about whatever is being looked at. (Woodiwiss, 2005, p. 14)

> The world exists independently of our knowledge of it. (Sayer, 1992, p. 5)

I ground this research in an ontological realism developed from my reading of Bhaskar (1998) and other advocates of critical realism (especially Archer, 1995, 1996 and Sayer, 1992), as well as through sustained reading of theorists who hold to a more general realist stance and have sought to dispense with the traditional opposition between structure and agency (Bourdieu, 1977, 1998; Morrow & Brown, 1994; Thompson, 1990). Holding to realist assumptions means that my attempt to learn something about China in part by inquiring into the perspectives of parents does not signal adherence to either ontological voluntarism or epistemological subjectivism. Rather, I suggest that what is called "perspective" might better be labelled "structured experience." In this connexion, I validate the importance of subjective experience and at the same time hold that to "experience" implies something outside of the self. To the extent that an individual lives an internal, personal life, he or she does so in relation to things

METHODOLOGICAL PRELIMINARIES AND SPECIFICATIONS

external to him or herself. Indeed, in this research, the very idea that human beings are classifiable in terms of a national-cultural identity (they are "Mainland Chinese"), class (they are "middle-class"), and geographic location ("a particular kind of contemporary Chinese city") betrays a further premise. While people enjoy a significant degree of autonomy in terms of what they think and do from day to day, they are nevertheless *situated actors* who go about their business in a sociocultural sphere that pre-exists their perceptions of it. Corollary to this view, social worlds also consist of non-human elements (e.g., institutions, geographies, policy regimes, discourses) that retain powers and potentialities irreducible to the "saying, making, and doing" (Bhaskar, 1998, p. 37) of their creators, though it cannot be said that they are completely resistant to those efforts. Human agents are, put simply, always only relatively free and imperfectly efficacious in terms of their ability to realize their plans and projects.

Working from these assumptions about human beings, social worlds, and the relations that bind them, I commit myself to understanding the current state of affairs in China by, first, making an analytical distinction between, (a), a particular structural, cultural, and ineluctably real social context and, (b), the actively formulated concerns of those who think and live, plan and cope with and within that context; and, second, by emplacing the former within the latter so as to give their due the relations that bind one to the other (Bhaskar, 1998; Denzin & Lincoln, 2005; Flick, von Kardoff, & Steinke, 2004; Kipnis, 2011). Recalling Mills' (1959) conception of sociology as a concern with the ways in which "the life of an individual" and "the history of a society" are intertwined (p. 3), I seek to "know" about Chinese society by exploring what people *think* it is like and striving toward a closer approximation of what it is *actually* like.

> People, in their conscious activity, for the most part unconsciously reproduce (and occasionally transform) the structures governing their substantive activities of production. (Bhaskar, 1998, p. 38)

METHODOLOGICAL SPECIFICATIONS

Ethnography is the work of describing a culture. (Spradley, 1979, p. 3)

Given these metatheoretical preliminaries, it follows that my concern with the educational culture of Shijiazhuang City will proceed as a *critical ethnography*. Ethnography presented itself to me as a way to make sense of a particular part of contemporary Chinese society given that, prior to my decision to take it up as an object of social scientific research, I had been fortunate enough to both experience personally and observe that society at close hand (O'Reilly, 2005). If ethnography seems a curiously active noun in the previous sentence, it is because I came to the understanding that I was – or wanted to be – doing ethnography long before I *decided* to do so. Having said this, the manner in which I have gone about this research has from the outset fulfilled the principal criteria of "conventional ethnography" (Taylor, 2005, p. 1), that is, I have pursued this research by placing myself in the

APPENDIX A

study site for an extended period of time. Doing so is, I would suggest, unavoidable if one is to "respect the irreducibility of human experience" (p. 3). But fealty to the "truth of the insider" and the context within which he/she lives comes at a price; a relatively unstructured data collection process has been costly in terms of time as it has not involved "following through a fixed and detailed research design specified at the start" (Hammersley & Atkinson, 2007, p. 3). Indeed, constant assessment and adjustment replaced predictable plans as I immersed myself in the lives and worlds of Shijiazhuang's parents in order to collect first-hand data in a setting as "natural" as possible (p. 4).

Conceived in this way as an immersive practice, ethnography – particularly that which does not attempt to be covert – involves more than mere presence. Rather, it entails a "presence plus" commonly known as participant observation. Before formally beginning this research, I had lived in Shijiazhuang for extended periods of time over six years, meaning that I had been practicing a kind of informal participant observation for some time. I have now lived and worked there for parts of 11 years, occupying a number of roles that have allowed me to watch, listen, ask questions, and generally gather "whatever data [were] available to throw light on the issues" that emerged and, through a process of reflection on these experiences and observations, became my central scholarly concerns (Hammersley & Atkinson, 2007, pp. 3–4, 15). During one uninterrupted stretch of two years from 2002 to 2004, I worked as a textbook compiler, editor, and teacher trainer in a Shijiazhuang-based publishing company. A seven month stay in 2005 allowed me to complete field work for my master's thesis study into the perspectives of Chinese teachers on their lives in the context of market economic reform (Yochim, 2006, 2012). In the years since 2006, I have spent parts of each year ranging from one to five months working and socializing, interviewing and observing Chinese friends and work associates. The latter half of this period has coincided with my entry as a member into a Chinese family and, significantly, as father to an only-grandson.

Prolonged engagement in the research site and emergent design have allowed me to collect a wide variety of data using an inclusive "family of methods" (Willis & Trondman, 2000, p. 5). I describe and justify these in detail below, but mention them here to indicate the congruence of ethnography and the realist metatheoretical foundations above. As a general methodology, ethnography has allowed me to take into account what I referred to above as the "emplacement" (Kipnis, 2011) of social actors, to "[recognize] and [record] how experience is *entrained* in the flow of contemporary history, large and small" (Willis & Trondman, 2000, p. 6). This recognition of emplacement/entrainment is one of the features of a *critical* ethnography. In this connexion, "critical" refers to the capacity of ethnography for depth interpretation, that is, for investigation of the non-human and non-discursive aspects of the social world that structure the thoughts and activities of its human inhabitants.

There is a second sense in which this is a *critical* methodology. While critical ethnography is at present most commonly associated with empirical inquiries that attempt to make a "contribution to equity, freedom, and justice" (Madison, 2005, p. 4), such critical *normative* stances toward, for example, social exclusion, are often less skeptical with respect to *epistemological* questions. This lack of criticality is most obvious with respect to the accuracy imputed to an agent's explanatory account of his social positioning. The critical eye, in other words, ought also to be turned toward matters of ontology and methodology, those discussed under *Metatheoretical Preliminaries*. In this sense, "criticality" is an extension of those efforts at social theoretical "underlabouring" that attempt to establish the metatheoretical foundations of "practical social theory" (Archer, 1995).

Important as these are, in this work I focus on third and fourth senses of *critical*, neither of which is obviously connected to the alleviation of particular social ills or the pursuit of immediate political causes (Morrow & Brown, 1994). With the third sense of critical I hold that where ethnography is critical, it has a capacity for "ideology critique and defamiliarization" (Morrow & Brown, 1994, p. 256). Defamiliarization is concerned not with the kind of cultural critique suggested in the critical normative stances of an alien other suggested above but, rather, with "a form of cultural critique" of that which is most familiar to the researcher (Marcus & Fischer, 1999, p. 1). It is self-reflection of this kind that I model in the opening paragraphs of this chapter.

A final claim to criticality lies in the practice of an epistemic reflexivity most closely associated with Bourdieu's reflexive sociology, but also of a kind considered central to critical realism. For Bourdieu and Wacquant (Bourdieu, 2003, 2004a, 2007; Bourdieu & Wacquant, 1993) there is more than one mode of inquiry commonly described as reflexive, but it is those concerned with the social conditions of knowledge production that ought to be of most concern to critical researchers. Reflexivity of this kind is different from "narcissistic" and "egological" varieties central to "postmodern anthropology" and phenomenology, taking as its objects "not only…the private person of the enquirer but also…the anthropological field itself and…the scholastic dispositions and biases it fosters and rewards in its members" (Bourdieu, 2003, p. 281). Woodiwiss (2005) also promotes epistemic reflexivity as the most crucial form of reflexivity, but describes it in a less daunting manner: "The three main…reasons for engaging in reflexive activity are: to spot gaps and jumps in one's reasoning…; to check the consistency of one's reasoning; and to understand the relations between theoretical work and power" (p. 89). For critical realists, epistemic reflexivity is fundamental to the work they do as "it performs a crucial underlabourer role," pointing "the researcher to ways of conceptualising what there is to study and for setting up productive and exciting research designs" (Sharp in Archer, Sharp, Stones, & Woodiwiss, p. 12). In this research, I see myself as practicing this kind of reflexivity both in the field – most consciously and obviously at moments when I use field notes to work through problems like those in Woodiwiss' list – and afterward during the production of this manuscript. By tying one chapter to the next with personal reflections, I attempt to represent not only the experience of doing the research, but also the epistemological significance of my positioning in the field.

APPENDIX A

Data Sources

Social theory is not simply an intellectual means of manipulating visualities but also a process of work involving things, namely tools, materials, instruments, and workplaces. (Woodiwiss, 2005, p. 69)

Guided by the concept of "data triangulation" (Denzin, 1978; see also Flick, 2006; Hammersley & Atkinson, 2007; Stake, 2005) and consistent with a realism that "counts a far wider range of materials as observations" (Woodiwiss, 2005, p. 37), I collected data from a number of different data sources. The aim of doing so was to produce a detailed and accurate portrait of Shijiazhuang's educational culture that takes into account its "embeddedness" or entrainment in a broader structural and cultural environment. I relied on personal engagement in the field, combining participant observation with probing methods such as semi- and un-structured interviews and documentary research. In addition to descriptive adequacy, triangulating data in this manner helped me to clarify meaning by locating and including diverse perspectives (Stake, 2005). It also helped me to "tease out what deserves to be called experiential knowledge from what is opinion and preference" (pp. 453–454, 455). The "truth" of the case was revealed through an iterative process of data analysis as I looked for "relationships across the entire corpus" (Hammersley & Atkinson, 2007, p. 163). The following sections provide detail and rationale for the use of particular data sources.

Fieldnotes. I kept a written account of the things I saw, heard, and experienced while gathering and reflecting on data in the field work phase of the study (Bogdan & Biklen, 2007). For Bogdan and Biklen, the category of "fieldnotes" in participant observation is given the broadest possible definition, taking in all data, including hand written notes, interview transcripts, documents, photos, and other materials (p. 119).

Popular press, policy documents, & public statements: I compiled a time-based series of corpora consisting of magazine articles, policy documents, speeches, editorials, posters – any material that contained guidance to its consumer in terms of what kinds people might be considered "good," what forms of knowledge and activities ought to be pursued in order to rear such people, and how the fostering of a population comprising them could bring about a developed, just society. I constructed four corpora, each comprising documents in and around the years 1950–1955, 1966–1975, 1978–1989, and 2000–present, that is, articles published within a few years of the expressions of *jianfu* statements discussed in Chapter 2. The normative orders I propose in this section are the result of an investigation that is partial due to its reliance on documentary sources. Using Raymond Williams' (1998) term, what I access is a "selective tradition" (p. 54), and the insight provided is necessarily limited by the biases and absences that obtain in any selection of documents.

METHODOLOGICAL PRELIMINARIES AND SPECIFICATIONS

One of these sources was back issues of *China Reconstructs/China Today*, a propaganda/current affairs magazine largely intended for consumption outside of China. The choice of this publication might seem unusual given the intended audience, but it proved valuable for a number of reasons. First of all, the purpose of this component of the research was not to ascertain the actual state of Chinese society at a given point in time. Rather, it was to develop a sense of the prevailing vision of what Chinese society and its constituent parts ought to be like at a given moment in time. Detailing this image that the nation sought to project outwardly was as useful as the actual ways and means it employed to create that society. Second, many of the documents, stories, and exemplars presented in these magazines were also used internally, so they can be seen as indicative of the kinds of materials used inside China to promote particular conceptions of the good. I read through all issues of each of these long-running magazines, the former comprising thirty-eight volumes (366 issues in microform and print), the latter thirty-six volumes to date (~400 issues). I identified articles that addressed educational matters. Some of these, such as "In a Peking Primary School" (Staff Reporter, 1954), deal explicitly with formal schooling and take some aspect of school reform as their topic. Others are less explicitly focused on educational matters, but have an overtly pedagogical aim, as in "My Husband is a 'Model'" (G. D. Liu, 1954).

I found other documents in a wide range of venues. Many policy documents included in the four corpora are available on official websites of the Chinese government (*e.g.*, www.moe.edu.cn) or through educational research organizations (*e.g.*, China Education and Research Network – www.edu.cn). Others have been published in translation, such as those made available by Hu and Seifman (1987) or indirectly in the form of analyses by others (e.g., Andreas, 2002, 2004; Pepper, 1978, 1996). Given the importance of the formal representations of Mao's thought (Martin, 1982), *The Selected Works of Mao Zedong* (Mao, 1957, 1966, 1967 [1942], 1977 [1957], 1997 [1953]) also provided insight.

Photographs, media reports, and urban planning documents: In order to document and interpret the process transforming Shijiazhuang, I took photos of public places, construction sites, da zi bao (大字报 – big character posters) announcing san nian da bianyang, and of the many posters and billboards advertising housing and commercial developments. With these data sources, I was concerned with recording san nian da bianyang in terms of both spectacle – i.e., the massive scale and scope of change and the impact on the city's residents – and visual indications of the city as re-imagined in planning documents. Figures 4.4 and 4.5, for example, provide a sense of the sheer scale of redevelopment, particularly when one considers that the photo captures only one of the hundreds of projects of this kind. Figure 4.8 shows the importance of cultural facilities to the aspirational city, but also indicates the tight connections between public investments and private commercial development.

I also collected maps of the city at different points in time, some available publicly, others supplied by contacts. Most of the latter were of proposed developments or

APPENDIX A

those underway but incomplete. Finally, I collected news stories detailing plans for and discussing the progress of *san nian da bianyang*. These artefacts helped me develop a sense of the aims, nature, scope, and material effects of the process of the redevelopment of Shijiazhuang, as well as the connections between redevelopment in general and the precepts and propositions of the aspirational cité.

Interviews: Following completion of informed consent procedures, individual respondents were engaged in an informal interview whose purpose was to establish a trusting relationship, to sensitize me to their life circumstances, and to spur my thinking on productive lines of inquiry in subsequent interviews. Each of the respondents was interviewed on at least one further occasion about a range of topics that preliminary reading, observations, and interviews suggested might be of concern to parents, as well as matters of theoretical interest. The locations of these interviews varied. Some were conducted in private rooms in tea shops, where the interviewee and I shared tea and snacks. Others were conducted in the homes of the interviewees. One was conducted in my apartment.

Subsequent interviews were semi-structured and aimed to gain insight into the beliefs and activities of parents with regard to the *education* of their child. Other lines of inquiry related to the *schooling* of children. Still others probed for conceptual and/or evaluative responses. Finally, respondents were engaged in discussions of concepts drawn from existing literature of relevance to contemporary educational culture, what Bogdan and Biklen (2007) refer to as "[trying] out ideas and themes on informants" (p. 165).

Handwritten notes were taken during the initial interviews. Subsequent interviews were recorded and transcribed. Later, follow-up interviews were conducted on line using synchronous internet video/chat software, a technique that was particularly helpful in conducting member checks after recorded interviews were fully transcribed.

Sampling, Key Informants, and Recruitment

This study was designed to explore the thoughts and activities of parents in only one urban setting. But its implicit claim is that the observations I make are "transferable" (Guba, 1981; Denzin & Lincoln, 2005) to other similar urban contexts. Therefore, it is worth pausing to dwell on the kinds of restrictions that the phrase "similar urban contexts" implies. Such limitations flow in part from the multiple meanings ascribed to "urban" in contemporary China. Popular exposure to all things China in recent years has led to a relatively high awareness of that country, including the fact that it is fundamentally split along urban-rural lines. Yet to recognize this and to make too simple a division between the two is to fundamentally misunderstand that "urban" might designate, inter alia, distinctions of governance, where it implies "city," a level of government that includes provincial capitals as well as those urban centres one step below; size of a locale (a "big" or "small" place) in terms of population or, more importantly, economic development and/or political influence; residence status,

METHODOLOGICAL PRELIMINARIES AND SPECIFICATIONS

where one's hukou (户口 – residence permit) literally inscribes a semi-permanent gradation of citizenship and the place(s) where the rights associated with *xiang xia* (乡下 – countryside/rural) and *chengshi* (城市 – city/urban) status obtain more or less fully; and/or a more generally implied social status, where the suggestion of or even proximity to rural origin can be particularly damning. As lived experience, these distinctions shift and increase in complexity as rural to urban migration proceeds apace, effects not diminished by the temporary status of much of the staggeringly large migrant labour population. The population of any given Chinese city is now surprisingly hybridized and undergoing constant change as a result.

For the purposes of this study, "urban" designates parents who live in Shijiazhuang, a city of moderate economic development and political influence on the national scene, and, thus, a not-prestigious but, on the whole, typical non-internationalized Chinese city. To the residents of Beijing, Tianjin, Shanghai, or Guangzhou, even to residents of second-tier eastern coastal cities such as Dalian or Wuhan, Shijiazhuang is rather tu (土 – literally "soil" or "earth," but inflected as a slight it connotes backwardness) and, by implication, much closer to "rural" than they see themselves to be. Yet it is, at the same time, the capital of a province of roughly seventy-million and the largest of that province's eleven cities. By 2004, the city proper housed a relatively modest two million, but, as the centre of its own prefecture, it now governs more than nine million people. While it does provide a range of educational opportunities to the residents of Hebei, its post-secondary institutions are not in the same class as the relatively few well-known and nationally supported comprehensive institutions located in cities like Beijing, Shanghai, and Xi'an. For all intents and purposes, then, while Shijiazhuang is most definitely a "city" and certainly not "rural" by the objective standards set out above, it nonetheless can be seen to be so by the subjective criteria described in the fourth of the categories of distinction. Put differently, for Shijiazhuang's most aggressively upwardly mobile, true urbanity exists elsewhere, in Beijing, Shanghai, or overseas.

In contemporary, market-oriented China, class is an important dimension of unification and differentiation (Wang, Davis, & Bian, 2006). Taking into account "ownership of property, skill, and authority in the workplace" (p. 322), China's emergent

Table A.1. Class-occupational structure of contemporary China (adapted from Bian, 2002; Wang, Davis, & Bian, 2006, p. 326)

Control over property	Control over organizations	Skilled & semi-skilled labour	Structurally disempowered
Private owners Administrative staff	Enterprise managers Government officials Party officials	Professionals White-collar administrative staff Blue collar production workers Service workers	Laid-off labour Retired labour Rural to urban migrant labour

141

social structure can be seen to comprise three categories and eight subdivisions. Two of the eight, "private owners and administrative staff," imply "control over property" (as opposed to ownership); two, "enterprise managers and government/Party officials," indicate "control of organizations"; and four, "professionals, white-collar administrative staff, blue collar production workers, and service workers," require "some kind of skill" (p. 322/326). Unfortunately, these three categories and their subdivisions exclude a crucial feature of the post-Mao urban landscape: the downward mobility and dispossession that is an outcome of processes of differentiation and disempowerment of the Mao-era urban proletariat (Bian, 2002). This once-privileged, now-fragmented proletariat significantly includes "a new urban poverty stratum" that has emerged from within the ranks of "layoff…and retired labor" (Bian, 2002, p. 96), not to mention from the ranks of employed or casually employed rural to urban migrant labourers. Inclusion of a fourth category of "structurally disempowered" gives one a fuller picture of the nature of contemporary urban society.

This class-occupational structure suggests a more highly variegated social configuration than that implied in the research questions listed above. Having said this, in those questions, the term "middle-class" is a convenient placeholder at once suggested by the common sense self-positioning of respondents, popular literature that encourages people to examine themselves in terms of relative "middle-classness,"[2] and the public discourse of the state and its research organs. Respondents were not purposefully recruited with respect to this typology, but sampling was "purposive" (Patton, 1990) in the sense that I aimed to recruit a group of respondents with the capacity to compile an information rich case "from which…a great deal about issues…central…to the purpose of the research" (p. 169). With respect to the aims of the research, the principal need was to assemble data representative of a broad range of Shijiazhuang parents' views and experiences. The strategy of "convenience sampling," like purposive sampling associated with "theoretical sampling" (Glaser & Strauss, 1967), was also important (Patton, 1990). I identified parents of children currently in the midst of their nine years of *yiwu jiaoyu* (义务教育 – compulsory education) as well as those of children about to enter these years. When I initially interviewed them, they were parents to children ranging from *youeryuan* (幼儿园 – preschool/kindergarten) to *chu san* (初三 – Lower Middle School Year Three/Grade 9), or approximately three to fifteen years of age. By the end of the period of study, the youngest of these children was in her last year of *youeryuan*, the oldest in the midst of writing *gaokao* (高考 – high school exit exams). Initial informants were drawn from an existing group of contacts that included past work colleagues and research collaborators. Subsequent informants were identified through referrals from this initial group, i.e., through "snowball" or "respondent-driven sampling," an approach that provided access to respondents whose occupations, e.g., government/Party officials, made their recruitment problematic (Heckathorn, 1997).[3] I recruited informants representing a total of fifteen families. Those introduced by name below were key to the data generation as I was able to interview them most thoroughly and spend the most time observing them.

METHODOLOGICAL PRELIMINARIES AND SPECIFICATIONS

Table A.2. Objects, data sources, and modes of analysis

Chapter	Object (order)	Data sources	Mode of analysis
2–3	*Jianfu* (cultural system)	• Field notes/reflections • Popular press • Policy	Corpus Analysis
4	Shijiazhuang City (*cultural system*)	• Maps • Planning documents • Photographs • *da zi bao* • Advertisements	Corpus Analysis
5	Parents' beliefs and activities (*socio-cultural interaction*)	• Observation (fieldnotes/reflections) • Interviews	Close listening/reading Focussed Coding

DATA ANALYSIS

Three distinct modes of analysis were used to deal with the different kinds of data collected for the study. These forms correspond to the focus of each of Chapters 2 through 5. Tables A.2 and A.3 provide a brief overview of the structure of this tripartite analysis, including the objects of study, data sources, and modes of analysis.

Table A.3. Comparison of codes in different modes of analysis

Code family	Code used in "scoping orders of worth"	Code used in "scoping the city"	Code used in "scoping parents' beliefs and practices"
Process	• De-ruralization • Modernization	• De-ruralization • Modernization • Beautification • Culturalization	• Cultivating suzhi • Family education
Relationship and social structure	• Common good • Relations between persons	• Common good • Relations between persons	• Treating others well • Mianzi/lian • Fairness
Ways of thinking about people and objects	• Good persons • Valued Knowledge • Modes of Learning	• Beautiful places • The good life • Good schools	• Good persons • Valued knowledge • Modes of learning • Beautiful places • Good places to eat • The good life • Good schools

143

APPENDIX A

Before presenting the analysis of *jianfu*, I provide a reminder about data sources and methods of analysis. As discussed above, I compiled four discrete corpora comprising materials in broad circulation within a few years of the time that *jianfu* was formally proclaimed. I read these materials looking for indicators of the kinds of people, social relations, knowledge, and learning represented as valuable or praiseworthy at that time. Taken together, each of these collections of normative criteria comprise a more or less distinct order of worth, providing guidance to people on how to govern themselves publicly and privately, and especially to parents on how to proceed with respect to educating and getting an education for their children.

SCOPING ORDERS OF WORTH

In this chapter and again in Chapter 3, I construct a history of orders of worth of China's Communist state. The analysis is grounded in Boltanski & Thévenot's (2006) and Boltanski & Chiapello's (2007) concept of "order of worth." An order of worth comprises a comprehensive set of criteria by which judgements are made about the value or "goodness" of people, things, and social arrangements and, at the same time, can provide justification for one's participation in extant social order. Propaganda of various kinds are the primary vehicle by which an officially sanctioned order of worth is proposed and promoted, whereby "a series of novel political-cultural forms" is created to fulfill "the pressing need of the CCP…to consolidate its hold on China, justify its legitimacy, and instill a new socialist culture in the nation" (Hung, 2011, p. 2). An order of worth is also a set of precepts or prescription that orients – imperfectly, to be sure – the thoughts and activities of people who live in a given socio-cultural environment.

To maintain legitimacy – i.e., to be effective in providing justification – a order of worth must fulfill three criteria. First, it must provide for excitement or challenge, for "attractive, exciting life prospects" (Boltanski & Chiapello, 2007, p. 24). With respect to Chinese parents' educational projects, the pursuit of educational success/ attainment is in and of itself an extreme challenge in a system characterized by a scarcity – both perceived and real – of high quality opportunities and governed by an entrance/examination system with a significant degree of selective power. But for those not motivated by pure challenge, one finds all kinds of exciting promises on offer in contemporary Chinese schools, international travel/study, for example. Second, an order of worth must supply "guarantees of security" (p. 25) to those who engage with the world it aims to govern. For the middle-class urban parents who are the subjects of this study, the order of worth that orients their activities holds out the promise of success through dedication and hard work, that is, it offers the possibility of good jobs and happiness to those who readily submit themselves to the barriers it places before them. Third, an order of worth must provide a conception of the common good, some sense that one's educational pursuits are not harmful to others, indeed, that the drive to competition and self-betterment characteristic of today's educational culture somehow contributes to the good of the wider community to which one belongs. Justification of this kind can be seen most clearly, perhaps, in proposals that seek to identify, advance, and disproportionately reward "special talents" despite the manifest developmental imbalances (e.g. lack of social skills, physical frailty, etc.) such individuals might display. Where special talents are able to contribute to the overall development of society (e.g., a musician capable of uplifting the spirits of the people at large, a scientist with the intellectual capacity required to bring to market discoveries that improve the health of all), balanced or overall development can be set aside.

To specify the relevant orders of worth, I identified four distinct collections of documents as *corpora* grouped around the occurrence of a policy directive – *jianfu* – repeatedly forwarded as the solution to perceived flaws in the revolutionary state's educational processes and systems. These calls to *jianfu* coincide with epochal moments in the history of the People's Republic, some of them more with epochal moments in the history of the People's Republic, some of them more familiar and, therefore, more easily recognized – such as the founding of the PRC or the launching of the Great Proletarian Cultural Revolution – and others less so, such as the present period, which coincides roughly with the elevation of Jiang Zemin's *Three Represents* as a core component of the guiding philosophy of the Chinese Communist Party. I have not attempted to identify every potential order of worth. For example, the decade of the 1990s followed a crucial moment of transition following the shock of Tiananmen and the demise of European communism, not to mention Deng's highly significant southern tour, but I have not attributed to this important decade its own order of worth and given it the detailed treatment it likely deserves. However, I would suggest that the orders I do present are sufficient for the purposes of explication and comparison.

As discussed above, the resources through which one can discern a distinctive order of worth are nearly inexhaustible. Put simply, one could discover, compile, read, and analyze for years on end without exhausting the quantity and range of available materials. I began to read through any materials I could find that seemed to bear on *education* of one form or another, especially that which offered explicit or implicit guidance for people on how to train and/or educate themselves well. Those that leant themselves to discerning the order of worth of a given period were added to the corpus. For example, some texts comment on the intolerable workload of students:

> at present the classes in junior middle schools take too much of the students' time, and it would be preferable if they were cut down to suitable proportions. (Mao, 1997 [1953], p. 97)

Others are concerned with the kinds of knowledge that ought to be valued and the places within which such knowledge ought to be produced and transmitted:

145

APPENDIX A

Table A.4. Coding used in "scoping orders of worth"

Code family	Codes used in "scoping orders of worth"	Examples of coded data
Process	De-ruralization	"The All-China Federation of Trade Unions survey suggested that the children of migrant workers newly graduated from high school are not confident or competent in setting concrete career goals, or handling the complex and fluctuating information and social environments" (Hou, 2010, p. 12)
	Modernization	"As a rising modern country with an ancient civilization, it is fitting for China to make a special effort to develop its higher education… and to in turn improve the quality of world education" (CWI, 2011, p. 4).
Relationship and social structure	Common good	"We do not really belong to cities. When we're old we'll go back to our village to live. In cities we just serve the people, and everything else is provisional. But we're glad to do so, and have no regrets, since in many ways we are doing better than back on the farm" (Hou, 2010, p. 12).
	Relations between persons	• "Many fighters of this peoples' army are writing today….The most gifted and experienced writers in the country help them with lectures and criticism" (CWI, 1952c, p. 41). • See Figures 2.1, 2.2, 2.3, 3.1, 3.3
Ways of thinking about people and objects	Good persons	"The questions were difficult, for with only three years of schooling I lacked real theoretical knowledge….He determined to work hard to make up what he lacked in theory" (Kao, 1966, p. 28).
	Valued Knowledge	• "Most of the 2006 Hong Kong graduates that have found work are with international investment banks, consultancy firms and transnational companies" (Lu, 2006a, p. 41). • See Figures 2.2, 2.4, 2.6, 2.7
	Modes of Learning	"Theoretical and technical knowledge is learned through combining study, productive labor and scientific experimentation" (Staff Reporter, 1975, p. 2).

Theoretical and technical knowledge is learned through combining study, productive labor and scientific experimentation. This is in sharp contrast to the old universities under the revisionist line where the students were divorced from proletarian politics, labor, and the workers and peasants. (Staff Reporter, 1975, p. 2)

Still others describe the qualities of a good teacher and the ways in which "good" teachers and pupils ought to relate to one another:

Gone were the authoritarian, self-centred pedagogues I remembered from my own schooldays. Gone too was the reticence of the children toward the teachers…, based on fear of authority, and the individualistic spirit among the pupils themselves. In their place were warm friendliness and an atmosphere of cooperation and good teamwork. (Pan, 1955, p. 13)

Once the various corpora were compiled, I began the process of discerning the dominant order of worth of each period. As I engaged in a "close reading" (Hammersley & Atkinson, 2007) of the documents, I made notes of frequently recurring words and phrases. Some of these (e.g., modernization) were identified as spontaneous codes in subsequent analysis. I created other codes (e.g., de-ruralization) to describe themes that emerged during analysis. I then used *HyperResearch* qualitative analysis software to code the entire corpus. I conducted keyword searches using the spontaneous codes, the purpose of which was to identify occurrences of a topic or theme and develop a rich understanding of it. Spontaneous codes were designated as a list of initial codes. As this process continued, a set of dominant codes emerged, that is, they occurred more often than others and aligned with one or the other of the aspects of Boltanski & Chiapello's framework.

Of these aspects, the four identified in Chapters 2 and 3 emerged as powerful indicators of the shape and texture of orders of worth as they concern matters of education: reference to common good; reference to good persons and relations between persons; reference to knowledge; and reference to teaching/learning styles. To be sure, no order of worth is eternal, and the combination of excitement, security, and "moral reasons" (Boltanski & Chiapello, 2007, p. 25) that legitimate social arrangements at the same time provide for the possibility of its delegitimization. Indeed, the ways in which parents talked about rearing and educating their children in Shijiazhuang indicated that their relation to the dominant order of worth of their time is far from secure. It also confirms Boltanski & Chiapello's claims of the special role of critique to the eventual demise of that order. An order of worth, that is, is at once an expression of the preferred way to live life and a critique or dismissal of some other, no longer desirable way of life. An order of worth offers a critique of the order it aims to supplant, pointing out how the kinds of people, relations between people, forms of education, and/or notion of common good proposed in the past is somehow insufficient. But it is also a normative template, a vision of the future by which the mistakes of the past can be corrected and a more desirable future realized. As a more or less comprehensive guide to living, a

APPENDIX A

set of cultural resources that every day people live in relation to, and a collection of omnipresent and accessible exemplars, these orders of worth provide some indication of the moral universe within which every day people go about their lives.

SCOPING THE CITY

Maps of Shijiazhuang, government planning documents, photographs, and notes of my observations and experiences of construction and re-development in the city helped me create the descriptions presented in this chapter. In terms of the general precepts of *san nian da bianyang*, I read through speeches and news reports looking for repeated terms, exhortations of residents to embrace *san nian da bianyang*, and evaluations of initiatives proposed or underway, especially for those explicitly linked to improvements for the common good and/or to the creation of an urban environment capable of nurturing good people and positive relations amongst citizens.

"Process" codes (Bogdan & Biklen, 2007, p. 176) such as "de-ruralization," "modernization," and "beautification" were used to code data linked to notions of how the city ought to change. In development plans, I paid attention to potential changes in "spatial relations" produced in planners' visions, in particular the ways in which these plans made private vehicle ownership a necessary condition of living the good life. In photos of advertisements on construction walls, I looked for indicators – both textual and visual – of "the good life" and the kinds of people who could be produced by this good life. The photos were categorized using codes belonging to the "relationship and social structure codes" (Bogdan & Biklen, 2007, p. 177) family, such as "common good" and "relations between persons." These codes are discussed separately in the subsections under *Tangible Effects of Renovation* in Chapter 4, but are also linked to codes commonly used with interview transcripts. Table A.5 shows the relationships between these codes.

Following these more generalized processes of change, I focus on a specific instance of change in the form of one new neighbourhood currently under construction. Linyin Dayuan is a large new neighbourhood taking the place of Beijiao Village in north central Shijiazhuang. What makes this development an interesting object of analysis is the particularly heavy layer of promotion taking place around it in the form of advertising. These advertisements provide examples of the kinds of promotional materials on display throughout the city, whether on the construction walls of new developments or in the hallways of shopping malls throughout the city. The images and slogans contained in the ads were compiled and coded using the same code families and specific codes as other documents in this section and are included to given a sense of the kinds of projects that residents of the city are confronted by on a daily basis.

For the third part of Chapter 4, *Educational Institutions for the Aspirational City*, I conducted a corpus analysis of the kind described above using materials available on the websites of Shijiazhuang Foreign Language School (SFLS) and *Jinbaobei/ Gymboree China*. Because my interest was in connecting elements of Shijiazhuang's

Table A.5. Coding used in "scoping the city"

Code family	Codes used in "scoping the city"	Examples of coded data
Process	De-ruralization	See Figures 4.7, 4.9, 4.13, 4.15
	Modernization	See Figures 4.1, 4.8, 4.11, 4.18
	Beautification	• See Figures 4.5, 4.10 • "Each landscape, green belt, and even street and neighbourhood – each should project 'ingenuity' so as to become a work of art" (ido.3mt.com.cn, 2009)
Relationship and social structure	Common good	"In order to accelerate the process of urbanization with the consequence of building a moderately prosperous [*xiaokang* – 小康] society in our province as a whole in the long-term, we must continuously emancipate our mind and develop innovative new ideas, initiatives, and leadership" (Hebei People's Government, 2007, "Promote Urbanization and Institutional Renovation")
	Relations between persons	
Ways of thinking about people and objects	Good persons	"We set it our goal to educate our students to be qualified personnel who are patriotic, sociable, cooperative, polite, healthy and creative and who can meet the global challenges of the world" (SFLEG, 2013d).
	Valued Knowledge	"Students energetically use brooms to sweep leaves and scrape off the small ad stickers. See how much our small labour can accomplish? See how the residential environment can be changed with only our small hands?" (SFLEG, 2013a).
	Modes of Learning	"…the development of children's language, art, science exploration, group games,… the ability to help your baby learn to be independent and live in groups" (Gymboree, 2013).

educational institutions to the order of worth identified in the Chapter 4 corpus analysis, I focused on materials that addressed the domains of common good, good persons and relations between persons, knowledge, and teaching/learning styles. These schools' promotional/communication materials proved particularly useful in

APPENDIX A

this regard as they provided insight into how the school and its staff wishes to be viewed by parents, teachers, and visitors. For example, I looked at descriptions of its facilities to get a sense of what kinds of knowledge are valued as well as what kind of students the school aims to produce. I read through dozens of staff introductions and compiled a list of characteristics that describe the kinds teachers seen as "good" and worthy of teaching at such a school. I read articles on student volunteer activities looking for depictions of model students, including the personal qualities such students are expected to exhibit, how they ought to dress and address teachers, and what the purpose of such students might ultimately be. Finally, I looked carefully at how the school conceives of "good parents," including the kinds of knowledge it views as essential for good parenting, how it attempts to establish good relations between parents and the school, and the kinds of parent role models the school publicizes.

SCOPING PARENTS' BELIEFS AND PRACTICES

Hammersley and Atkinson (2007) recommend "close reading" of data as a way of finding concepts with which to understand what is "going on" and as a way to develop fresh insight into the phenomena under investigation (p. 162). For me, this process began in a slightly different way – with repeated close *listening* during the period in which I conducted interviews. I loaded interview recordings into a portable listening device and listened to them repeatedly over an extended period of time. From a purely practical perspective, repeated listening both relieved the pressure of immediate transcription and made eventual transcription easier. More importantly, I developed a familiarity with the interview recordings that allowed me to, (1) remain attuned to prosodic[4] elements not easily represented in transcriptions[5]; (2) to pick up on potentially productive lines of inquiry while still in the field; and (3) to expedite the process of "initial coding" (Lofland, Snow, Anderson, & Lofland, 2006, p. 201). Together with close reading of transcripts, close listening helped me to think with the data; to search for "interesting patterns" and "surprising or puzzling elements"; to make connections to expectations based on "common sense knowledge, official accounts, or previous theory"; and to seek out variations and contradictions in the views, beliefs, and attitudes of individuals or within groups, or between what people say and what they do (Hammersley & Atkinson, 2007, p. 163).[6]

During repeated listening and reading, both "spontaneous" (i.e., taken from the usage of participants) and "observer-identified" (i.e., created by me) concepts arose (p. 163). The former – such as *jiating jiaoyu, suzhi, zonghe/pingheng fazhan,* and *mianzi* – are discussed in Chapter 5, as are examples of the latter (e.g., negotiating, navigating). In identifying these concepts, I drew on common sense, personal experience, and pertinent theory (p. 163).[7] Concept formation of this kind is typically imprecise, akin to Blumer's "sensitizing concepts" (in Hammersley & Atkinson, 2007, p. 164). Such concepts are a contingent product of a preliminary analysis

Table A.6. *Coding used in "scoping parents' beliefs and practices"*
All quoted material is from interview data

Code family	Codes use in "scoping parents beliefs and practices"	Examples of coded data
Process	Cultivating suzhi	"I taught my child, when he finishes something to just keep the garbage and take it home to throw out. So now he remembers 'Don't throw it on the ground, mama! Take it home for me and throw it in the garbage!" I think that shows one's suzhi."
	Family education (*jiating jiaoyu*)	"First, it involves simple living, looking after basic needs. Another is to teach him to know his environment and society, not only how to get dressed, how to study things…not only those things. Another thing is to teach him a way of thinking, like how to tackle problems he faces, how to think."
Relationship and social structure	Treating others well	"Like when we are on the bus, I teach him to give up his seat to old people."
	Mianzi/lian	"I think I am the kind of person that cares a lot about what others think of me and my child. If she does well, it makes me look good."
	Fairness	"For example, look at how highly students in Hebei or Henan have to score on the exams. For students from Beijing, it's much easier."
Ways of thinking about people and objects	Good persons	"I think a good person is someone is useful, who has value to society."
	Valued knowledge	"She should learn some technical knowledge, but also learn how to solve problems."
	Modes of learning	"I just want him to do well in the end, and that will be good enough. In the end, if he can test in the better half, that is good enough for me."
	Beautiful places	"One thing I do is try to take her to scenic areas so she will understand that the world is full of different kinds of places, not just the city."
	The good life	"There is a little girl who lives next door to us, and I guess she has probably never even been to KFC for a meal."
	Good schools	"For primary school, I think a common school nearby is good enough. Later, I hope he can go to a better one, like SFLS."

APPENDIX A

that "suggest directions along which to look," to give "a general sense of what is relevant," and to provide "reference and guidance" (Blumer, 1954, p. 7).

With repeated readings, certain topics and concepts came to the fore as they were either, (a), repeatedly returned to and/or imbued with explanatory significance by interviewees, or (b), because they offered insight with respect to the research questions. These initial topics and concepts were the foundation of an initial list of "coding categories" (Bogdan & Biklen, 2007, p. 173). One family of codes, for example, dealt with the concept of *pingheng fazhan* (all-around/balanced development), and comprised discrete codes such as *facilities needed for balanced development, schooling is about teaching-learning creativity,* and *schooling is about teaching-learning to be cooperative.* These categories and codes organized subsequent rounds of "focused coding" (Lofland et al., 2006) during which all of the interview transcripts were coded using the QR software *HyperResearch*. I used the software to perform manual and automated key word searches.

The types of codes of most concern in this research are usefully described by Bogdan and Biklen (2007) under a number of family names. Crucially, interview data yielded insight into "perspectives held by subjects" (p. 175) in terms of their understandings of the purposes and aims of "education." In terms of considering how parents go about getting the kind of education they envision for their children, a number of the codes that emerged to organize the data belong to the family of "strategy codes," those that refer to the "tactics, methods, techniques, maneuvers, ploys, and other conscious ways people accomplish various things" (p. 177). They also revealed "subjects' ways of thinking about people and objects" (p. 175), perspectives that helped me explore links between informants' perspectives and the aspirational cité.

NOTES

[1] The divide I refer to is the Catholic-Public/Protestant division in Alberta's government funded school system. While changes to funding formulas, demographics, and a group of policies that allow for "choice" have to some extent broken down the barriers that once made crossing sectarian boundaries rare, the objective fact that only one school exists in many small communities means that the "right to choose" remains a limited and largely abstract possibility.
[2] The best of example of this literature is Xu Haifeng's (2003) *ni "zhong chan" le ma?* (你中产了吗? – *Are you part of the middle-class?*).
[3] Questions such as those that follow will helped me to identify further respondents. To whom do you go for to help you make decisions about your child's education? What kinds of people and sources do you trust/respect (or not)? Do you know others who might be interested in discussing these topics with me?
[4] Here I refer to elements such as pitch and stress (Prosodic, 1998). More generally, recognizing that an informant was angry or joking, i.e., recognizing the *spirit* of an utterance, is greatly enhanced by access to original recordings.
[5] For the same reason, I later transcribed the interviews using *Transcriva* (http://transcriva.en.softonic.com/mac), software that allows for synchronized listening and reading.
[6] In Glaser and Strauss (1970) this process is described as a search for "categories and properties" (p. 105).
[7] In Glaser and Strauss (1970), these are categories the researcher "has constructed himself" and "those that have been abstracted from the language of the researcher situation" (p. 107).

APPENDIX B

DOCUMENTS USED IN CORPUS ANALYSIS

CORPUS 1 – THE EARLY REVOLUTIONARY PERIOD

1952

Chang, W.-S. (1952, July–August). Doctors serve, teach and learn. *China Reconstructs, 1*(4).
Chen, S.-M. (1952, March–April). A place the children love. *China Reconstructs, 1*(2).
Chien, C. (1952, November–December). Private enterprise grows. *China Reconstructs, 1*(6).
Ching, C.-H. (1952, September–October). Clearing the decks for industrialization. *China Reconstructs, 1*(5).
Fei, X. (1952, May–June). China's multi-national family. *China Reconstructs, 1*(3).
How Workers. (1952, January–February). How workers move industry forward. *China Reconstructs, 1*(1), 24–25.
Hu, H.-C. (1952, January–February). University trade union. *China Reconstructs, 1*(1).
Jen, T.-Y. (1952, January–February). The children's own theatre. *China Reconstructs, 1*(1).
Marriage Law. (1952, July–August). Marriage Law brings happiness. *China Reconstructs, 1*(4), 46.
Mei, L.-F. (1952, September–October). Old art with a new future. *China Reconstructs, 1*(5).
New City New People. (1952, May–June). New City New People. *China Reconstructs, 1*(3).
News of CWI. (1952, January–February). News of CWI. *China Reconstructs, 1*(1).
Shih, C.-C. (1952, July–August). Worker's clubs and cultural groups. *China Reconstructs, 1*(4).
Soldier Writer. (1952, May–June). Kao Yu-Pao Soldier Writer. *China Reconstructs, 1*(3).
Soong, C. L. (1952, January–February). Welfare work and world peace. *China Reconstructs, 1*(1).
Sports Athletics. (1952, September–October). Sports and Athletics for all. *China Reconstructs, 1*(5), 16–17.
Workers' Inventions. (1952, May–June). Workers' Inventions and innovations. *China Reconstructs, 1*(3), 12.

1953

A Teacher. (1953, May–June). A Teacher housewife. *China Reconstructs, 2*(3).
Chien, T.-S. (1953, September–October). Higher education takes a new path. *China Reconstructs, 2*(5).
Ching, C. (1953, July–August). World's biggest elections. *China Reconstructs, 2*(4).
Chou, J. (1953, May–June). Women workers and their children. *China Reconstructs, 2*(3).
Hinton, W. (1953, September–October). Two ordinary girls. *China Reconstructs, 2*(5).
Li, P.-T. (1953, March–April). New day in child care. *China Reconstructs, 2*(2).
Liu, N.-I. (1953, May–June). What Chinese trade unions do. *China Reconstructs, 2*(3).
Liu, O.-S. (1953, November–December). My experience as an industrialist. *China Reconstructs, 2*(6).
Lo, C. (1953, March–April). Women are equals. *China Reconstructs, 2*(2).
The Peasants Get. (1952, May–June). The Peasants Get new implements. *China Reconstructs, 1*(3), 10–12.
Three Children. (1952, November–December). Three Children and a cow. *China Reconstructs, 1*(6).
TOC. (1952, January–February). Table of contents. *China Reconstructs, 1*(1).
TOC. (1952, March–April). Table of contents. *China Reconstructs, 1*(2).
TOC. (1952, May–June). Table of contents. *China Reconstructs, 1*(3).

APPENDIX B

TOC. (1952, July–August). Table of contents. *China Reconstructs, 1*(4).
TOC. (1952, September–October). Table of contents. *China Reconstructs, 1*(5).
TOC. (1952, November–December). Table of contents. *China Reconstructs, 1*(6).
Travels in China. (1952, July–August). Travels in China (new culture). *China Reconstructs, 1*(4).
Tze, K. (1952, March–April). Chinese women and children. *China Reconstructs, 1*(2).
Village Teacher. (1952, March–April). A Village Teacher fights illiteracy. *China Reconstructs, 1*(2).
Weapon Against. (1952, September–October). Weapon Against illiteracy. *China Reconstructs, 1*(5).
Workers Education. (1952, November–December). Workers' Education. *China Reconstructs, 1*(6).
Workers Get. (1952, November–December). Workers Get new homes. *China Reconstructs, 1*(6).

1954

Chen, C.-H. (1954, September–October). Wide horizons for students. *China Reconstructs, 3*(5).
Chi, F.-Y. (1954, July–August). Peasant girl to farm leader. *China Reconstructs, 3*(4).
China Reconstructs. (1954, November–December). China Reconstructs moves to monthly issues. *China Reconstructs, 3*(6).
Huang, T.-P. (1954, November–December). Peasant hunters of fukien province. *China Reconstructs, 3*(6).
Li, P.-T. (1954, May–June). Wang Chung-Lun who out-distanced time. *China Reconstructs, 3*(3).
List of China. (1954, November–December). List of china reconstructs worldwide distributors. *China Reconstructs, 3*(6).
Liu, G. D. (1954, September–October). My husband is a 'model.' *China Reconstructs, 3*(5).
Liu, S.-T. (1954, March–April). At the ferry. *China Reconstructs, 3*(2).
Lu, P. (1954, November–December). Labour party delegation. *China Reconstructs, 3*(6).
Lu, Y.-S. (1954, November–December). One peaceful night. *China Reconstructs, 3*(6).
Pai, H. (1954, November–December). What the hani girl said to me. *China Reconstructs, 3*(6).
Staff Reporter. (1954, July–August). In a Peking primary school. *China Reconstructs, 3*(4).
Sun, H.-C. (1954, March–April). Girl dispatcher. *China Reconstructs, 3*(2).
TOC. (1954, January–February). Table of contents. *China Reconstructs, 3*(1).
TOC. (1954, March–April). Table of contents. *China Reconstructs, 3*(2).
TOC. (1954, May–June). Table of contents. *China Reconstructs, 3*(3).
TOC. (1954, July–August). Table of contents. *China Reconstructs, 3*(4).
TOC. (1954, September–October). Table of contents. *China Reconstructs, 3*(5).
World Youth. (1954, November–December). World Youth in Peking. *China Reconstructs, 3*(6).
Yang, G. T. (1954, July–August). Books and people. *China Reconstructs, 3*(4).

1955

Alley, R. (1955, March). At the school again. *China Reconstructs, 4*(3), 18–20.
Li, S.-M. (1955, May). The Hui people's academy. *China Reconstructs, 4*(5), 12–13.
Lin, T. K. (1955, August). Broadcasting for the people. *China Reconstructs, 4*(8), 2–5.
Pan, Y.-J. (1955, June). A school that leads the way. *China Reconstructs, 4*(6), 13–15.
Tien, T. (1955, February). Better books for children. *China Reconstructs, 4*(2), 25–27.
TOC. (1955, March). Table of contents. *China Reconstructs, 4*(3).
TOC. (1955, May). Table of contents. *China Reconstructs, 4*(5).

1956

Chen, H.-S. (1956, September). Training teachers for middle schools. *China Reconstructs, 5*(9), 18–19.
Pan, Y. (1956, April). Meeting new needs in education. *China Reconstructs, 5*(4), 2–5.
Yang, K. T. (1956, June). Growing boy. *China Reconstructs, 5*(6), 24–26.

DOCUMENTS USED IN CORPUS ANALYSIS

1965

Epstein, I. (1965, August). Biggest export fair at Canton. *China Reconstructs, 14*(8), 9–12.
Ho, C.-C. (1965, October). China builds her own chemical fibre industry. *China Reconstructs, 14*(10), 40–41.

CORPUS 2 – THE GREAT PROLETARIAN CULTURAL REVOLUTION

1966

Books. (1966, April). Books for the countryside. *China Reconstructs, 15*(4), 20–20.
Animated Cartoon. (1966, March). Animated Cartoon films teach the young. *China Reconstructs, 15*(3), 24–24.
Chang, C. (1966, January). Open-book examinations bring good results. *China Reconstructs, 15*(1), 14–15.
Chen, C.-H. (1966, February). Across the grasslands with a mobile theatre. *China Reconstructs, 15*(2).
Chin, P.-S. (1966, August). Making a transistorized ultrasonic thickness gauge. *China Reconstructs, 15*(2).
Chu, P.-C. (1966, April). Boxwood carvings of children. *China Reconstructs, 15*(4), 36–37.
Fang, C. (1966, June). Weaver who looks behind the cloth. *China Reconstructs, 15*(6), 36–38.
Fighting Spirit. (1966, February). Fighting Spirit in songs. *China Reconstructs, 15*(2).
Four New. (1966, June). Four New track and field records. *China Reconstructs, 15*(2).
Ho, W. (1966, April). Commerce serves the countryside. *China Reconstructs, 15*(2).
Hsin, P. (1966, May). A young fighter-Wang Chieh. *China Reconstructs, 15*(5), 10–13.
Kao, H.-C. (1966, March). Man with fortitude. *China Reconstructs, 15*(3), 26–28.
Kao, Y.-W. (1966, April). Revolution in machine designing. *China Reconstructs, 15*(4), 26–32.
Kumara, A. (1966, September). My third visit to China. *China Reconstructs, 15*(2).
Lake, R. (1966, February). A day in Yenan. *China Reconstructs, 15*(2), 25–28.
Li, P.-Y. (1966, October). Serving the mountain people. *China Reconstructs, 15*(2).
Man of Iron. (1966, May). The 'Man of Iron' Wang Chi-Hsi. *China Reconstructs, 15*(5), 2–5.
Mu, C. (1966, May). County party secretary-Chiao Yu-Lu. *China Reconstructs, 15*(5), 6–9.
Pa, C. (1966, May). Defeating the U.S. flying bandits. *China Reconstructs, 15*(2).
Peng, H.-C. (1966, April). A model reservoir manager. *China Reconstructs, 15*(4), 24–25.
Shi, T. (1966, July). Land wrested from the sea. *China Reconstructs, 15*(2).
Soong, C. L. (1966, January). Sixteen years of liberation. *China Reconstructs, 15*(1), 2–9.
Tai, S.-E. (1966, April). Mass efforts to extend improved seed. *China Reconstructs, 15*(4), 18–19.
Tao, T.-C. (1966, March). Ancient corner towers. *China Reconstructs, 15*(2).
The Old Woman. (1966, November). The Old Woman and the needle. *China Reconstructs, 15*(2).
The Students Go. (1966, January). The students go to the peasants. *China Reconstructs, 15*(1), 39–41.
TOC. (1966, July). Table of contents. *China Reconstructs, 15*(7), 1.
Wang, K.-C. (1966, March). The 100,000 whys. *China Reconstructs, 15*(3), 16–17.
Yu, C.-H. (1966, April). We don't turn down a difficult order! *China Reconstructs, 15*(4), 12–14.
Yu, W.-H. (1966, February). How I won the peasants' trust. *China Reconstructs, 15*(2), 16–18.
Yuen, H.-Y. (1966, July). Our summer vacation. *China Reconstructs, 15*(7), 55.

1967

A Long March. (1967, February). A Long March to Peking. *China Reconstructs, 16*(2), 11–14.
Chang, P. (1967, May). Wipe out the poisonous influence of the book on self-cultivation. *China Reconstructs, 16*(5), 9.
Chen, Y.-K. (1967, March). How we won the bumper harvest. *China Reconstructs, 16*(3), 20–21.
Chi, T. (1967, February). 'The east is red' rings out over Shanghai. *China Reconstructs, 16*(2), 10.

APPENDIX B

Ching, C. (1967, March). Speech by comrade Chiang Ching. *China Reconstructs, 16*(3), 5–6.
Jutseniu Long March Detachment. (1967, March). Not a single comrade fell behind. *China Reconstructs, 16*(3), 34–34.
Li, J.-N. (1967, January). We bend nature to our will. *China Reconstructs, 16*(1), 36–39.
Liu, S.-J. (1967, January). Heroic drilling team battles a sea of fire. *China Reconstructs, 16*(1), 26–31.
Pien, H.-T. (1967, February). The red guards – Shock force of the great proletarian cultural revolution. *China Reconstructs, 16*(2), 6–9.
Red Guards. (1967, January). Red Guards on a trolley bus. *China Reconstructs, 16*(1), 43–43.
TOC. (1967, January). Table of contents. *China Reconstructs, 16*(1), 1–1.

CORPUS 3 – REFORM AND OPENING UP

1975

A Lesson. (1975, April). A Lesson for the teacher. *China Reconstructs, 24*(4), 46–46.
CCP Central Committee. (1983). Circular of the CCP Central Committee and the state council on some questions concerning the strengthening and reform of rural school education (1983)*. *Chinese Education and Society, 12*(12), 71–76.
CCP Central Committee. (1985). *Reform of China's educational structure – Decision of the CPC Central Committee: Higher Education* (p. 22). Beijing: Foreign Languages Press.
Chang, T.-L. (1975, November). A factory-college graduate. *China Reconstructs, 24*(11), 6–8.
China Reconstructs Correspondents. (1975, February). Graduates from three year medical school. *China Reconstructs, 24*(2), 29–31.
China Reconstructs Correspondents. (1975, April). Higher education in Shanghai 'walks on two legs.' *China Reconstructs, 24*(4), 42–45.
Chu, H.-Y. (1975, March). How I acted a boy revolutionary hero. *China Reconstructs, 24*(3), 32–33.
Chung, T. (1975, December). Sports in new China. *China Reconstructs, 24*(12), 2–10.
Cover. (1975, February). Cover. *China Reconstructs, 24*(2).
Hsiao, P. (1975, November). The children's own newspaper. *China Reconstructs, 24*(11), 9–11.
Hsin, H.-W. (1975, May). A new type of college. *China Reconstructs, 24*(5), 6–10.
Hu, S., & Seifman, E. (1987). *Education and socialist modernization: A documentary history of education in the people's republic of China, 1977–1986* (p. 229). New York, NY: AMS Press.
Soong, C. L. (1975, April). Confucianism and modern China. *China Reconstructs, 24*(4), 2–4.
Staff Reporter. (1975, November). Factories run their own colleges. *China Reconstructs, 24*(11), 2–8.
The Shining. (1975, March). The Shining red star. *China Reconstructs, 24*(3), 27–31.
They Battle. (1975, February). They Battle with their poems. *China Reconstructs, 24*(2), 32–33.
Yung, H. (1975, May). Education in China today. *China Reconstructs, 24*(5), 2–5.

State Education Commission, 1987–1999

State Education Commission. (1994). 国家教委关于全面贯彻教育方针，减轻中小学生过重课业负担的意见 [State Education Commission Commentary on a Comprehensive Approach to Reducing Primary and Secondary Students Heavy Schoolwork Burden]. *China Education and Research Network*. Retrieved May 13, 2011, from http://www.chinalawedu.com/news/1200/22598/22615/22794/2006/3/we407315187121360028310-0.htm
State Education Commission. (2004 [1998]). Provisional regulations on schooling for migrant children. *Chinese Education & Society, 37*(5), 7–9.
State Education Commission. (2005a [1987]). 国家教委 1987 年工作要点 [Main Working Points of the State Education Commission for 1987]. *China Education and Research Network*. Retrieved May 13, 2011, from http://www.edu.cn/moe_gong_zuo_493/20060323/t20060323_135938.shtml

DOCUMENTS USED IN CORPUS ANALYSIS

State Education Commission. (2005b [1988]). 国家教委 1988 年工作要点 [Main Working Points of the State Education Commission for 1988]. *China Education and Research Network*. Retrieved May 13, 2011, from http://www.edu.cn/jybgz_9336/20100121/t20100121_443600.shtml
State Education Commission. (2005c [1989]). 国家教委 1989 年工作要点 [Main Working Points of the State Education Commission for 1989]. *China Education and Research Network*. Retrieved May 13, 2011, from http://www.edu.cn/moe_gong_zuo_493/20060323/t20060323_135957.shtml
State Education Commission. (2005d [1990]). 国家教委 1990 年工作要点 [Main Working Points of the State Education Commission for 1990]. *China Education and Research Network*. Retrieved May 13, 2011, from http://www.edu.cn/moe_gong_zuo_493/20060323/t20060323_135965.shtml
State Education Commission. (2005e [1991]). 国家教委 1991 年工作要点 [Main Working Points of the State Education Commission for 1991]. *China Education and Research Network*. Retrieved May 13, 2005, from http://www.edu.cn/moe_gong_zuo_493/20060323/t20060323_135970.shtml
State Education Commission. (2005f [1992]). 国家教委 1992 年工作要点 [Main Working Points of the State Education Commission for 1992]. *China Education and Research Network*. Retrieved May 13, 2011, from http://www.edu.cn/jybgz_9336/20100121/t20100121_443596.shtml
State Education Commission. (2005g [1993]). 国家教委 1993 年工作要点 [Main Working Points of the State Education Commission for 1993]. *China Education and Research Network*. Retrieved May 13, 2011, from http://www.edu.cn/jybgz_9336/20100121/t20100121_443595.shtml
State Education Commission. (2005h [1994]). 国家教委 1994 年工作要点 [Main Working Points of the State Education Commission for 1994]. *China Education and Research Network*. Retrieved May 13, 2011, from http://www.edu.cn/moe_gong_zuo_493/20060323/t20060323_135985.shtml
State Education Commission. (2005i [1995]). 国家教委 1995 年工作要点 [Main Working Points of the State Education Commission for 1995]. *China Education and Research Network*. Retrieved May 13, 2011, from http://www.edu.cn/moe_gong_zuo_493/20060323/t20060323_135999.shtml
State Education Commission. (2005j [1996]). 国家教委 1996 年工作要点 [Main Working Points of the State Education Commission for 1996]. *China Education and Research Network*. Retrieved May 13, 2011, from http://www.edu.cn/moe_gong_zuo_493/20060323/t20060323_136004.shtm
State Education Commission. (2005k [1997]). 国家教委 1997 年工作要点 [Main Working Points of the State Education Commission for 1997]. *China Education and Research Network*. Retrieved May 13, 2011, from http://www.edu.cn/moe_gong_zuo_493/20060323/t20060323_136008.shtml
Ministry of Education. (2005f [1999]). 教育部 1999 年工作要点 [Main Points of the Ministry of Education for 1999]. *China Education and Research Network*. Retrieved May 13, 2011, from http://www.edu.cn/jybgz_9336/20100121/t20100121_443590.shtml

CORPUS 4 – POST-2000

2006

CWI. (2006, November). China to introduce overseas academic talents. *China Today, 55*(11), 9–9.
Gao, S. (2006, October). Parental love cures net addiction. *China Today, 55*(10), 44–45.
Lu, R. (2006, April). High scores: Low ability. *China Today, 56*(4), 45–49.
Lu, R. (2006, October). Vying for the cream of China's academic crop. *China Today, 55*(10), 40–42.
Xu, X. (2006, August). Advocate of cultural integration. *China Today, 55*(8), 64–65.

2007

CWI. (2007, June). Font of music prodigies. *China Today, 56*(6), 10–11.
CWI. (2007, June). Great expectations. *China Today, 56*(6), 4–4.
Dornian, P. (2007, June). Music education advances through sino-foreign exchanges. *China Today, 56*(6), 22–23.
Huo, J. (2007, December). Three pillars of traditional rudimentary education. *China Today, 56*(12), 60–67.

APPENDIX B

Li, Y. (2007, June). Musical upward mobility. *China Today, 56*(6), 15–17.
Liu, Q. (2007, October). Recharge before advancing. *China Today, 56*(10), 26–29.
Lu, R. (2007, October). Time to learn. *China Today, 56*(10), 14–17.
Lu, R., & Luo, Y. (2007, June). Music is a calling not a work skill. *China Today, 56*(6), 12–14.

2008

Cadieux, L., & Hu, Y. (2008, March). A devoted music educator. *China Today, 57*(3), 64–65.
CWI. (2008, February). China plans to send 12,000 state-funded students abroad in 2008. *China Today, 57*(2), 8–8.
Hou, R. (2008, June). The booming baby business. *China Today, 57*(6), 30–31.
Zeng, P. (2008, May). A sound principal underlying a good education. *China Today, 57*(5), 47–49.

2009

Chambers, R. E. (2009, August). Model students. *China Today, 58*(8), 54–55.
Jiang, P., & Feng, J. (2009, October). Adhering to the values of an intellectual. *China Today, 58*(10), 24–27.
Lu, R. (2009, February). How to guide children: Family education consultancies take off. *China Today, 58*(2), 38–40.
Liu, Q. (2009, March). University graduates suffer "employment anxiety." *China Today, 58*(3), 32–34.
Lu, R. (2009, May). A top Chinese university reaches out to migrant workers. *China Today, 58*(5), 55–57.
Liu, Q. (2009, August). Where's my job? Job shortage for grads a national concern. *China Today, 58*(8), 15–18.
Liu, Q. (2009, September). Yu Shufan And her "children." *China Today, 57*(9), 54–55.
Zhao, Y. (2009, August). When the office seems chilly, school seems hot. *China Today, 57*(8), 33–35.
Zhou, Xi. (2009, February). My neighbour's American kids. *China Today, 58*(2), 41–41.

2010

Cheng, W. (2010, July). For the children of the grasslands. *China Today, 59*(7), 58–59.
CWI. (2010, February). The firm, the enduring, the simple, and the modest are near to virtue. *China Today, 59*(2), 70–71.
CWI. (2010, April). Educational funding to rise. *China Today, 59*(4), 8–8.
CWI. (2010, April). Xinjiang to exempt tuition and fees for teacher training. *China Today, 59*(4), 8–8.
Grossman, S. (2010, January). The world as classroom. *China Today, 59*(1), 70–72.
Hou, R. (2010, October). The in-between world: New-wave migrants. *China Today, 59*(10), 11–14.
Lu, R. (2010, August). Zhang Kailang: Putting the pop in popular science education. *China Today, 59*(8), 46–47.
Meng, Q., & Zhou, Y. (2010, April). An industry loses its shine. *China Today, 59*(4), 48–50.
Ministry of Education. (2010). *Outline of China's national plan for medium and long-term education reform and development, 2010–2020*. Beijing: Ministry of Education.
Zhang, H. (2010, June). Brains unchained: Chinese education devolves to evolve. *China Today, 59*(6), 49–50.
Zhao, Y. (2010, August). Scholars on the run. *China Today, 59*(8), 50–51.
Zhao, Y. (2010, August). The price of parenthood. *China Today, 59*(8), 44–46.

2011

Admin. (2010). 究意什么是全职妈妈. *www.qzmama.org*. Retrieved May 9, 2012, from http://www.qzmama.org/article-1-1.html
CWI. (2011, September). Chinese education influences the world. *China Today, 60*(9), 4–4.
CWI. (2011, November). Private capital in kindergartens encouraged. *China Today, 60*(11), 8–8.
Hou, R. (2011, September). Chinese universities embracing the world. *China Today, 60*(9), 20–24.
Ling, J. (2011, September). Xi'An Jiaotong-Liverpool university: Exploring a new educational model. *China Today, 60*(9), 25–27.
Lu, R. (2011, September). Approach to higher education reform. *China Today, 60*(9), 16–20.
Lu, R. (2011, September). To build world-class universities calls for restructuring higher education. *China Today, 60*(9), 28–30.
O'Mahony, T., & Bravery, B. (2011, September). From gaokao to knowhow. *China Today, 60*(9), 40–41.
Ouyang, H. (2011, February). Top ten concerns of 2010. *China Today, 60*(2), 38–43.
Wu, W. (2011, March). Our expectations for education. *China Today, 60*(3), 35–35.
Xu, Y. (2011, January). Changchun invests in people. *China Today, 60*(1), 52–55.
Xu, Y. (2011, September). Daqing: Science giant. *China Today, 60*(9), 78–79.
Zhang, H. (2011, July). Changing education: One Tibetan family's experience. *China Today, 60*(7), 49–50.
Zhao, D. (2011, April). Special love for a special individual. *China Today, 60*(4), 54–56.

2012

CWI. (2012, April). Free schooling for demobilized servicemen. *China Today, 61*(4), 9–9.
Ding, X. (2012, April). Remote county of abundant education. *China Today, 61*(4), 60–61.
Shen, H. (2012, June). Give children what is most valuable. *China Today, 61*(6), 28–30.
Zhang, H. (2012, June). Labor of love: Embracing the volunteer spirit in education. *China Today, 61*(6), 26–27.

China Ministry of Education, 2000–2010

Ministry of Education. (2005a [2001]). 教育部 2001 年工作要点 [Main Points of the Ministry of Education for 2001]. *China Education and Research Network*. Retrieved May 13, 2011, from http://www.edu.cn/moe_gong_zuo_493/20060323/t20060323_136016.shtml
Ministry of Education. (2005b [2000]). 教育部 2000 年工作要点 [Main Points of the Ministry of Education for 2000]. *China Education and Research Network*. Retrieved May 13, 2011, from http://www.edu.cn/20051229/3168313.shtml
Ministry of Education. (2005c [2003]). 教育部 2003 年工作要点 [Main Points of the Ministry of Education for 2003]. *China Education and Research Network*. Retrieved May 13, 2005, from http://www.edu.cn/20050819/3147525.shtml
Ministry of Education. (2005d [2005]). 教育部 2005 年工作要点 [Main Points of the Ministry of Education for 2005]. *China Education and Research Network*. Retrieved May 13, 2011, from http://www.edu.cn/20050819/3147527.shtml
Ministry of Education. (2005e [2004]). 教育部 2004 年工作要点 [Main Points of the Ministry of Education for 2004]. *China Education and Research Network*. Retrieved May 13, 2011, from http://www.edu.cn/20040105/3096860.shtml
Ministry of Education. (2005g [2002]). 教育部 2002 年工作要点 [Main Points of the Ministry of Education for 2002]. *China Education and Research Network*. Retrieved May 13, 2011, from http://www.edu.cn/moe_gong_zuo_493/20060323/t20060323_136017.shtml
Ministry of Education. (2010). *Outline of China's national plan for medium and long-term education reform and development, 2010–2020*. Beijing: Ministry of Education.

APPENDIX B

San nian da bianyang (一年一大步, 三年大变样) *Documents*

Hebei People's Government. (2007). *hebei sheng renmin zhengfu guanyu jiakuai tuijin chengzhenhua jin cheng de ruogan yijian* [Hebei people's government opinion on the acceleration of urbanization] (Ji Zheng [2007] No. 138). Retrieved from http://www.hebjs.gov.cn/zfxx/flfg/xgwj/200712/t20071223_88759.htm

Yao, Y. (Ed.). (2009, July 15). "一年一大步, 三年大变样" 石家庄迎来大发展 ["One year one big step forward, three years total change": Shijiazhuang ushers in major development]. *CRI Online*. Retrieved from http://gb.cri.cn/27824/2009/07/15/3785s2563458.htm

REFERENCES

Adams, M. (2006). Hybridizing the habitus: Towards an understanding of contemporary identity? *Sociology, 40*(3), 511–528. Retrieved from http://soc.sagepub.com/cgi/content/abstract/40/3/511

Adamson, B. (1995). The 'four modernizations' programme in China and English language teacher education: A case study. *Compare: A Journal of Comparative Education, 25*(3), 197–210.

Allaire, J. (2007). *China and bicycle: The end of the story?* Retrieved from http://webu2.upmf-grenoble.fr/iepe/textes/JA_poster-Velocity-juin2007.pdf

A Long March. (1967). A long march to Peking. *China Reconstructs, 16*(2), 11–14.

Althusser, L. (1970). *Ideology and ideological state apparatuses*. Retrieved from http://www.marxists.org/reference/archive/althusser/1970/ideology.htm

Anagnost, A. A. (1997). *National past-times: Narrative, representation, and power in modern China*. Durham, NC: Duke University Press.

Anagnost, A. A. (2004). The corporeal politics of suzhi. *Public Culture, 16*(2), 189–208.

Andreas, J. (2002). Battling over political and cultural power during the Chinese cultural revolution. *Theory and Society, 31*, 463–519. Retrieved from http://link.springer.com/article/10.1023%2FA%3A1020949030112?LI=true

Andreas, J. (2004). Leveling the little pagoda: The impact of college examinations, and their elimination, on rural education in China. *Comparative Education Review, 48*(1), 1–47. Retrieved from http://www.jstor.org/discover/10.1086/379840

Andreas, J. (2009). *Rise of the red engineers: The cultural revolution and the origins of China's new class*. Stanford, CA: Stanford University Press.

Appleton, S., & Song, L. (2008). The myth of the "new urban poverty"? Trends in urban poverty in China, 1988–2002. In J. R. Logan (Ed.), *Urban China in transition* (pp. 48–65). Oxford: Blackwell Publishing.

Archer, M. S. (1985). The myth of cultural integration. *British Journal of Sociology, 36*(3), 333–353. Retrieved from http://www.jstor.org/stable/590456

Archer, M. S. (1993). Bourdieu's theory of cultural reproduction: French or universal? *French Cultural Studies, 4*(12), 225–240. Retrieved from http://frc.sagepub.com

Archer, M. S. (1995). *Realist social theory: The morphogenetic approach*. New York, NY: Cambridge University Press.

Archer, M. S. (1996). *Culture and agency: The place of culture in social theory* (Rev. ed.). New York, NY: Cambridge University Press.

Archer, M. S. (2000). *Being human: The problem of agency*. New York, NY: Cambridge University Press.

Archer, M. S. (2003). *Structure, agency, and the internal conversation*. New York, NY: Cambridge University Press.

Archer, M. S. (2007). *Making our way through the world: Human reflexivity and social mobility*. New York, NY: Cambridge University Press.

Archer, M., Sharp, R., Stones, R., & Woodiwiss, T. (1998). Critical realism and research methodology. *Journal of Critical Realism, 2*(1), 12–16.

Arrighi, G. (2007). *Adam Smith in Beijing: Lineages of the twenty-first century*. London: Verso Books.

Bakken, B. (1988). Backwards reform in Chinese education. *The Australian Journal of Chinese Affairs, 19*(20), 127–163. Retrieved from http://www.jstor.org/stable/2158543

Barboza, D. (2008, November 9). China unveils sweeping plan for economy. *The New York Times*. Retrieved from http://www.nytimes.com/2008/11/10/world/asia/10china.html

Barendsen, R. D. (1975). *The educational revolution in China*. Washington, DC: U.S. Office of Education, Institute of International Studies.

Beck, U., Giddens, A., & Lash, S. (1994). *Reflexive modernity: Politics, tradition, and aesthetics in the modern social order*. Stanford, CA: Stanford University Press.

REFERENCES

Bellamy, L. A. (1994). Capital, habitus, field, and practice: An introduction to the work of Pierre Bourdieu. In L. Erwin & D. MacLennan (Eds.), *Sociology of education in Canada* (pp. 120–136). Toronto: Copp Clark Longman.

Bergesen, A. (1982). The emerging science of the world-system. *International Social Science Journal, 34*, 23–36.

Bhaskar, R. (1998). *The possibility of naturalism: A philosophical critique of the contemporary human sciences.* London: Routledge.

Bian, Y. (2002). Chinese social stratification and social mobility. *Annual Review of Sociology, 28*(1), 91–116. Retrieved from http://www.annualreviews.org/doi/abs/10.1146/annurev.soc.28.110601.140823?journalCode=soc

Bian, Y., & Gerber, T. P. (2008). Class structure and class inequality in urban China and Russia: Effects of institutional change or economic performance? In J. R. Logan (Ed.), *Urban China in transition* (pp. 66–88). Oxford: Blackwell Publishing.

Blumer, H. (1954). What is wrong with social theory? *American Sociological Review, 19*(1), 3–10. Retrieved from http://www.jstor.org/stable/2088165

Bogdan, R. C., & Biklen, S. K. (2007). *Qualitative research for education: An introduction to theories and methods* (5th ed.). New York, NY: Pearson Education Group.

Boltanski, L., & Chiapello, E. (2007). *The new spirit of capitalism* [Le nouvel esprit du capitalisme] (G. Elliot, Trans.). New York, NY: Verso Books.

Boltanski, L., & Thévenot, L. (2006). *On justification: Economies of worth* [De la justification] (C. Porter, Trans.). Princeton, NJ: Princeton University Press.

Boulding, E. (1983). Familia faber: The family as maker of the future. *Journal of Marriage and the Family, 45*(2), 257–166. Retrieved from http://www.jstor.org/stable/351505

Bourdieu, P. (1977). *Outline of a theory of practice.* New York, NY: Cambridge University Press.

Bourdieu, P. (1986). The forms of capital. In J. E. Richardson (Ed.), *Handbook of theory for the sociology of education* (pp. 241–258). Westport, CT: Greenword Press.

Bourdieu, P. (1990). *The logic of practice.* Stanford, CA: Stanford University Press.

Bourdieu, P. (1991). The peculiar history of scientific reason. *Sociological Forum, 6*(1), 3–26. Retrieved from http://link.springer.com/article/10.1007%2FBF01112725?LI=true

Bourdieu, P. (1998). *Practical reason: On the theory of action.* Stanford, CA: Stanford University Press.

Bourdieu, P. (2003). Participant objectivation. *Journal of the Royal Anthropological Institute, 9*, 281–294.

Bourdieu, P. (2004a). *Science of science and reflexivity.* Chicago, IL: University of Chicago Press.

Bourdieu, P. (2004b). The peasant and his body. *Ethnography, 5*(4), 579–599. Retrieved from http://eth.sagepub.com/content/5/4/579.short

Bourdieu, P. (2007). *Sketch for a self-analysis.* Cambridge: Polity Press.

Bourdieu, P., & Passeron, J. C. (1990). *Reproduction in education, society and culture.* London: Sage Publications.

Bourdieu, P., & Wacquant, L. J. D. (1992). *An invitation to reflexive sociology.* Chicago, IL: University of Chicago Press.

Bourdieu, P., & Wacquant, L. J. D. (2001). Neoliberal newspeak: Notes on the new planetary vulgate. *Radical Philosophy, 105*, 2–5. Retrieved from http://www.radicalphilosophy.com/commentary/newliberalspeak

Bowles, S., & Gintis, H. (1976). *Schooling in capitalist America: Educational reform and the contradictions of economic life.* New York, NY: Basic Books.

Bray, M., & Borevskaya, N. (2001). Financing education in transitional societies: Lessons from Russia and China. *Comparative Education, 37*(3), 345–365.

Broadman, H. G. (2001). The business(es) of the Chinese state. *The World Economy, 24*, 849–875.

Burns, G. E. (2001). *Toward a redefinition of formal and informal learning: Education and the Aboriginal people* (WALL Working Paper No. 28). Retrieved from https://tspace.library.utoronto.ca/bitstream/1807/2742/2/28towardanewdef.pdf

Carles, P. (Director). (2001). *La sociologie est un sport du combat* [Web]. Retrieved from http://www.youtube.com/watch?v=Csbu08SqAuc&list=PL9D719A804757CA17

Castells, M. (1997). *The power of identity.* Malden, MA: Blackwell Publishing.

REFERENCES

CERNET. (2001). *Zhongguo jiaoyu bainian dashi* [Key moments in 20th century Chinese education]. Retrieved February 14, 2008, from http://www.edu.cn/20010903/3000035.shtml

CERNET. (2005). *Number of students enrollment by level and type of school, 1978–2002*. Retrieved April 17, 2008, from http://www.edu.cn/education_1384/20060323/t20060323_115821.shtml

Chan, D., & Mok, K. H. (2001). Education reforms and coping strategies under the tidal wave of marketisation: A comparative study of Hong Kong and the mainland. *Comparative Education, 37*(1), 21–41. Retrieved from http://www.tandfonline.com/doi/abs/10.1080/03050060020020417

Chang, L. T. (2008). Gilded age, gilded cage: China's sudden prosperity brings undreamed-of freedoms and new anxieties. *National Geographic, 213*(5), 78–97. Retrieved from http://ngm.nationalgeographic.com/print/2008/05/china/middle-class/leslie-chang-text

Chang, P. (1967). Wipe out the poisonous influence of the book on self-cultivation. *China Reconstructs, 16*(5), 9.

Channel 4 News. (2013, February 28). *Apocalypse now in China's most polluted city*. Retrieved March 13, 2013, from http://news.linktv.org/videos/airpocalypse-now-in-chinas-most-polluted-city

Chen, Y. (1967). How we won the bumper harvest. *China Reconstructs, 16*(3), 20–21.

Chen, Z. L. (2000). *qie shi jianqing xuesheng guozhong fudan quan mian tuijin suzhi jiaoyu* [Emphasize lightening student workload and comprehensively promote quality education]. Retrieved from http://www.edu.cn/20010827/208908.shtml

Cheng, K. M. (1990). Financing education in mainland China: What are the real problems? In B. Lin & L. Fan (Eds.), *Education in mainland China: Review and evaluation* (pp. 218–239). Taipei: Institute of International Relations.

Cheng, Y. (1952). Thirteen years in Chungking. *China Reconstructs, 1*(3), 45–49.

Cheng, Y., & Manning, P. (2003). Revolution in education: China and Cuba in global context, 1957–1976. *Journal of World History, 14*(3), 359–391. Retrieved from http://muse.jhu.edu/journals/jwh/summary/v014/14.3cheng.html

China Daily. (2004, January 7). *China high school students low in imagination?* Retrieved February 16, 2008, from http://www.china.org.cn/english/culture/84131.htm

China Daily. (2007, March 23). *Debate over education reforms*. Retrieved February 12, 2008, from http://www.china.org.cn/english/education/204093.htm

china.org.cn. (2004). *Mothers as family educators*. Retrieved from http://www.china.org.cn/english/2004/Jun/97510.htm

China Reconstructs Correspondents. (1975). Higher education in Shanghai 'walks on two legs.' *China Reconstructs, 24*(4), 42–45.

chineseposters.net. (2013). *New socialist things*. Retrieved from http://chineseposters.net/themes/new-socialist-things.php

Ching, C. (1967). Speech by comrade Chiang Ching. *China Reconstructs, 16*(3), 5–6.

Chua, A. (2011). *Battle hymn of the tiger mother* [Kindle DX version]. Retrieved from http://www.Amazon.com

Chua-Rubenfeld, S. (2011, January 17). Why I love my strict Chinese mom. *New York Post*. Retrieved from http://www.nypost.com/p/entertainment/why_love_my_strict_chinese_mom_uUvfmLcA5eteY0u2KXt7hM

Chung, T. (1975). Sports in new China. *China Reconstructs, 14*(12), 2–10.

Cleverley, J. (1991). *The schooling of China: Tradition and modernity in Chinese education*. Sydney: Allen & Unwin.

Cochran, A. (2011, January 19). Amy Chua's "tiger daughter" responds to critics. *CBS News*. Retrieved from http://www.cbsnews.com/8301-504744_162-20028893-10391703.html

Cohen, S. (1972). *Folk devils and moral panics: The creation of the mods and rockers*. London: MacGibbon & Kee Ltd.

Coleman, J. S. (1988). Social capital in the creation of human capital. *The American Journal of Sociology, 94*, S95–S120.

Coleman, J. S., & Hoffer, T. (2010). Schools, families, and communities. In R. Arum, I. R. Beatty, & C. Ford (Eds.), *The structure of schooling: Readings in the sociology of education* (pp. 50–58). Thousand Oaks, CA: Pine Forge Press.

REFERENCES

CPP. (1949). *The common program of the Chinese people's political consultative conference*. Retrieved December 5, 2012, from http://www.e-chaupak.net/database/chicon/1949/1949e.pdf

CPP. (1966, August 8). Decision of the central committee of the Chinese communist party concerning the great proletarian cultural revolution. *Peking Review, 9*(33), 6–11. Retrieved January 21, 2013, from http://www.marxists.org/subject/china/peking-review/1966/PR1966-33g.htm

Crotty, M. (1998). *The foundations of social research: Meaning and perspective in the research*. London: Sage Publications.

CWI. (1952a). How workers move industry forward. *China Reconstructs, 1*(1), 24–25.

CWI. (1952b). A village teacher fights illiteracy. *China Reconstructs, 1*(2), 12–13.

CWI. (1952c). Kao Yu-Pao, soldier-writer. *China Reconstructs, 1*(3), 40–41.

CWI. (1952d). Sports and athletics for all. *China Reconstructs, 1*(5), 40–42.

CWI. (1952e). Weapon against illiteracy. *China Reconstructs, 1*(5), 49–50.

CWI. (1952f). Workers get new homes. *China Reconstructs, 1*(6), 16–17.

CWI. (1955). A school that leads the way. *China Reconstructs, 4*(6), 13–15.

CWI. (1975). Cover. *China Reconstructs, 24*(2).

CWI. (2008, February). China plans to send 12,000 state-funded students abroad in 2008. *China Today, 57*(2), 8–8.

CWI. (2011, September). Chinese education influences the world. *China Today, 60*(9), 4.

Davies, G. (2007). *Worrying about China: The language of Chinese critical inquiry*. Cambridge, MA: Harvard University Press.

Davis, D. S. (2003). From welfare benefit to capitalized asset: The re-commodification of residential space in urban China. In R. Forrest & J. Lee (Eds.), *Housing and social change: East-west perspectives* (pp. 183–198). London: Routledge.

Debord, G. (1994 [1967]). *The Society of the spectacle*. Cambridge, MA: Zone Books.

De Certeau, M. (1984). *The practice of everyday life*. Berkeley, CA: University of California Press.

Deng, X. P. (1987 [1978]). Speech at the national conference on education. In S. M. Hu & E. Seifman (Eds.), *Education and socialist modernization: A documentary history of education in the people's republic of China, 1977–1986* (pp. 74–78). New York, NY: AMS Press.

Denzin, N. K. (1978). *The research act: A theoretical introduction to sociological methods*. New York, NY: McGraw-Hill.

Denzin, N. K., & Lincoln, Y. S. (Eds.). (2005). *The Sage handbook of qualitative research* (3rd ed.). Thousand Oaks, CA: Sage Publications.

Durkheim, E. (1984 [1893]). *The division of labour in society*. London: Macmillan.

Dynon, N. (2008). "Four civilizations" and the evolution of post-Mao Chinese socialist ideology. *The China Journal, 60*, 83–109. Retrieved from http://www.jstor.org/stable/20647989

Eagleton, T., & Bourdieu, P. (1992). Doxa and common life. *New Left Review, 191*, 111–121. Retrieved from http://dajialai.org/ziliao1/%CE%F7%B7%BD%D0%C2%D7%F3%C5%C9/New%20Left%20Review/EAGLETON/8.pdf

Edgar, D. (2003). Globalization and western bias in family sociology. In J. Scott, J. Treas, & M. Richards (Eds.), *The Blackwell companion to the sociology of families* (pp. 3–16). Oxford: Blackwell Publishing. Retrieved from http://www.blackwellreference.com.login.ezproxy.library.ualberta.ca/subscriber/tocnode.html?id=g9780631221586_chunk_g97806312215863

Elder-Vass, D. (2007). Reconciling Archer and Bourdieu in an emergentist theory of action. *Sociological Theory, 25*(4), 325–346.

Engels, F. (1884). *The origin of the family, private property and the state*. Retrieved from http://www.marxists.org/archive/marx/works/1884/origin-family/

Fan, G. (2006). Critical review of theoretical research on education adjustments to the market economy. *Chinese Education and Society, 39*(5), 17–37.

Fan, L. (1990). Secondary education in mainland China. In B. Lin & L. Fan (Eds.), *Education in mainland China: Review and evaluation* (pp. 111–129). Taipei: Institute of International Relations.

Fei, X. (1992 [1947]). *From the soil: The foundations of Chinese society*. Berkeley, CA: University of California Press.

Flick, U. (2009). *An introduction to qualitative research*. London: Sage Publications.

REFERENCES

Flick, U., von Kardoff, E., & Steinke, I. (Eds.). (2004). *A companion to qualitative research*. London: Sage Publications.
Fong, V. L. (2007). Morality, cosmopolitanism, or academic attainment? Discourses on "quality" and urban Chinese-only-children's claims to ideal personhood. *City & Society, 19*(1), 86–113.
Foucault, M. (1996). What is critique? In J. Schmidt (Ed.), *What is enlightenment? Eighteenth-century answers and twentieth-century questions* (pp. 382–398). Berkeley, CA: University of California Press.
Fraenkel, J. R., & Wallen, N. E. (1996). *How to design and evaluate research in education* (3rd ed.). New York, NY: McGraw-Hill.
Frank, A. (1998). *Reorient: Global economic in the Asian age*. Berkeley, CA: University of California Press.
Geertz, C. (1973). Thick description: Toward an interpretive theory of culture. In C. Geertz (Ed.), *The interpretation of cultures: Selected essays* (pp. 3–30). New York, NY: Basic Books.
Giddens, A. (1986). *The constitution of society: Outline of the theory of structuration*. Cambridge: Polity Press.
Giroux, H. A. (1983). Theories of reproduction and resistance in the new sociology of education: A critical analysis. *Harvard Educational Review, 53*(3), 257–293.
Glaser, B. G., & Strauss, A. L. (1967). *The discovery of grounded theory: Strategies for qualitative research*. New York, NY: Aldine de Gruyter.
Grossman, S. (2010). The world as classroom. *China Today, 59*(1), 70–72.
Guba, E. G. (1981). Criteria for assessing the trustworthiness of naturalistic inquiries. *ECTJ, 29*(2), 75–91. Retrieved from http://link.springer.com/article/10.1007%2FBF02766777?LI=true
Guo, L. (2012). The impact of new national curricular reform on teachers. *Canadian and International Education, 41*(2), 87–105. Retrieved from http://login.ezproxy.library.ualberta.ca/login?url=http://search.proquest.com/docview/1355923414?accountid=14474
Guo, S. (2005). Exploring current issues in teacher education in China. *Alberta Journal of Educational Research, 51*(1), 69–84. Retrieved from http://ajer.synergiesprairies.ca/ajer/index.php/ajer/article/view/499/488
Guo, S. (2012). Globalization, market economy and social inequality in China: Exploring the experience of migrant teachers. *Canadian and International Education, 41*(2), 8–27. Retrieved from http://login.ezproxy.library.ualberta.ca/login?url=http://search.proquest.com/docview/1355923417?accountid=14474
Guo, S., Guo, Y., Beckett, G., Li, Q., & Guo, L. (2013). Changes in Chinese education under globalisation and market economy: Emerging issues and debates. *Compare: A Journal of Comparative and International Education, 43*(2), 244–264. Retrieved from http://dx.doi.org/10.1080/03057925.2012.721524
Guo, Y. (2012). Teaching English for economic competitiveness: Emerging issues and challenges in English education in China. *Canadian and International Education, 41*(2), 28–50. Retrieved from http://login.ezproxy.library.ualberta.ca/login?url=http://search.proquest.com/docview/1355923419?accountid=14474
Gymboree. (2013). *Curriculum*. Retrieved from http://www.gymboree.com.cn/kecheng/
Hammersley, M., & Atkinson, P. (2007). *Ethnography: Principles in practice*. New York, NY: Taylor & Francis.
Han, T. (1975). Leadership made up of the old, middle-aged and young. *China Reconstructs, 24*(9), 2–5.
Hanser, A. (2005). Made in the P.R.C.: China's consumer revolution (People's Republic of China) (Author Abstract). *Current History, 683*, 272–277. Retrieved from http://login.ezproxy.library.ualberta.ca/login?url=http://search.ebscohost.com/login.aspx?direct=true&db=edsgao&AN=edsgcl.135815486&site=eds-live&scope=site
Hanser, A. (2007). Is the customer always right? Class, service and the production of distinction in Chinese department stores. *Theory and Society, 36*(5), 415–435. Retrieved from http://login.ezproxy.library.ualberta.ca/login?url=http://search.ebscohost.com/login.aspx?direct=true&db=edsjab&AN=edsjab.10.2307.40213591&site=eds-live&scope=site
Harvey, D. (1988). *Social justice and the city*. Oxford: Blackwell Publishing.
Harvey, D. (1989). *The condition of post-modernity: An enquiry into the origins of social change*. Cambridge, MA: Blackwell Publishing.

REFERENCES

Harvey, D. (2000). *Spaces of hope*. Berkeley, CA: University of California Press.
Harvey, D. (2001). *Spaces of capital: Toward a critical geography*. New York, NY: Routledge.
Harvey, D. (2003). *Paris, capital of modernity*. London: Routledge.
Harvey, D. (2005). *The new imperialism*. Oxford: Oxford University Press.
Harvey, D., Arrighi, G., & Andreas, J. (2008). *Symposium on Giovanni Arrighi's Adam Smith in Beijing*. Baltimore, MD: Red Emma's. Retrieved from http://youtu.be/nLdNKf0vAhg
Hebei People's Government. (2007). *hebei sheng renmin zhengfu guanyu jiakuai tuijin chengzhenhua jin cheng de ruogan yijian* [Hebei people's government opinion on the acceleration of urbanization] (Ji Zheng [2007] No. 138). Retrieved from http://www.hebjs.gov.cn/zfxx/flfg/xgwj/200712/t20071223_88759.htm
Heckathorn, D. D. (1997). Respondent-driven sampling: A new approach to the study of hidden populations. *Social Problems, 44*(2), 174–199. Retrieved from http://www.jstor.org/stable/3096941
Henze, J. (1987). Educational modernization as a search for higher efficiency. In R. Hayhoe & M. Bastid (Eds.), *China's education and the industrialized world* (pp. 252–270). New York, NY: M. E. Sharpe.
Henze, J. (1992). The formal education system and modernization: An analysis of developments since 1978. In R. Hayhoe (Ed.), *Education and modernization: The Chinese experience* (pp. 103–139). Oxford: Pergamon Press.
Ho, D. Y. (1976). On the concept of face. *American Journal of Sociology, 81*(4), 867–884. Retrieved from http://www.jstor.org/stable/2777600
Hofstede, G., & Bond, M. S. (1988). The Confucius connection: From cultural roots to economic growth. *Organizational Dynamics, 16*(4), 5–21. Retrieved from http://www2.seminolestate.edu/falbritton/Summer%202009/FHI/Articles/Hofstede.confucious%20connection%20120505%20science%20direct.pdf
Hou, R. (2008). The booming baby business. *China Today, 57*(6), 30–31.
Hou, R. (2010). The in-between world: New-wave migrants. *China Today, 59*(10), 11–14.
Hsiao, P. (1975). The children's own newspaper. *China Reconstructs, 24*(11), 9–11.
Hsin, H. W. (1975). A new type of college. *China Reconstructs, 24*(5), 6–10.
Hsu, C. L. (2008). The city in the school and the school in the city: Ideology, imagery, and institutions in maoist and market socialist China. *Visual Studies, 23*(1), 20–33. Retrieved from http://www.tandfonline.com/doi/abs/10.1080/14725860801908510
Hu, H. C. (1944). The Chinese concepts of "face." *American Anthropologist, 46*, 45–64. Retrieved from http://onlinelibrary.wiley.com/doi/10.1525/aa.1944.46.1.02a00040/abstract
Hu, S. M., & Seifman, E. (Eds.). (1987). *Education and socialist modernization: A documentary history of education in the people's republic of China, 1977–1986*. New York, NY: AMS Press.
Huang, F. (2004). Curriculum reform in contemporary China: Six goals and seven strategies. *Journal of Curriculum Studies, 36*(1), 101–115. Retrieved from http://dx.doi.org/10.1080/0022027030200004742000174126
Huang, Y. (2008). *Capitalism with Chinese characteristics: Entrepreneurship and the state*. Cambridge: Cambridge University Press.
Huang, Y., & Low, S. M. (2008). Is gating always exclusionary? A comparative analysis of gated communities in American and Chinese cities. In J. R. Logan (Ed.), *Urban China in transition* (pp. 182–202). Oxford: Blackwell Publishing.
Hung, C. (2011). *Mao's new world: Political culture in the early people's republic*. Ithaca, NY: Cornell University Press.
Hwang, K. K. (1987). Face and favor: The Chinese power game. *American Journal of Sociology, 92*(4), 944–974. Retrieved from http://www.jstor.org/stable/2780044
Hwang, K. K. (2012). Face and morality in Confucian society. In K. K. Hwang (Ed.), *Foundations of Chinese psychology: Confucian social relations* (pp. 265–295). London: Springer.
Ianzelo, T., & Richardson, B. (1980). *North China factory* [Web]. Retrieved from http://www.nfb.ca/film/north_china_factory
ido.3mt.com.cn. (2009). *yuji san nian da bianyang hou, san huan zhi nei fangjia nan da yu 4000 yuan mei ping* [Forecast for post-san nian da bianyang, real estate prices inside the third ring road under 4,000 yuan per square meter will be scarce]. Retrieved April 25, 2012, from http://ido.3mt.com.cn/Article/200901/show1251292c35p1.html

REFERENCES

Jiang, P., & Feng, J. (2009). Adhering to the values of an intellectual. *China Today, 58*(10), 24–27.
Johnson, I. (2015, July 19). As Beijing becomes a supercity, the rapid growth brings pains. *The New York Times*. Retrieved from https://www.nytimes.com/2015/07/20/world/asia/in-china-a-supercity-rises-around-beijing.html?ref=asia&_r=3
Jones, A. (2002). Politics and history curriculum reform in Post-Mao China. *International Journal of Educational Research, 37*(6), 545–566. Retrieved from http://dx.doi.org/10.1016/S0883-0355(03)00050-8
Kao, H.-C. (1966, March). Man with fortitude. *China Reconstructs, 15*(3), 26–28.
Kent, A. (1981). Red and expert: The revolution in education at Shanghai teachers' university, 1975–1976. *The China Quarterly, 86*, 304–321.
Khan, A. R., Griffin, K., Riskin, C., & Zhao, R. (1992). Household income and its distribution in China. *The China Quarterly, 132*, 1029–1061. Retrieved from http://dx.doi.org/10.1017/S0305741000045525
Khan, A. R., & Riskin, C. (1998). Income and inequality in China: Composition, distribution and growth of household income, 1988 to 1995. *The China Quarterly, 154*, 221–253. Retrieved from http://dx.doi.org/10.1017/S0305741000002022
King, A. Y., & Myers, J. T. (1977). *Shame as an incomplete conception of Chinese culture: A study of face*. Hong Kong: The Chinese University of Hong Kong, Social Research Center. Retrieved from http://hkhiso.itsc.cuhk.edu.hk/history/system/files/Shame%20as%20an%20incomplete%20conception%20of%20Chinese%20culture.pdf
Kipnis, A. (2006). Suzhi: A keyword approach. *The China Quarterly, 186*, 295–313. Retrieved from http://journals.cambridge.org/action/displayAbstract?fromPage=online&aid=449702
Kipnis, A. (2011). *Governing educational desire: Culture, politics, and schooling in China*. Chicago, IL: University of Chicago Press.
Kipnis, A. (2012). Private lessons and national formations: National hierarchy and the individual psyche in the marketing of Chinese educational programs. In A. B. Kipnis (Ed.), *Chinese modernity and the individual psyche* (pp. 187–202). New York, NY: Palgrave McMillan.
Kleinman, A., Yan, Y., Jun, J., Sing, L., Zhang, E., Pan, T., Wu, F., & Guo, J. (2011). *Deep China: The moral life of the person: What anthropology and psychiatry tell us about China today*. Berkeley, CA: University of California Press.
Kong, S. (2005). *Consuming literature: Best sellers and the commercialization of literary production in contemporary China*. Stanford, CA: Stanford University Press.
Kuan, T. (2008). *Adjusting the bonds of love: Parenting, expertise and social change in a Chinese city* (Ph.D. thesis). University of Southern California, Los Angeles, CA.
Kuan, T. (2011). "The heart says one thing but the hand does another": A story about emotion-work, ambivalence and popular advice for parents. *The China Journal, 65*, 77–100. Retrieved from http://www.jstor.org/stable/10.2307/25790558
Kuhn, T. S. (1970). *The structure of scientific revolutions* (2nd ed.). Chicago, IL: University of Chicago Press.
Lammana, M. A. (2002). *Emile Durkheim on the family*. Thousand Oaks, CA: Sage Publications.
Law, W. W. (2007). Legislation and educational change: The struggle for social justice and quality in China's compulsory schooling. *Education and the Law, 19*(3–4), 177–199. Retrieved from http://www.tandfonline.com/doi/abs/10.1080/09539960701751493
Levenson, E. V. (2002, July 1–2). Harvard Girl. *Harvard Magazine*. Retrieved from http://harvardmagazine.com/2002/07/harvard-girl.html
Li, J. (1967). We bend nature to our will. *China Reconstructs, 16*(1), 36–39.
Li, Q. (2012). Disparities between urban and rural teachers under China's market economy: A case study of Hunan province. *Canadian and International Education, 41*(2), 71–86. Retrieved from http://login.ezproxy.library.ualberta.ca/login?url=http://search.proquest.com/docview/1355923406?accountid=14474
Li, S., & Zhao, R. (2011). Market reform and the widening of the income gap. *Social Sciences in China, 32*(2), 140–158.
Liang, G. Y. (2007). *pinglun: weihe zhongguo yi "jianfu" shangdi bian fa xiao?* [Comment: Why is that when China tries to "lighten students' heavy burden" God laughs?]. Retrieved February 14, 2008, from http://www.edu.cn/te_bie_tui_jian_1073/20070914/t20070914_254809.shtml

REFERENCES

Liang, Z., Luong, H. V., & Chen, Y. P. (2008). Urbanization in China in the 1990s: Patterns and regional variations. In J. R. Logan (Ed.), *Urban China in transition* (pp. 205–225). Oxford: Blackwell Publishing.

Lin, Y. (2000). *My country and my people*. Beijing: Foreign Languages Teaching & Research Press.

Ling, J. (2011). Xi'An Jiaotong-liverpool university: Exploring a new educational model. *China Today, 60*(9), 25–27.

Liu, G. D. (1954). My husband is a 'model.' *China Reconstructs, 3*(5).

Liu, S. (1967). Heroic drilling team battles a sea of fire. *China Reconstructs, 16*(1), 26–31.

Lofland, J., Snow, D., Anderson, L., & Lofland, L. H. (2006). *Analyzing social settings: A guide to qualitative observation and analysis*. Belmont, CA: Wadsworth Thompson.

Löfstedt, J. I. (1980). *Chinese educational policy*. Atlantic Highlands, NJ: Humanities Press.

Lu, R. (2006a). Vying for the cream of China's academic crop. *China Today, 55*(10), 40–42.

Lu, R. (2006b). High scores – low ability. *China Today, 56*(4), 45–49.

Lu, R. (2009a). How to guide children: Family education consultancies take off. *China Today, 58*(2), 38–40.

Lu, R. (2009b). A top Chinese university reaches out to migrant workers. *China Today, 58*(5), 55–57.

Lu, R. (2010). Zhang Kailang: Putting the pop in popular science education. *China Today, 59*(8), 46–47.

MacFarquhar, R., & Schoenals, M. (2006). *Mao's last revolution*. Cambridge, MA: Belknap Press of Harvard University Press.

Madison, D. S. (2012). *Critical ethnography: Method, ethics, and performance*. Los Angeles, CA: Sage Publications.

Mahmood, S. (2004). *Politics of piety: The Islamic revival and the feminist subject*. Princeton, NJ: Princeton University Press.

Malcolm, J., Hodkinson, P., & Colley, H. (2003). The interrelationships between informal and formal learning. *Journal of Workplace Learning, 15*(7–8), 313–318. Retrieved from Retrieved from http://login.ezproxy.library.ualberta.ca/login?url=http://search.proquest.com/docview/198448063?accountid=14474

Malinowski, B. (1944). *A scientific theory of culture and other essays*. New York, NY: Routledge.

Mao, Z. D. (1957, March 12). Speech at the Chinese communist party's national conference on propaganda work. *The selected works of Mao Tse-Tung, Volume V*. Beijing: Foreign Languages Press. Retrieved from http://www.marxists.org/reference/archive/mao/selected-works/volume-5/mswv5_59.htm

Mao, Z. D. (1966, May 7). Notes on the report of further improving the army's agricultural work by the rear service department of the military commission. *The selected works of Mao Tse-Tung, Volume IX*. Beijing: Foreign Languages Press. Retrieved from http://www.marxists.org/reference/archive/mao/selected-works-volume-9/mswv9_57.htm

Mao, Z. D. (1967 [1942], May). Talks at the Yenan forum on literature and art. *The selected works of Mao Tse-Tung, Volume III*. Beijing: Foreign Languages Press. Retrieved from http://www.marxists.org/reference/archive/mao/selected-works/volume-3/mswv3_08.htm

Mao, Z. D. (1977 [1957], October 9). Be activists in promoting the revolution. *The selected works of Mao Zedong, Volume V*. Beijing: Foreign Languages Press. Retrieved from http://www.marxists.org/reference/archive/mao/selected-works/volume-5/mswv5_67.htm

Mao, Z. D. (1997 [1953], June 30). The youth league in its work must take the characteristics of youth into consideration. *The selected works of Mao Tse-Tung, Volume V*. Beijing: Foreign Languages Press. Retrieved from http://www.marxists.org/reference/archive/mao/selected-works/volume-5/mswv5_29.htm

Marcus, G. E., & Fischer, M. M. J. (1999). *Anthropology as cultural critique: An experimental moment in the human sciences* (2nd ed.). Chicago, IL: University of Chicago Press.

Marriage Law. (1975 [1950]). *The marriage law of the people's republic of China*. Peking: Foreign Languages Press. Retrieved December 5, 2012, from http://www.paulnoll.com/China/Mao/Marriage-01.html

Martin, H. (1982). *Cult & canon: The origins and development of state maoism*. Armonk, NY: M. E. Sharpe.

Marx, K. (1973 [1857]). *Outline of the critique of political economy*. London: Penguin. Retrieved from http://www.marxists.org/archive/marx/works/1857/grundrisse/index.htm

REFERENCES

Marx, K., & Engels, F. (1848). *The communist manifesto*. Retrieved from http://www.marxists.org/archive/marx/works/1848/communist-manifesto/index.htm

Mills, C. W. (1959). *The sociological imagination*. New York, NY: Oxford University Press.

Ministry of Education. (1980 [1955]). *Chinese educational policy*. Atlantic Highlands, NJ: Humanities Press.

Ministry of Education. (2010). *Outline of China's national plan for medium and long-term education reform and development, 2010–2020*. Beijing: Ministry of Education.

Morrow, R. A., & Brown, D. D. (1994). In deconstructing the conventional discourse of methodology: Quantitative versus qualitative methods. *Critical theory and methodology* (pp. 199–225). Thousand Oaks, CA: Sage Publications.

Murphy, R. (2004). Turning peasants into modern Chinese citizens: "Population quality" discourse, demographic transition and primary education. *China Quarterly, 177*, 1–20. Retrieved from http://journals.cambridge.org/action/displayAbstract?fromPage=online&aid=219841

Musgrove, F. (1966). *The family, education, and society*. London: Routledge & Keegan Paul Ltd.

OECD. (2013). *Skills beyond schools: Recognition of non-formal and informal learning*. Retrieved from http://www.oecd.org/education/skills-beyond-school/recognitionofnon-formalandinformallearning-home.htm

O'Mahony, T., & Bravery, B. (2011). From gaokao to knowhow. *China Today, 60*(9), 40–41.

Ong, A., & Zhang, L. (2008). Powers of the self, socialism from afar. In L. Zhang & A. Ong (Ed.), *Privatizing China: Socialism from afar* (pp. 1–22). Ithaca, NY: Cornell University Press.

O'Reilly, K. (2005). *Ethnographic methods*. New York, NY: Routledge.

Paine, L. (1990). The teacher as virtuoso: A Chinese model for teaching. *Teachers College Record, 92*(1), 50–81.

Paine, L. (1992). Teaching and modernization in contemporary China. In R. Hayhoe (Ed.), *Education and modernization: The Chinese experience* (pp. 183–209). New York, NY: Pergamon Press.

Pan, T. (2011). Place attachment, communal memory, and the moral underpinnings of gentrification in postreform Shanghai. In A. Kleinman, Y. Yan, J. Jun, L. Sing, E. Zhang, T. Pan, F. Wu, & J. Guo (Eds.), *Deep China: The moral life of the person: What anthropology and psychiatry tell us about China today* (pp. 152–176). Berkeley, CA: University of California Press.

Pan, Y. (1955). A school that leads the way. *China Reconstructs, 4*(6), 13–15.

Patton, M. Q. (1990). *Qualitative evaluation and research methods* (2nd ed.). Newbury Park, CA: Sage Publications.

Peng, D. (1997). Does Confucianism matter? The role of the oriental tradition in economic development in East Asia. In A. Ikeo (Ed.), *Economic development in twentieth century East Asia: The international context* (pp. 170–189). Florence, KY: Routledge.

People's Daily. (2000). Family education tends to be more mature and sensible. *People's Daily Online*. Retrieved from http://english.people.com.cn/english/200005/26/print20000526_41709.html

Pepper, S. (1978). Education and revolution: The "Chinese model" revised. *Asian Survey, 18*(9), 847–890. Retrieved from http://www.jstor.org/discover/10.2307/2643600?uid=3739392&uid=2129&uid=2134&uid=2&uid=70&uid=3737720&uid=4&sid=21101898675341

Pepper, S. (1996). *Radicalism and education reform in twentieth-century China*. New York, NY: Cambridge University Press.

Pien, H. (1967). The red guards: Shock force of the great proletarian cultural revolution. *China Reconstructs, 16*(2), 6–9.

Prosodic. (1998). *The Oxford dictionary of English grammar*. Oxford: Oxford University Press. Retrieved March 2, 2012, from http://www.oxfordreference.com.login.ezproxy.library.ualberta.ca/views/ENTRY.html?subview=Main&entry=t28.e1197

Putnam, R. D. (2000). *Bowling alone: The collapse and revival of American community*. New York, NY: Simon & Schuster.

Qin, H. (2008). School choice in China. *Frontiers of education in China, 3*(3), 331–345. Retrieved from http://link.springer.com/article/10.1007%2Fs11516-008-0022-6?LI=true

Red Guards. (1967). Red guards on a trolley bus. *China Reconstructs, 16*(1), 43.

Ren, X. (2013). *Urban China*. Cambridge: Polity Press.

REFERENCES

Reuters. (2008). *Factbox: China's property market cooling measures*. Retrieved from http://www.reuters.com/article/2008/01/20/us-property-china-factbox-idUSHKG5334920080120
Rosen, S. (1984). New directions in secondary education. In R. Hayhoe (Ed.), *Contemporary Chinese education* (pp. 65–92). Worcester: Billings & Sons.
Rosen, S. (2004). The victory of materialism: Aspirations to join China's urban moneyed classes and the commercialization of education. *The China Journal, 51*, 27–51. Retrieved from http://www.jstor.org/discover/10.2307/3182145?uid=3739392&uid=2129&uid=2134&uid=2&uid=70&uid=3737720&uid=4&sid=21101898675341
Sautman, B. (1991). Politicization, hyperpoliticization, and depoliticization of Chinese education. *Comparative Education Review, 35*(4), 669–689. Retrieved from http://www.jstor.org/discover/10.2307/1188111?uid=3739392&uid=2129&uid=2134&uid=2&uid=70&uid=3737720&uid=4&sid=21101898675341
Sayer, R. A. (1992). *Method in social science: A realist approach* (2nd ed.). New York, NY: Routledge.
Schugurensky, D. (2000). *The forms of informal learning: Towards a conceptualization of the field* (WALL Working Paper No. 19). Retrieved from https://tspace.library.utoronto.ca/bitstream/1807/2733/2/19formsofinformal.pdf
Schumacher, S., & McMillan, J. U. (1993). Literature review. *Research in education* (pp. 112–146). New York, NY: Harper Collins.
Schumpeter, J. A. (2003 [1943]). *Capitalism, socialism, and democracy*. London: George Allen & Unwin Publishers Ltd.
SFLEG. (2012a). *zai xuexiao pengren jiaoshi li de fuxiang* [Daydreaming in a culinary arts classroom]. Retrieved from http://www.sjzfls.com/show.aspx?id=2163
SFLEG. (2012b). *haizi guodu nifan shi fumu yazhi de jieguo* [A child's excessive rebellion is the fruit of parents' repression]. Retrieved from http://www.sjzfls.com/show.aspx?id=1808
SFLEG. (2012c). *jiayuan gong yu jian chengxiao* [Parent-school collaborative education bears fruit]. Retrieved from http://www.sjzfls.com/show.aspx?id=2150
SFLEG. (2012d). *jiangjiu piping yishu, zuo zhihui jiazhang* [Pay attention to the art of criticism, be a wise parent]. Retrieved from http://www.sjzfls.com/show.aspx?id=1676
SFLEG. (2012e). *wo de jiating jiaoyu xinde* [What I learned about family education]. Retrieved from http://www.sjzfls.com/show.aspx?id=1308
SFLEG. (2013a). *liucun jiyi shen chu de shequ shijian – chu yi (16) ban shehui shijian huodong xiao fendui zoufang huai dong shequ* [Preserving the memory of the depths of the social/community practice squad – The first day (16) class social practice squad visited East Huai neighbourhood]. Retrieved from http://www.sjzfls.com/show.aspx?id=2182
SFLEG. (2013b). *women rang tian geng lan shui geng qing – chu yi (11) ban "luse huanbao xiao fendui" zai hang dong* [We make the sky bluer and the water clearer – Grade 7 (class 11) "green squad" in action]. Retrieved from http://www.sjzfls.com/show.aspx?id=2181
SFLEG. (2013c). *ganxie shi en, women zhiyuan zhe zai hang dong* [Thanking our teachers, our volunteers in action]. Retrieved from http://www.sjzfls.com/show.aspx?id=2012
SFLEG. (2013d). *Introduction to SFLS*. Retrieved from http://www.sjzfls.com/en/about/show-Introduction%20to%20SFLS.html
Shen, A. P. (1994). Teacher education and national development in China. *Journal of Education, 176*(2), 57–71.
Shen, Y. (1952). New developments in culture and art. *People's China, 22*, 29–33. Retrieved January 1, 2013, from http://chineseposters.net/resources/shen-yen-ping-new-developments.php
Shijiazhuang Daily. (2009, April). 三年大变样拆迁改造规划图 [Three Years Big Change Demolition and Renovation Plan]. *Shijiazhuang Daily*. Retrieved from http://www.sjzdaily.com.cn/zhuanti/2009-04/14/content_1356081.htm
Smith, D. G. (2008). "The farthest west is but the farthest east": The long way of oriental/occidental engagement. In C. Eppert & H. Wang (Eds.), *Cross-cultural studies in curriculum: Eastern thought, educational insights* (pp. 1–34). New York, NY: Lawrence Erlbaum Associates.
Soong, Ching Ling. (1975 [1937]). Confucianism and modern China. *China Reconstructs, 24*(4), 2–4.

REFERENCES

Spradley, J. P. (1979). *The ethnographic interview*. New York, NY: Holt, Rinehart & Winston.
Spring, J. H. (2006). *Pedagogies of globalization: The rise of the educational security state*. New York, NY: Lawrence Erlbaum Associates.
Staff Reporter. (1954). In a Peking primary school. *China Reconstructs, 3*(4).
Staff Reporter. (1975). Factories run their own colleges. *China Reconstructs, 24*(11), 2–8.
Stake, R. (2005). Qualitative case studies. In N. K. Denzin & Y. S. Lincoln (Eds.), *The Sage handbook of qualitative research* (3rd ed., pp. 443–466). Thousand Oaks, CA: Sage Publications.
Sutherland, D., & Yao, S. (2011). Income inequality in China over 30 years of reforms. *Cambridge Journal of Regions, 4*, 91–105. Retrieved from http://cjres.oxfordjournals.org/content/4/1/91
Taylor, S. (2005). Researching the social: An introduction to ethnographic research. In S. Taylor (Ed.), *Ethnographic research: A reader* (pp. 1–12). London: Sage Publications.
Thompson, J. B. (1990). *Ideology and modern culture: Critical social theory in the era of mass communication*. Cambridge: Polity Press.
Wang, H. (1998). Contemporary Chinese thought and the question of modernity. *Social Text, 55*, 9–44. Retrieved from http://www.upf.edu/materials/huma/central/historia/lite/bibli/arti/art_50.pdf
Wang, J., & Paine, L. W. (2003). Learning to teach with mandated curriculum and public examination of teaching as contexts. *Teaching and Teacher Education, 19*, 75–94. Retrieved from http://dx.doi.org/10.1016/S0742-051X(02)00087-2
Wang, S., Davis, D., & Bian, Y. (2006). The uneven distribution of cultural capital: Book reading in urban China. *Modern China, 32*, 315–348. Retrieved from http://mcx.sagepub.com/cgi/content/abstract/32/3/315
Wang, Y. P. (2003). Urban reform and low-income communities in Chinese cities. In R. Forrest & J. Lee (Eds.), *Housing and social change: East-west perspectives* (pp. 240–263). London: Routledge.
Warner, M. (1996). Chinese enterprise reform, human resources and the 1994 labour law. *The International Journal of Human Resource Management, 7*(4), 779–796.
Weber, M. (1951). *The religion of China: Confucianism and Taoism*. New York, NY: Free Press.
Weber, M. (1999 [1922]). Class, status, party. In C. Lemert (Ed.), *Social theory: The multicultural and classic readings* (pp. 115–125). Boulder, CO: Westview Press.
Wee, S. (2012, October 23). China hints at reform by dropping Mao wording. *The Globe and Mail*. Retrieved October 25, 2012, from http://www.theglobeandmail.com/news/world/china-hints-at-reform-by-dropping-mao-wording-from-recent-statements/article4630711/
Werquin, P. (2007). *Terms, concepts and models for analysing the value of recognition programmes*. Retrieved from http://www.oecd.org/education/skills-beyond-school/41834711.pdf
White, M. J., Wu, F., & Chen, Y. P. (2008). Urbanization, institutional change, and sociospatial inequality in China, 1990–2001. In J. R. Logan (Ed.), *Urban China in transition* (pp. 115–139). Oxford: Blackwell Publishing.
Whitehouse, D. (2009). Crisis and class struggle in China. *International Socialist Review*, p. 67. Retrieved from http://isreview.org/issue/67/crisis-and-class-struggle-china
Whyte, M. K. (1973). The family. *Proceedings of the Academy of Political Science, 31*(1), 175–192. Retrieved from http://www.jstor.org/stable/1173493
Whyte, M. K. (1992). Introduction: Rural economic reforms and Chinese family patterns. *The China Quarterly, 130*(2), 317–322. Retrieved from http://www.jstor.org/stable/654403?origin=JSTOR-pdf
Whyte, M. K. (1996). The Chinese family and economic development: Obstacle or engine? *Economic Development and Cultural Change, 45*(1), 1–30. Retrieved from http://www.jstor.org/stable/1154365
Williams, R. (1983). *Keywords: A vocabulary of culture and society*. Glasgow: Flamingo.
Williams, R. (1998). The analysis of culture. In J. Storey (Ed.), *Cultural theory and popular culture: A reader* (pp. 48–56). Athens, GA: The University of Georgia Press.
Williams, R. (2002 [1958]). Culture is ordinary. In B. Highmore (Ed.), *The everyday life reader* (pp. 91–100). London: Routledge.
Willis, P. (1977). *Learning to labour: How working class kids get working class jobs*. New York, NY: Columbia University Press.
Willis, P., & Trondman, M. (2002). Manifesto for ethnography. *Cultural Studies Critical Methodologies, 2*(3), 394–402. Retrieved from https://www.dur.ac.uk/resources/anthropology/willis.pdf

REFERENCES

Wong, S. (1985). The Chinese family firm: A model. *The British Journal of Sociology, 36*(1), 58–72. Retrieved from http://www.jstor.org/stable/590402

Woodiwiss, A. (2005). *Scoping the social: An introduction to the practice of social theory.* New York, NY: Open University Press.

Woronov, T. (2008). Raising quality, fostering "creativity": Ideologies and practices of education reform in Beijing. *Anthropology & Education Quarterly, 39*(4), 401–422. Retrieved from http://onlinelibrary.wiley.com/doi/10.1111/j.1548-1492.2008.00030.x/abstract

Wu, Q. L., Zhu, H. B., Chen, F., & Liu, G. L. (n.d.). Parents as partners: A case study from China, Chuzho city. *Scottish School Board Association.* Retrieved from http://www.schoolboard-scotland.com/conference/China.htm

Wu, W., & Rosenbaum, E. (2008). Migration and housing: Comparing China with the United States. In J. R. Logan (Ed.), *Urban China in transition* (pp. 250–268). Oxford: Blackwell Publishing.

Xinhua. (1987). Requirements for 1987 college enrollment. In S. M. Hu & E. Seifman (Eds.), *Education and socialist modernization: A documentary history of education in the people's republic of China, 1977–1986* (pp. 78–79). New York, NY: AMS Press.

Xinhua. (2001, June 25). The "three represents" theory. *Xinhua News Agency.* Retrieved from http://news.xinhuanet.com/english/20010625/422678.htm

Xinhua. (2004a). *Children need holistic, not specialty education: Experts.* Retrieved February 11, 2008, from http://www.china.org.cn/english/culture/84125.htm

Xinhua. (2004b). *China not to pursue profit-oriented education: Official.* Retrieved February 13, 2008, from http://www.china.org.cn/english/government/84137.htm

Xinhua. (2007). *Zhong Nanshan calls for educational system to reform to improve Chinese youngsters' health.* Retrieved from http://www.china.org.cn/english/education/202116.htm

Xu, H. (2003). *ni zhongchan le ma?* [Are you part of the middle-class?]. Beijing: Economics Daily Press.

Yacine, T. (2004). Pierre Bourdieu in Algeria at war: Notes on the birth of an engaged ethnosociology. *Ethnography, 5*(4), 487–509.

Yan, Y. (2010). The Chinese path to individualization. *The British Journal of Sociology, 63*(3), 489–512. Retrieved from http://dx.doi.org/10.1111/j.1468-4446.2010.01323.x

Yan, Y. (2011). The individualization of the family in rural China. *Boundary 2, 38*(1), 203–229. Retrieved from http://boundary2.dukejournals.org/content/38/1/203.full.pdf+html

Yang, D. P. (2006). Pursuing harmony and fairness in education. *Chinese Education and Society, 39*(6), 3–44. Retrieved from http://mesharpe.metapress.com/link.asp?id=570213x452103754

Yang, F. (2002). Education in China. *Educational Philosophy and Theory, 34*(2), 135–144. Retrieved from http://dx.doi.org/10.1111/j.1469-5812.2002.tb00292.x

Yao, Y. (Ed.). (2009, July 15). *"yi nian yi da bu, san nian da bianyang" shijiazhuang yinglai da fazhan* ["One year one big step forward, three years total change": Shijiazhuang ushers in major development]. *CRI Online.* Retrieved from http://gb.cri.cn/27824/2009/07/15/3785s2563458.htm

Ying, H. (2012). *haizi de xinli pilao burong hushi* [Children's mental fatigue can not be ignored]. Retrieved from http://www.sjzfls.com/show.aspx?id=1687

Yochim, L. (2006). *Hindsight hermeneutics: Critical reflections on research with middle school teachers in mainland China* (Master's thesis). University of Alberta, Edmonton, Canada. (MR22202).

Yochim, L. (2012). 'Headmasters become noblemen': Mainland Chinese teachers' perspectives on changes in education under the socialist market economy. *Canadian and International Education, 41*(2), 106–126.

Yu, H. (2012). *China in ten words.* New York, NY: Anchor Books.

Yung, H. (1975). Education in China today. *China Reconstructs, 24*(5), 2–5.

Yusuf, S., & Nabeshima, K. (2008). Two decades of reform: The changing organization dynamics of Chinese industrial firms. In J. R. Logan (Ed.), *Urban China in transition* (pp. 27–47). Malden, MA: Blackwell Publishing.

Zeng, P. (2008). A sound principal underlying a good education. *China Today, 57*(5), 47–49.

Zeng, T., Deng, Y., Yang, R., Zuo, X., Chu, Z., & Li, X. (2007). Balanced development of compulsory education: Cornerstone of education equity. *Frontiers of Education in China, 2*(4), 469–493. Retrieved from http://link.springer.com/content/pdf/10.1007%2Fs11516-007-0037-4.pdf

REFERENCES

Zhang, H. (2010). Brains unchained: Chinese education devolves to evolve. *China Today, 59*(6), 49–50.
Zhang, H. (2012). Labor of love: Embracing the volunteer spirit in education. *China Today, 61*(6), 26–27.
Zhang, L. (2010). *In search of paradise: Middle-class living in a Chinese metropolis.* Ithaca, NY: Cornell University Press.
Zhang, X. (2008). *Postsocialism and cultural politics: China in the last decade of the twentieth century.* Durham, NC: Duke University Press.
Zhang, Y. (2013, June 12). Across China, strong itch to spend. *The Wall Street Journal.* Retrieved from http://library.pressdisplay.com
Zhao, D. (2011). Special love for a special individual. *China Today, 60*(4), 54–56.
Zhao, Y. (2010). Scholars on the run. *China Today, 59*(8), 50–51.
Zhou, M., & Cai, G. (2008). Trapped in neglected corners of a booming metropolis: Residential patterns and marginalization of migrant workers in Guangzhou. In J. R. Logan (Ed.), *Urban China in transition* (pp. 226–249). Oxford: Blackwell Publishing.
Zhu, M. (1999). The views and involvement of Chinese parents in the children's education. *Prospects, 29*(2), 233–238.
Zhu, S. (2011). Modernizing Chinese law: The protection of private property in China. *ProtoSociology, 28*, 73–86.

Printed in the United States
By Bookmasters